Wanstead House

Wanstead House

East London's Lost Palace

Hannah Armstrong

Dearest Stefanie,
Thank you for all
your support.
With love,
Hannah
x

 Historic England

Published by Liverpool University Press on behalf of Historic England, The Engine House, Fire Fly Avenue, Swindon SN2 2EH
www.HistoricEngland.org.uk

Historic England is a Government service championing England's heritage and giving expert, constructive advice.

The views contained in this book are those of the author alone and not Historic England or Liverpool University Press.

First published 2022

ISBN: 978-1-80085-609-7 cased

British Library Cataloguing in Publication data
A CIP catalogue record for this book is available from the British Library.

Typeset in Charter 9/11

Page layout by Carnegie Book Production

Printed in Turkey via Akcent Media Limited

Contents

Preface

When I was just a few days old, my mother and father took me for what was the first of many visits to Wanstead Park. As a child, I was too young to understand the historic significance of the landscape through which I rambled, but the crumbling ruin of the Grotto Boathouse and word of a former palace struck a chord with me. When my family and I left the United Kingdom, my early memories of the park faded. It was not until studying for my Masters in Decorative Arts and Design History at the University of Glasgow that I was reminded of Wanstead by reoccurring references to its renowned classic design and lavish interiors, immortalised in William Hogarth's portrait of the Child family standing in the Grand Ballroom.

The demolition of the house and the dispersal of its evidence across the country only made my quest for uncovering Wanstead's history more compelling. In 2013, I was awarded a grant from the Arts and Humanities Research Council to write my PhD thesis on Wanstead House and its landscape at Birkbeck College, University of London, under the supervision of Dr Kate Retford. Over the next four years, I investigated the historic landscape and the lost interiors of the house. I pieced together a range of evidence, trawled through archives, encountered building fragments and met several wonderful historians who generously shared their knowledge of this lost Georgian estate.

It was an honour to be approached by the Friends of Wanstead Parklands to write the first fully illustrated monograph on Wanstead House and its landscape. Writing this book has enabled me to further my research and I am delighted to share these findings, alongside a fantastic archive of visual material, to a wide readership. It is my sincere hope that this book will advance historic understanding and public appreciation for this significant heritage site and ensure Wanstead's preservation for future generations.

Acknowledgements

There are many people without whom this book would not have been possible. First, I would like to express my deepest gratitude to the Friends of Wanstead Parklands for providing me with the opportunity to write this book. I would like to express special thanks to Nigel Franceschi for his support throughout and whose encouragement spurred me on at the most challenging of times. It has been a privilege to work with you. Thank you to the team at Historic England, especially John Hudson who supported the book's initial conception. I owe a debt of gratitude to the team at Liverpool University Press, in particular Sarah Warren, Rachel Chamberlain, Catherine Pugh and Alison Welsby, who took on this project and offered such valuable guidance throughout.

This book developed from my PhD thesis undertaken at Birkbeck College, University of London. I want to thank my PhD supervisor Kate Retford; I feel enormously privileged to have worked with you and am forever grateful for your generosity and wisdom – without you, I would never have made it this far. Thank you to John Bonehill of the University of Glasgow, who encouraged me to explore Wanstead for a PhD thesis. There are many historians who I have learnt from and who have generously shared their research with me. I would like to thank Richard Arnopp, whose knowledge of Wanstead cannot be overstated, and who kindly provided invaluable comments on the manuscript and was always at hand to answer my questions. Sally Jeffery, for her expertise on Wanstead's landscape; Geraldine and Greg Roberts, for their knowledge on William and Catherine Pole-Tylney-Long-Wellesley, as well as Tim Couzens, Stephen Pewsey, Dennis Keeling, Georgina Green, Ray Weakes, Chris O'Donnell, Joanne O'Hara, John Harris and Diana Davis. Their knowledge and research have made a valuable contribution to this study.

One of the great pleasures of a work of this kind is the opportunity to visit archives. I would like to express thanks to the staff at Essex Record Office, Wiltshire and Swindon Archives, Redbridge Museums and Heritage Centre, Newham Archives, the National Archives, the British Library, Heinz Archive, Witt Library and Bibliothèque Nationale de France, as well as Bryan Maggs at Sir Paul Getty's Library and Pamela Kingsbury at Hoares Bank Archive. Thank you to Rosie France for providing me with access to the largest known collection of Wanstead's building fabric at Hills Road, Cambridge.

Finally, I would like to express my deepest gratitude and love to my family, who have continuously expressed enthusiasm towards my research. To my siblings, may this book remind you of our happy childhood. My husband, Tim, who has been alongside me during these last eight years of research and whose love and support I could not be without. Our daughters, Orla and Phoebe, who arrived into the world as this book came together. Last but by no means least, I would like to thank my mother and father, Moira and Brendan Armstrong. It is because of you that Wanstead holds a special place in my heart. I dedicate this book to you both.

Illustration credits

Illustrations are reproduced by kind permission as follows:

The British Library Board Figs 1.2, 1.3, 1.4, 3.7, 5.1

© The Trustees of the British Museum Figs 8.2, 8.4, 8.5, 10.2

Courtesy of Burton Constable Hall Fig 4.6

Courtesy of Carlton Hobbs LLC Fig 4.10

Reproduced by permission of Chatsworth Settlement Trustees/Bridgeman Images Fig 10.1

© Christie's Images/Bridgeman Images Figs 4.3, 4.13, 9.1

© Crown Copyright and database rights 2021 OS 100047474 Fig 0.1

© The Devonshire Collections, Chatsworth. Reproduced by permission of Chatsworth Settlement Trustees Fig 4.7

© Environment Agency copyright and database right 2021. All rights reserved Fig 0.8

Reproduced by courtesy of the Essex Record Office Figs 0.3, 5.3, 6.2, 9.9

© Fairfax House, York Civic Trust Fig 4.12

By courtesy of Geraldine Roberts Fig 8.1

© Historic England Archive Fig 0.2

Courtesy of John Harris Fig 6.5

The John Howard McFadden Collection, 1928 Fig 4.8

Photograph by Ardon Bar Hama © Sir John Soane's Museum, London. Fig 6.8

Courtesy of Joseph Bacon Fig 4.4

© London Metropolitan Archives (City of London) Fig 5.2

Mike Booth/Alamy Stock Photo Fig 5.5

Abbreviations

Bibliothèque Nationale de France	BNF
British Library	BL
Essex Record Office	ERO
Lewis Walpole Collection Online	LWL
National Archives	NA
National Art Library	NAL
Newham Archive, Hiram Stead Collection	Stead
Redbridge Museums and Heritage Centre	RHC
Sir Paul Getty's Library, Wormsley Estate	PGL
Wiltshire and Swindon History Centre	WSHC

Family tree

Child/Tylney Family Tree

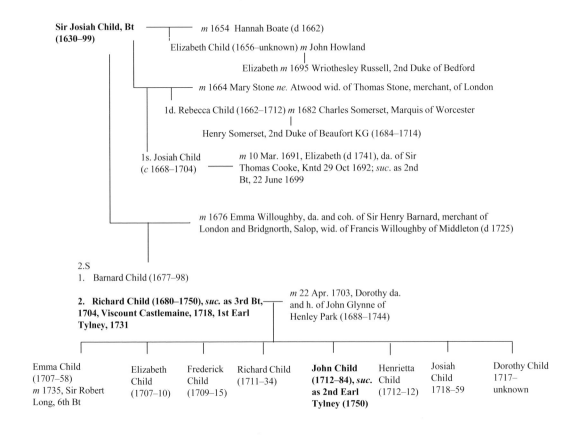

Sir Josiah Child, Bt
(1630–99) — *m* 1654 Hannah Boate (d 1662)

Elizabeth Child (1656–unknown) *m* John Howland

Elizabeth *m* 1695 Wriothesley Russell, 2nd Duke of Bedford

m 1664 Mary Stone *ne.* Atwood wid. of Thomas Stone, merchant, of London

1d. Rebecca Child (1662–1712) *m* 1682 Charles Somerset, Marquis of Worcester

Henry Somerset, 2nd Duke of Beaufort KG (1684–1714)

1s. Josiah Child
(*c* 1668–1704) — *m* 10 Mar. 1691, Elizabeth (d 1741), da. of Sir Thomas Cooke, Kntd 29 Oct 1692; *suc.* as 2nd Bt, 22 June 1699

m 1676 Emma Willoughby, da. and coh. of Sir Henry Barnard, merchant of London and Bridgnorth, Salop, wid. of Francis Willoughby of Middleton (d 1725)

2.S
1. Barnard Child (1677–98)

2. Richard Child (1680–1750), *suc.* as 3rd Bt, 1704, Viscount Castlemaine, 1718, 1st Earl Tylney, 1731

m 22 Apr. 1703, Dorothy da. and h. of John Glynne of Henley Park (1688–1744)

Emma Child
(1707–58)
m 1735, Sir Robert Long, 6th Bt

Elizabeth Child
(1707–10)

Frederick Child
(1709–15)

Richard Child
(1711–34)

**John Child
(1712–84), *suc.* as 2nd Earl Tylney (1750)**

Henrietta Child
(1712–12)

Josiah Child
1718–59

Dorothy Child
1717–
unknown

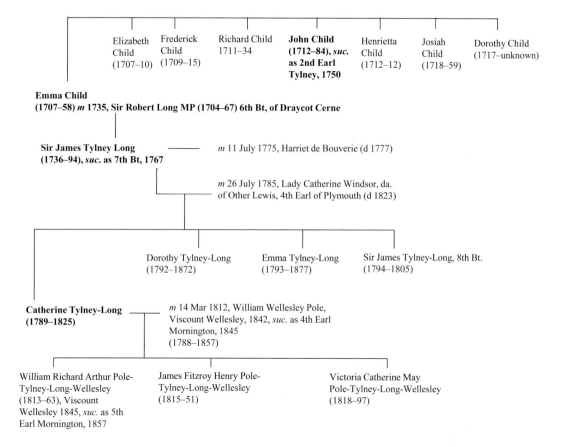

Elizabeth Child (1707–10)

Frederick Child (1709–15)

Richard Child 1711–34

John Child (1712–84), *suc.* as 2nd Earl Tylney, 1750

Henrietta Child (1712–12)

Josiah Child (1718–59)

Dorothy Child (1717–unknown)

Emma Child (1707–58) *m* 1735, Sir Robert Long MP (1704–67) 6th Bt, of Draycot Cerne

Sir James Tylney Long (1736–94), *suc.* as 7th Bt, 1767 ——— *m* 11 July 1775, Harriet de Bouverie (d 1777)

m 26 July 1785, Lady Catherine Windsor, da. of Other Lewis, 4th Earl of Plymouth (d 1823)

Dorothy Tylney-Long (1792–1872)

Emma Tylney-Long (1793–1877)

Sir James Tylney-Long, 8th Bt. (1794–1805)

Catherine Tylney-Long (1789–1825) ——— *m* 14 Mar 1812, William Wellesley Pole, Viscount Wellesley, 1842, *suc.* as 4th Earl Mornington, 1845 (1788–1857)

William Richard Arthur Pole-Tylney-Long-Wellesley (1813–63), Viscount Wellesley 1845, *suc.* as 5th Earl Mornington, 1857

James Fitzroy Henry Pole-Tylney-Long-Wellesley (1815–51)

Victoria Catherine May Pole-Tylney-Long-Wellesley (1818–97)

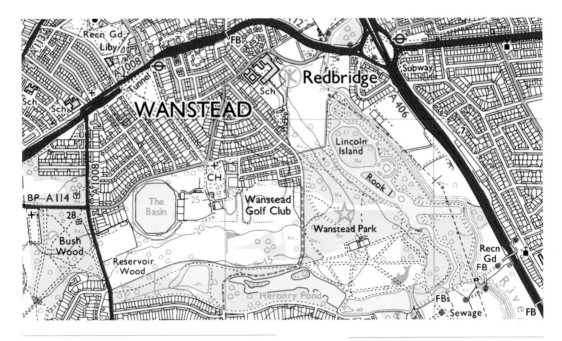

Fig 0.1
Ordnance Survey Map of Wanstead Park.
[Crown Copyright and database rights 2021 OS 100047474]

Fig 0.2
Aerial view of the park from the east.
[Historic England Archive]

Introduction: in search of East London's lost palace

Waenstede: an early history

The London suburb of Wanstead is situated eight miles north-east of the capital, straddling the A12, the former Roman route that connected London to Chelmsford and Colchester. The earliest records of Wanstead date back to the Domesday survey of 1086, when a small parish in the western fringes of Essex was recorded as Waenstede, deriving from the Old English *waen*, 'waggon' and *stede*, 'place'. Wanstead's development was slow, remaining as a village with large areas of woodland until the arrival of the Eastern Counties Railway in the mid-19th century. In 1937–8, Wanstead Underground station was built as part of the extension to the Central Line and, in 1965, the Essex suburb was incorporated into Greater London as part of the new borough of Redbridge. The construction during the mid-1990s of a major link road to connect the M11 to the Blackwall Tunnel under the Thames cut through the heart of Wanstead, but the area has nonetheless retained a village-like character with its green spaces and an attractive high street.

South of Wanstead High Street lies Wanstead Park and golf course, a Grade II* landscape of 129 hectares (Figs 0.1 and 0.2).[1] Archaeological discoveries of a tessellated Roman pavement, pottery and coins reveal that some form of settlement occupied the land here from as early as the 1st–4th centuries AD.[2] In 1086, the Domesday survey recorded a manor held by the Bishop of London near the north-west bank of Perch Pond, one of several historic waterworks in Wanstead Park. By the 16th century, the land belonged to the Crown and was used by King Henry VIII as a retreat from the capital and a base for hunting in nearby Epping Forest.

Fig 0.3
Detail of Map of Essex from
Speculum Britainiae (1594) by
John Norden.
[Essex Record Office]

1

In 1549, King Edward VI granted Wanstead to Lord Chancellor Richard Rich, who rebuilt the manor 'on higher ground several hundred paces to the north and east.'[3]

Robert Dudley, 1st Earl of Leicester and courtier to Queen Elizabeth I, purchased the manor built by Lord Rich in 1577. During Leicester's ownership, the house was extended and splendid gardens were created.[4] John Norden's map of 1594 records Leicester's 'statelye home' as a two-chimneyed gabled house at the centre of the enclosed park. The medieval church of St Mary the Virgin appears to the west of the manor (Fig 0.3).[5] To the east, the River Roding runs north to south with an arm running south-west of the park. Leicester's debts at the time of his death in 1588 were considerable and the manor was eventually seized by Queen Elizabeth I until 1593, when she released it to Robert Devereux, Earl of Essex, in exchange for other manors. Subsequent owners of Wanstead included Charles Blount, Lord Mountjoy, in 1598; George Villiers, Earl of Buckingham, in 1617; Sir Henry Mildmay (later master of the king's jewel house) in 1619; and Sir Robert Brooke, his son-in-law, in 1661.

'The noblest house in the kingdom': Wanstead House and the Child family[6]

By the late 17th century, Wanstead ranked among the largest houses in Essex.[7] Its rich Tudor history and grandeur is likely to have appealed to the wealthy, aspiring London merchant and later governor of the East India Company, Sir Josiah Child (c 1630–99) when seeking to acquire a family seat within easy reach of the capital. In 1673, Josiah purchased the house and grounds for £11,500. His acquisition marked the dawn of a new era at Wanstead.

In c 1713, Josiah's son and heir, Richard Child, later Viscount Castlemaine and 1st Earl Tylney (1680–1750), commissioned the architect Colen Campbell (1676–1729) to rebuild the family seat in a classical Italianate style (Fig 0.4). Its interior was fitted out by the leading designer of the early Georgian period, William Kent (1685–1748), and its grounds improved on several occasions by major landscape designers such as George London (d 1714) and Humphry Repton (1752–1818). Described by a contemporary as 'one of the most beautiful and magnificent private houses in Europe', Wanstead was equal to the great Georgian stately homes of Blenheim Palace, Wilton, Houghton and Holkham.[8]

For one hundred years, the estate passed through four generations, who fulfilled the role of custodian to varying degrees. Wanstead's glory days came to an abrupt end in 1822, when the severe financial debts accumulated by its owners, William and Catherine Pole-Tylney-Long-Wellesley, led to the sale of the entire contents of Wanstead House and its outbuildings (Fig 0.5).[9] The sale was a major event and made Wanstead 'the most attractive resort of the fashionable world, who have deserted the west end of the town in shoals, and made Whitechapel more travelled than Whitehall.'[10] Two years later, the house was demolished, its building fabric dispersed far and wide. Contemporaries lamented the event,

Fig 0.4

Wanstead House (undated) by Richard Westall, watercolour and graphite, 18.1 × 28.3 cm. [Yale Centre for British Art, New Haven]

with one newspaper reporting, '*sic transit gloria mundi*; thus passes the glory of the world.'[11] After the sale, the grounds fell into decline, trees were felled, and the land leased for grazing. In 1882, the Corporation of London purchased part of the park from Henry Wellesley, 1st Earl of Cowley (1804–84), to incorporate into Epping Forest. Land on the edge of the park was sold to developers, and in 1893, the remaining grounds, including the site of the former palace, were purchased by Wanstead Golf Club.

Sales and demolitions on the scale of Wanstead were not unusual during the long 18th century, nor were they associated with a particular period, geographical region or class of owner. In 1747, Cannons in Middlesex, the home to Richard Child's stepsister Cassandra Brydges, was demolished following the death of her husband, James Brydges, 1st Duke of Chandos, in 1744.[12] Philip Stanhope, 5th Earl Chesterfield's Eythorpe House in Buckinghamshire suffered a similar fate between 1810 and 1811.[13] In 1822, William Beckford arranged a sale of the contents of his home, Fonthill Abbey in Wiltshire (*c* 1745).[14] Although the Fonthill sale was eventually cancelled, contemporaries drew comparisons to Wanstead: 'the tide of public curiosity which at one time this summer flowed so uninterruptedly to Wanstead House … had no sooner run its course, than it found a new attraction – that of Fonthill Abbey.'[15] The demise and demolition of any of these houses was a poignant business, as these structures served as symbols of power and optimism, anticipating a lengthy future for the family's ownership.

Wanstead House: East London's Lost Palace demonstrates that although its magnificent edifice and gardens are lost, this Georgian estate

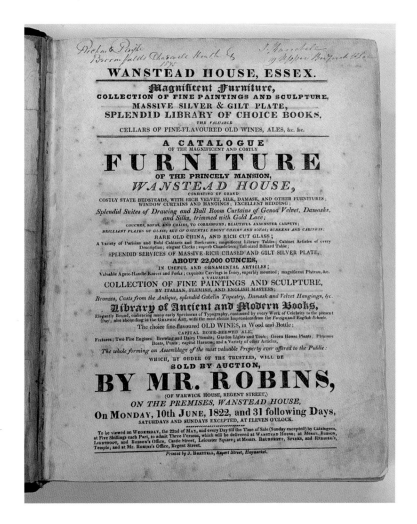

Fig 0.5
Wanstead House sale
catalogue (1822).
[Redbridge Museums and
Heritage Centre]

should by no means be lost to history. A study of Wanstead is important
for several reasons. First, Campbell's classical design for Wanstead
House in *c* 1713 was ground-breaking. Its publication in one of the most
important and well-known architectural publications of the era, *Vitruvius
Britannicus* (1715), catapulted Wanstead to fame and is widely credited
for sowing the seeds for the English Palladian movement.[16] Features such
as the Corinthian hexastyle portico, 'the first yet practiced in this manner
in the Kingdom', became ubiquitous, and notable English country houses
including Wentworth Woodhouse, Nostell Priory and Prior Park used
Wanstead's façade as a blueprint.[17]

Campbell's design for Wanstead was admired throughout the
18th century. In 1724, Daniel Defoe described it as 'extremely glorious
and magnificent' and, in 1800, *The Gentleman's Magazine* commented
'foreigners assign more architectural merit [to Wanstead House] than
to most others of our noblemen's residences.'[18] When the dismantling
of Wanstead House was underway in 1823–4, the public was urged to

rescue its renowned classic elements: 'it would be much deplored should this unrivalled portico not be perpetuated as a national specimen of architectural beauty and taste.'[19] Wanstead's demolition has consequently erased all traces of one of the 18th-century's most influential and admired houses from the landscape.

Second, the scale and grandeur of Wanstead House made it akin to a palace or country house. Cartographer John Rocque's 1746 survey of London shows how Wanstead, particularly in its scale, outshone other retreats built on the peripheries of London during this period such as Chiswick House (c 1729) and Marble Hill (1750–1) in Twickenham, Osterley Park, Middlesex (1763–80), Kenwood, Hampstead Heath (1767–9) and Syon Park, Middlesex (1784). Residences such as Chiswick and Marble Hill were designed to more closely conform to the 'villa ideology' introduced by Richard Boyle, 3rd Earl Burlington (1694–1753), and thus were smaller than Wanstead, which instead compared more closely with royal residences like Kensington Palace.[20]

Certainly, contemporaries regarded Wanstead's scale within the peripheries of London as unique. In 1813, Humphry Repton commented that the house 'must be classed with those royal and princely residences ... those who could treat this splendid Palace like the seat of an English country gentleman, at the distance of a hundred miles from the metropolis, would rob it of all its importance, and more than half its interest and beauty.'[21] Wanstead House is therefore best defined as an 18th-century suburban palace, of which few examples survive.

Third, Wanstead House is an important case study of an estate developed from a mercantile career, albeit one that we, from our 21st-century viewpoint, find objectionable in its exploitation and mistreatment of human beings. It is an unpalatable truth that the landscape developments initiated during the late 17th century were funded predominantly by Josiah's powerful role as governor of the expansionist East India Company and his direct involvement in the transatlantic slave trade. The building of Campbell's classical mansion in c 1713 would not have been possible without the substantial fortune Josiah bequeathed his son, Richard. Wanstead exemplifies the types of success and fortunes attainable through a mercantile career in the late 17th century and draws attention to the role that aggressive colonial expansion played in the development of many of Great Britain's monumental edifices.

Finally, the meteoric rise and fall of the Child dynasty at Wanstead House represents the challenges of inheritance, debt and estate management in a way not generally invited by success stories, by houses that have endured and survived through the centuries. An investigation into what has been lost is arguably of equal merit to those in situ, furthering our understanding of 18th-century estate management.

The absence of Wanstead House requires the author to examine all ownerships and pinpoint when improvements were made and why. This enables us to situate Wanstead within the wider context of 18th-century art, social, cultural and economic histories. Providing a chronological account also encourages us to examine periods of high and low activity.

There is often a tendency, particularly if presented with a rich archive for a specific ownership or stage of improvement, to focus on more active periods in the life of a country house, thereby neglecting those for which evidence is sparse and in which little activity occurred. But as country house historian Jeremy Musson states, focusing on certain periods of ownership can overlook 'the glorious oddities, along with the human story of the house.'[22]

Sources and historiography: reconstructing the lost Georgian estate

In the absence of a physical structure, this study of Wanstead has drawn on a variety of material evidence, including surviving examples of its building fabric and furniture, paintings, historic maps and surveys of the estate, drawings, prints, architectural plans, correspondence, visitor accounts, newspapers, sales catalogues, and even poetry. Evidence of the lost estate can also be found in the existing landscape, beginning at the junction of Overton Drive and Blake Hall Road, where a pair of early 18th-century Portland stone piers, bearing the inter-laced monogram 'RC', marks the formal approach towards Richard Child's 'princely mansion' (Fig 0.6).[23] East of the gate piers lies the Basin pond, which featured in many contemporary views of the approach (*see* Fig 4.1). Today it is a prominent feature of the golf course, where a large crater at the first tee marks the spot where the house once stood (Fig 0.7; *see* Fig 0.2). In front of the crater, the distinct outline of a parterre garden designed by Repton in 1813 can be identified. Nearby, the former stables accommodate the golf clubhouse.

East of the golf course, further remnants of the estate can be found in the Wanstead Parklands. Here are examples of late 17th- and early 18th-century avenues, as well as two garden follies: the Grotto Boathouse and Temple, both built in the 1760s. An archaeological Lidar survey of

Fig 0.6
Overton Drive stone pier.
[Hannah Armstrong]

Fig 0.7
Site of house, Wanstead Golf
Course.
[Nigel Franceschi]

Fig 0.8
Lidar scan of Wanstead Park
(2012).
[Environment Agency
copyright and database right
2021]

the park reveals evidence of early 18th-century landscape features, now buried beneath undergrowth, such as the Amphitheatre, Fortification and Mounts (Fig 0.8).[24] Five of the original seven lakes survive. Despite their critical condition, they are a reminder of the site's former splendour. The straight canal in the Ornamental Waters, for example, continues to guide our gaze towards where Wanstead House once stood (Fig 0.9).

The fragile state of the parkland (now on the Heritage at Risk Register) and ongoing efforts to implement conservation measures has resulted in several unpublished reports. Most notable is the report produced by the Debois Landscape Survey Group for the City of London

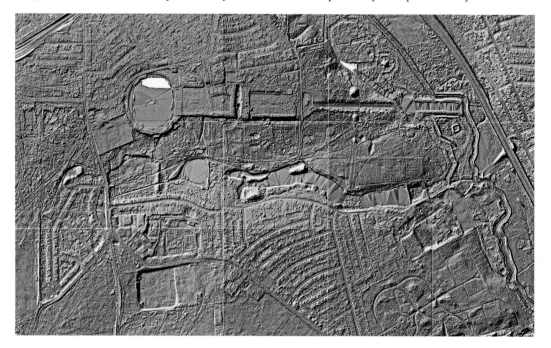

Fig 0.9
View from canal looking west.
[Nigel Franceschi]

Corporation in response to the damage caused to the park by the Great Storm of 1987, and the marginally less powerful storm of 1990.[25] The survey provided the basis for a management plan as well as serving as a stock take, documenting evidence of the historic landscape and the park's ecology. Particularly valuable is its cross-examination of the existing landscape with plans of the park by John Rocque in 1735. It is the most extensive and detailed analysis of the park to date and its value for the Wanstead historian cannot be overstated. Other surveys include Alan Cornish and James Berry's *The Lake System of Wanstead Park and the Mystery of the Heronry Pond* (1978), which summarised the history of the lakes and laid out proposals for their preservation, and Compass Archaeology's survey for English Heritage in 2013.[26]

The landscape has also inspired academic research. In 1999, the London Parks and Gardens Trust organised a study day on Wanstead for which landscape historian Sally Jeffery provided participants with a detailed overview of the park's 18th-century history.[27] In 2002, local historian Georgina Green made the significant discovery of Repton's 1813 report for Wanstead, which featured several of the landscape designer's 'before and after' watercolour views. The findings were presented in an article by Jeffery for *Country Life Magazine* and more recently in her chapter for *Repton in London*, published in 2018 to commemorate the bicentenary of his death.[28] Architectural historians John Harris and Andrew Skelton have published articles on the landscape, its outbuildings and follies for *Country Life Magazine* and the *Georgian Group Journal*.[29] Literature on the Georgian house is comparatively sparse. Where it does exist, it is predominantly concerned with Campbell's career and the designs published for Wanstead in *Vitruvius Britannicus* between 1715 and 1725, or in wider scholarship on William Kent.[30]

In 1996, A P Baggs' article, 'The After-Life of Wanstead', published for *The Georgian Group Journal*, alerted readers to an early 19th-century brick house in Cambridge where the largest known collection of surviving fragments from Wanstead House are located.[31] The whereabouts of Wanstead's building fabric, furniture and fine-art collection has inspired several local historians, eager to piece together how the house and its interior appeared. Richard Arnopp, Tim Couzens, Dennis Keeling and Stephen Pewsey have carried out valuable research, which has informed this study and made a major contribution to the current preservation and local understanding of the site's history.[32] In 2015, Geraldine Roberts published *The Angel and the Cad*, a thoroughly researched account of the scandalous story of the demise of Wanstead's final owners, Catherine and William Pole-Tylney-Long-Wellesley. Roberts' publication was well received, reflecting the interest in Wanstead's story.[33]

Given the enthusiasm and support surrounding Wanstead House, it seems curious that a monograph that brings together the wide range of evidence and existing literature for this influential estate has not come to fruition until now. *Wanstead House: East London's Lost Palace* will re-establish Wanstead's position among the leading houses of Georgian England.[34] By doing so, it serves as a case study for examining lost houses and the process of cross-examining a range of sources in the absence of a physical structure. Above all, this study not only aims to enhance our historical understanding of Wanstead, but hopefully will inspire others to go out in search of England's lost Georgian houses.

Notes

1. https://historicengland.org.uk/listing/the-list/list-entry/1000194, accessed 18 April 2021.
2. Morant 1768, ii; Lethieullier 1779, 73–4; Compass Archaeology 2014, 10.
3. Compass Archaeology 2013, 10.
4. For material relating to Robert Dudley, 1st Earl of Leicester, and Wanstead House, see Goldring 2014; Adams 1995; Goldring 2016, 16–21.
5. Compass Archaeology, Appendix II 2013, 3–4; Emmison and Skelton's analysis of Norden's *The Chorographical Description of Essex* (*c* 1594), states that maps by Norden are largely accurate in spatial representation and are a reliable pictorial source.
6. Young 1768, 199.
7. Parsons 1973, 318.
8. Shaw 1788, 28; Young 1768, 338.
9. See ERO SALE/B284, frontispiece.
10. *The Literary Chronicle and Weekly Review*, 15 June 1822, 379–80.
11. 'Chit-Chat', *The Kaleidoscope: or, Literary and Scientific Mirror*, 24 September 1822, 95–6.
12. *The Kaleidoscope*, 24 September 1822, 95–6; Johnson, 'Brydges, James'; 'A Catalogue of All the Materials of the Dwelling-house … Sold by Auction by Mr. Cock', 16 June 1747.

13 Colvin 1963, 219–27.
14 Richter 2008, 543–63; McConnell, 'Beckford, William Thomas'. For other literature on Georgian country house sales, see MacArthur and Stobart 2010, 175–95; Wall 1997, 1–26.
15 *The Mirror of Literature, Amusement & Instruction*, 16 November 1822, 33–5.
16 Harris 1981, 16.
17 Campbell 1715, I, 4.
18 Furbank and Owens 1991, 41; *The Gentleman's Magazine, and Historical Chronicle*, 1069.
19 Stead, 80.
20 For literature on the Georgian villa, see Arnold 1996; Ackerman 1990; Harris 1994.
21 Repton 1813, 8.
22 Musson 2005, 13.
23 See ERO SALE/B284, frontispiece. Photographic evidence reveals that the gate piers have been repositioned from their original location, suggesting that they originally flanked an alternative entrance to the estate. However, a study of historic maps and estate views verifies that this route formed the principal approach to Wanstead House. The piers have therefore been erected in a highly suitable setting.
24 Thanks to Rob Wiseman for sharing these research findings with me.
25 Debois Landscape Survey Group 1990.
26 Berry and Cornish 1978; Compass Archaeology 2014.
27 Jeffery 2003.
28 Jeffery 2005, 98–101; Jeffery 2018, 21–9.
29 Harris 1991, 60–2; Skelton 2010, 49–64.
30 See Summerson 1993; J Harris 1981; Stutchbury 1967; Colvin 2008; Harris 1986; O'Hara 2010; Weber 2013.
31 Baggs 1996, 131–3.
32 Keeling 1997; Keeling 1994; Keeling 2014; Keeling 2015. For articles on Wanstead House and its owners, see Arnopp, 'The owners of Wanstead Park'.
33 Roberts 2015.
34 This book has been inspired by the author's own PhD thesis. See Armstrong 2016.

Part 1

Sir Josiah Child, Bt, the 'Albion Croesus', 1673–99

Fig 1.1
Sir Josiah Child Bt (c 1683) by John Riley,
oil on canvas, 102.9 × 87.9 cm.
[National Portrait Gallery, London]

Establishing a mercantile estate in the late 17th century

On Sunday 14 May 1665, the diarist Samuel Pepys (1633–1703) took a coach from London to visit the politician Sir Robert Brooke's (1637–69) estate at Wanstead. Writing later about his visit, Pepys was underwhelmed, describing it as 'A fine seat, but an old-fashioned house; and being not full of people looks desolately'.[1] Wanstead's 'desolate' appearance can be explained by Brooke's recent retirement to France to escape political burdens and financial debts. Four years after Pepys' visit, Brooke's body was discovered drowned in the River Rhone at Avignon. His manors of Wanstead and nearby Stonehall were left in trust to his cousin, John Brooke, to pay off his debts.[2] During this period the house was leased to the wealthy London merchant Sir Josiah Child (Fig 1.1), who eventually bought the house for £11,500 in 1673.[3]

Soon after purchasing Wanstead, Josiah became one of the leading directors of the East India Company, an organisation formed in London during the early years of the 17th century for the exploitation of trade with east and south-east Asia and India. However, the East India Company was not a major source of Josiah's wealth until *after* the purchase of Wanstead. The acquisition was instead made possible by several business ventures carried out during Josiah's early career, as well as by advantageous marriages and civic positions.

As the second son of Richard Child, a merchant of Fleet Street, and Elizabeth Roycroft of Weston Wick, Shropshire, Josiah is likely to have grown up in a well-to-do middling family, and, as was common among his peers, to have begun his career as a merchant's apprentice.[4] Diarist John Evelyn (1620–1706) described Josiah in 1683 as being 'from an ordinary Merchant's Apprentice.'[5] Josiah's trajectory, however, was far from ordinary. From as early as 1650, he demonstrated entrepreneurial skill, working as a supercargo, whose duties included overseeing the transportation of provisions from Plymouth to Lisbon on behalf of the parliamentary fleet.[6] In 1653, he acted as agent for the Admiralty commissions and, in 1655, served as deputy to the Navy's treasurer of Portsmouth, arranging the provisioning and victualling of ships, a post he held until the Restoration in 1660.[7] Josiah also undertook several important civic jobs, becoming a burgess in 1655 and assistant to the mayor of Portsmouth in 1656. Between 1658 and 1659, he served as mayor of Portsmouth and as Member of Parliament for Petersfield. These civic duties were no doubt instrumental to his advancing social and political status.

In Portsmouth, Josiah married his first wife, Hannah (d 1662), the daughter of Edward Boate, a master shipbuilder, with whom he had one daughter, Elizabeth (b 1656). When Hannah died in 1662, Josiah returned to London in pursuit of new business opportunities and a second wife. Two years later, he married Mary Stone, the daughter of William Attwood of Hackney and widow of Thomas Stone, a wealthy

London merchant. Josiah's eagerness to remarry underlines the financial advantages to be gained from the London marriage market. Mary Stone's status as a widow provided him with a generous portion of £3,000, plus £250 worth of household goods.[8] The couple had two children, a son, Josiah (1668–1704), and a daughter, Rebecca (1662–1712).

Back in the capital, Josiah's career gathered pace. His expertise in business and mercantile affairs saw him appointed to the Select Committee on the State of Trade in 1667, the Commons Committee in 1668 and the House of Lords Committee in 1669.[9] The committees were designed to advise the government about how to restore England's economy after the catastrophic plague of 1665, the Great Fire of London of 1666, and the recent fall in the price of land. Josiah argued that a low rate of interest, as practised in Holland, was the prime requisite for an expanding economy. It would also enable England to compete against the increasingly powerful Verenigde Oost-Indische Compagnie (the Dutch East India Company). Josiah published his proposals in several political pamphlets, most notably, *Brief Observations Concerning Trade* (1668) and *Discourse about Trade* (1690).

Despite being a leading voice in many government committee discussions, some at court viewed Josiah as suspect, accusing him of putting forward proposals that served his own interest and those of his closest nonconformist business associates, Thomas Papillon, Thomas Littleton and William Love. Roger North (1631–1734) described Josiah's mercantile clique as the 'fanatic party', intent on making Parliament more powerful than the Crown by overseeing the flow of commerce and withholding power from King Charles II.[10]

During the early 1670s, Josiah made several investments that likely played a major role in contributing towards the Wanstead acquisition. In 1670, he purchased the Anchor Brewery on Park Street in Southwark. One contemporary reported that 'much of the beer was small and stinking, and the rest ill-tasted and unfit for the sea.'[11] Nonetheless, the 'stinking beer' was supplied to the navy, the East India Company, and even to the monarchy. In 1672, Josiah partnered with fellow merchants Papillon, Littleton and several others in a navy-victualling contract, transporting stores from London to naval bases in the provinces and importing timber masts from New England. This proved to be particularly profitable when the Third Anglo-Dutch War broke out later that year.[12]

In 1672, Josiah became a founding member of the Royal Africa Company (formerly the Company of Royal Adventurers Trading to Africa), which was the largest trading company to be granted a royal charter by King Charles II to set up forts and factories, exercise martial law and hold a monopoly on the British trade of gold, silver and slaves from West Africa. Josiah believed that investing in the colonies, when agricultural prices and rents were falling and taxes and land sales were rising, was critical if England wished to outdo their Dutch rivals, whose wealth was principally sourced from trade. That year, Josiah also invested in a sugar works plantation of 1,330 acres with merchant Samuel Bache, in Port Royal, Jamaica.[13] Josiah's role was to supply the necessary servants, slaves and supplies (presumably via his Royal Africa Company links), while Bache undertook the direction of the plantation. The profits made were to be shared equally, and both men entered penal bonds of £10,000.[14]

For those who invested in the Atlantic slave trade, competition was fierce. If successful, a colonial merchant typically earned an annual income of around £400, a comfortable sum that enabled one to rent or purchase a suburban villa.[15] The acquisition or construction of a country house, however, was more unusual. In 1688, the cost of a small country house was around £2,000 and a nobleman's around £6,000.[16] Further evidence regarding the profits gained from his investment in a plantation has yet to be uncovered, and although these figures postdate Josiah's acquisition they nonetheless reveal that his purchase of Wanstead for £11,500 was remarkable by all standards of the day. Evidently, Josiah was among a select few colonial merchants who was able to ruthlessly exploit the market; 'from this time on, Child began to enjoy the reputation of uncommon wealth.'[17] The profits made by Josiah's various business ventures meant that, by 1673, he had raised the necessary funds to purchase the old manor at Wanstead.

The Wanstead acquisition: 'where commonly these overgrown and suddenly monied men do for the most part seat themselves'

In 1683, Evelyn scathingly described Josiah's estate at Wanstead as 'where commonly these overgrown and suddenly monied men do for the most part seat themselves.'[18] Indeed, villages in the vicinity such as Woodford, Walthamstow and Leyton were popular among wealthy merchants eager to adopt a degree of the landed elite lifestyle in Essex while maintaining all-important links to the City of London and the East India Docks. Landed investments provided relatively modest financial returns and so it was sensible for a newly moneyed gentleman like Josiah to keep a close eye on business ties and activities. Moreover, there was a fear among the nouveaux riche of being too distant from the city when residing at a country seat, and the potential drain on one's capital that this may have caused.[19]

Contrary to Evelyn's remarks, Josiah is likely to have taken pride in Wanstead's proximity to the capital, perceiving it as symbolic of the rise of the mercantile class into the upper echelons of late 17th-century English society. Joseph Harris, a teacher at the Latin Boarding School in nearby Leytonstone, romanticised the popularity of the Essex setting among the mercantile elite in his 1702 poem, 'Leighton-Stone Air':

> Return'd from China, or the Indian Bay,
>   Of from the Frozen or Western Sea,
> Prosp'rous to bless his pleas'd expectant Fair,
> Delights to sip his Villa's lushious Air,
> And sit and count his golden Mass of Care.[20]

Wanstead's rich history may also have appealed to Josiah, most notably its associations with the Tudor monarchs and Robert Dudley, 1st Earl of Leicester, who had purchased the manor and its gardens in 1577. Leicester's residence on the Strand in London and Kenilworth Castle in Warwickshire provided him with the all-important properties of town and country house. Queen Elizabeth's preference for moving between the

Thames-side palaces made ownership of a suburban residence essential for those wishing to secure or enhance their political standing at court. The acquisition of Wanstead therefore provided Leicester with a suburban residence, suitable for royal visits and made his 'trio [of properties] complete.'[21]

At Wanstead, Leicester held court, entertained foreign dignitaries and received royal visits.[22] In May 1578, the gardens provided the setting for one of the most significant cultural events of the Elizabethan era, the staging of playwright Sir Philip Sidney's garden masque *The Lady of May*.[23] On this occasion, a 330ft coarse canvas was erected as part of the stage drop and the gardens themselves were used to dramatic effect. Sidney's description records that 'six shepherds and others were seen dragging the damsel who is designated as 'The Lady of May' towards the Queen from the Wanstead wood'. There is also a suggestion that Elizabeth partook in the performance, 'her most excellent Maiestie walking in Wanstead garden as she passed down the groue [grove].'[24] Later that year, Elizabeth made a second visit to Wanstead to mark the end of her summer tour through Cambridgeshire, Suffolk and Norfolk. On this occasion, the earl hosted a splendid feast for his royal guest, who dined in ignorance of the news that her favourite courtier had married Lettice Knollys two days earlier at Wanstead's chapel.[25]

Despite having no previous connections with Wanstead, Josiah was able to assert his significance through the acquisition of a historical site with royal associations. Aristocratic landowners had the luxury of inheriting family estates, heirlooms, familial ties, lineage and pre-existing wealth, to enforce and support their social standing and superiority. A newly moneyed landowner lacked such advantages, and the possibility of drawing on the pre-existing history of a recently acquired property as a means of establishing his position would surely have been attractive.

Rebuilding versus landscape improvements

A series of views produced by Flemish artist Leonard Knyff (1650–1722) and engraver Johannes Kip (1653–1722) in *c* 1708 are the only known depictions of the house purchased by Josiah (Figs 1.2–1.4). In the series of views, the manor appears at the centre of the estate, built in a traditional Elizabethan style and enclosed around a quadrangle. On the east elevation, a gabled arcade supports a long gallery on the first floor (*see* Fig 1.4). Leicester's household accounts for 1584–5 record several payments towards building activities.[26] These are likely to have been carried out to modernise Lord Rich's manor in order to accommodate royal visits and lavish entertainments. Although there are no known views of the manor's interior, a probate inventory made in 1588 reveals that it was of a considerable size, accommodating 20 bedrooms, a great chamber, chapel and a great gallery, where portraits of King Henry VIII, Queen Mary and Queen Elizabeth were displayed.[27]

The instability of ownerships after Leicester's death in 1588 meant that no further architectural improvements were made. By the late 17th

Fig 1.2
View of Wanstead to the east
(c 1708), Johannes Kip and
Leonard Knyff.
[The British Library, London]

Fig 1.3
View of Wanstead to the west
(c 1708), Johannes Kip and
Leonard Knyff.
[The British Library, London]

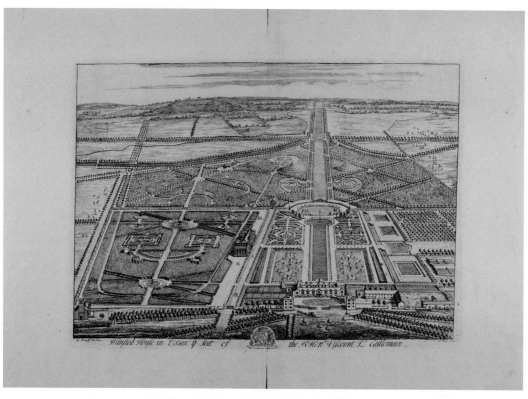

Wansted House in Essex ye Seat of the R.t Hon.ble Vicount L.d Castlemain

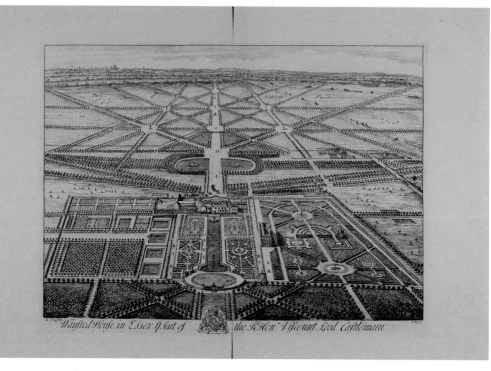

Wansted House in Essex ye Seat of the R.t Hon.ble Vicount Lord Castlemain

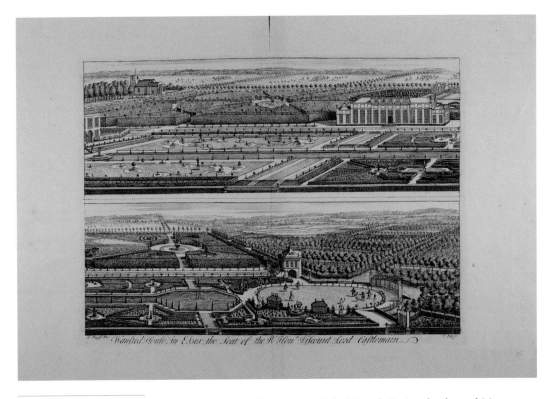

Wanstead House, in Essex, the Seat of the R. Hon. Viscount Lord Castlemain

Fig 1.4

View of Wanstead to the north (in two sections) (c 1708), Johannes Kip and Leonard Knyff.

[The British Library, London]

century, Wanstead appeared old-fashioned. Curiously, the ambitious Josiah did not attempt to modernise the manor. Instead he turned his attention to improving the surrounding landscape. This may have been a means of maintaining Wanstead's historic associations, but most probably it was because the costs of rebuilding were often unacceptably high for a newly moneyed owner. It was not unusual for building projects to be put on hold following the acquisition of an estate.[28] If Josiah believed in the longevity of country house ownership, then the improvement of the landscape may have been an attempt to prepare the property for his descendants, who, presumably, would have the funds to rebuild.

Josiah Child's landscape improvements, 1673–99

Kip and Knyff's views of Wanstead are the only known sources to provide information on the landscape improvements carried out by Josiah during the late 17th century (*see* Figs 1.2–1.4). This series of views, however, was produced in *c* 1708, several years after Josiah's death, and therefore not only record Josiah's late 17th-century scheme, but the gardens designed by George London (*c* 1640–1714) and Adam Holt (1691–1750) for his son, Richard Child (1680–1750), during the early 18th century. As a result, the engravings are complex sources, which conflate two different periods of ownership.

In addition, the views were produced on a commission basis and intended for publication. It is therefore necessary to interpret these pictorial sources with caution when investigating Josiah's improvements as they were subject to exaggeration in order to flatter the client and impress the viewer. The perspective and size of the landscape, for example, has been distorted. The *View to the west* presents an exaggerated view of the avenues and shows Leytonstone at a far greater distance than is geographically correct. The topography in the *View to the east* has been flattened and does not accurately depict the descent of the Long Walk (now the Glade) towards the straight canal and River Roding. Fortunately, several late 17th-century accounts of Wanstead survive. These include the description by Evelyn in 1683, a visitor account by John Gibson in 1691, and Joseph Harris's 1702 poem 'Leighton-Stone Air'. By cross-referencing these sources with the views by Kip and Knyff, we can establish, with some degree of confidence, which features can be attributed to Josiah, and which were created later.

Avenues

The earliest record of the planting of avenues appears in Evelyn's 1683 account: 'I went to see Sir Josiah Child's prodigious Cost in planting of Walnut trees, about his seate.'[29] Evelyn's use of the active verb 'planting' indicates that the plantation of trees for avenues was underway at the time of his visit. In 1691, Gibson described Josiah's plantations of walnuts, elms and ashes as 'more worth seeing than his gardens, which are but indifferent' and estimated their value to be around £10,000.[30] Further description of the avenues appear in 'Leighton-Stone Air' (1702), in which the author describes Wanstead as 'a pleasant Villa in the Forest near Leighton Stone made very delicious by the New Plantations Sir Josiah Child has honoured it with.'[31]

Avenues dominate Kip and Knyff's *View to the east* and *View to the west* (*see* Figs 1.2 and 1.3). However, because these views depict a landscape having undergone improvements by two of Wanstead's owners, it can be difficult to distinguish which of these avenues were planted by Josiah. The 1990 survey by the Debois Landscape Group has helped to establish dating for those depicted by Kip and Knyff. Among the avenues attributed to Josiah is that which forms the principal approach to Wanstead (*see* Fig 1.3). This avenue lies on the main axis of the estate and must have been completed by the time Gibson made his account in 1691, probably with elm.[32] The avenue began at the village of Wanstead (its western end survives as Bush Road) and continued eastwards, terminating at two large semicircular fishponds (now the Basin), where Josiah's plantations of 'Grotts: Chestnuts and Abel-trees', could be seen 'projecting their beauty in the Water.'[33] Projecting off the approach are several counter walks running to the north and south. Survivors from this period include the sweet chestnuts on cross avenues in the area now known as Bushwood.[34] St Mary's Avenue, which lies north of the Basin and now connects Wanstead High Street with the park, is likely to have formed part of Josiah's network of avenues recorded to the north but none of the first plantings survive.[35]

East of the house, an avenue continues along the main axis towards the River Roding (*see* Fig 1.2). This avenue is likely to have been created in conjunction with the approach, but appears wider, with a triple

Fig 1.5
View of the Glade looking
west, Wanstead Park.
[Hannah Armstrong]

plantation on its north and south sides. Commonly known by locals as the Glade, it remains a notable feature of the landscape (Fig 1.5). It is unknown which species were originally planted along this avenue; they seem to have been removed after the rebuilding of Wanstead House in c 1713 and do not appear in later views (*see* Figs 5.1 and 5.5–5.6). A bank in the earth, however, marks the original inside line of this avenue.[36]

The plantation of avenues at Wanstead formed an important basis for the late 17th-century landscape. Although Evelyn's *Sylva: or a discourse of Forest Trees* (1664) is credited for introducing the term 'avenue' as 'the principal walk to the front of the house or Seat' into the English language, the avenue was by no means a new feature of the English garden.[37] Tree-lined drives, much like avenues, were associated with ceremonial routes, and were a feature of Tudor palaces such as Nonsuch and Twickenham Park.[38] The plantation of avenues to create such an approach to Josiah's manor at Wanstead is likely to have been intended to build anticipation and evoke a sense of drama, while displaying the level of grandeur associated with the great Tudor palaces of England.

The avenues at Wanstead are also likely to have been influenced by European garden design. Italian Renaissance architect Andrea Palladio (1508–80), for example, paid close attention to tying the building with its surroundings by creating a strong central axis running through the landscape.[39] Such techniques can be seen at the Villa Emo at Fanzolo, built between 1555 and 1565, where the avenue appears to run straight through the landscape into the house. In France, baroque gardens adopted similar features, most notably at the Château de Versailles where André Le Nôtre's (1613–1700) designs for the Tapis Vert proved highly successful. Indeed, many French landscape designers advocated the use of avenues. André Mollet's (d 1665) *Jardin de Plaisir* (*Garden of Pleasure*) (1670) described the avenue as 'most necessary to adorning houses' and in 1672, René Rapin praised their use, stating 'for nothing without them is pleasant made.'[40] Such European splendour is sure to have inspired Josiah's decision to introduce avenues at Wanstead.

Crucially, an avenue helped to emphasise the house as a pivotal point in the landscape and, by doing so, illustrated the exceptional wealth and power of the owner. They are among the earliest examples of the Child family expressing their dominance over the land. Furthermore, the avenues provided visitors to the grounds with impressive views of the house from various points within the landscape. Among a series of anonymous views produced *c* 1730 and formerly attributed to Charles Catton the Elder (1728–98), is an aerial perspective of the estate taken from the east (*see* Fig 5.5).[41] This view shows how the central avenue planted by Josiah played an important part in the 18th-century landscape experience, guiding a visitor's gaze from the foot of the straight canal towards Wanstead's east elevation.

Alternatively, avenues provided long vistas from the house. Mollet's *Garden of Pleasure* describes the prospect of the landscape provided by avenues: 'when the doors of the house are open'd, one may see from one end to the other, as far as our sight will extend.'[42] Avenues could thus frame and lead the eye towards particular landscape monuments designed to serve as 'eye catchers'.[43] The central avenue in Kip and Knyff's *View to the east*, for example, leads the visitor's eye towards the canal and River Roding (*see* Fig 1.2). In the anonymous view from the east, an avenue on the right leads towards the Fortification Island and Ornamental Waters, while that on the left runs towards where the Grotto Boathouse was erected in the 1760s (*see* Fig 5.5). Although these 'eye catchers' were later additions to the landscape, Josiah's introduction of avenues made it possible for such developments to occur.

A comparison between Kip and Knyff's views of Wanstead and a plan produced by John Roque in 1735 indicates that Campbell's mansion, begun *c* 1713, stood directly on the site of Josiah's Elizabethan manor (*see* Figs 1.2–1.4 and Fig 5.1). This is likely to have been because the new plantations of avenues leading up to the old building dictated where the new house should be built. Josiah's plantations can therefore be interpreted as his way of leaving his mark on Wanstead. By effectively preparing the grounds for his descendants, Josiah was ensuring that any new house was built in what was considered the ideal location by the estate's founder.

Fishponds

Kip and Knyff's *View to the west* and *View to the east* depict ponds on both sides of the house. However, as these views postdate Josiah's ownership, we must remember that some may be later additions. The four small rectangular ponds on the east side of the house, for example, seem more in keeping with the formal gardens created by George London in *c* 1706. The two semicircular fishponds flanking the approach to the former manor in Kip and Knyff's *View to the west* are sure to be those mentioned in contemporary accounts by Evelyn, Gibson and Harris (*see* Fig 1.3).

John Evelyn commented on Josiah's 'making of fishponds' in 1683; but it is possible that these ponds existed in some form during Leicester's ownership. Leicester's household accounts for 9 April 1585 record a payment made to 'the fisherman at Wanstead'.[44] Evelyn's comments may therefore refer to a feature that Josiah modernised, improved and expanded, rather than an entirely new one.[45]

Visitors' inclusion of them in their accounts of Josiah's gardens suggests that they were considered noteworthy features. Fishponds served several important roles, all of which were integral to the reputation of Josiah and the estate. Traditionally, fishponds primarily served a utilitarian function, providing the estate with a source of food. In 1691, Gibson estimated that the fish stock at Wanstead was worth £5,000, suggesting that the ponds at this property could provide copious amounts of fish.[46] Roger North's *A Discourse of Fish and Fish-Ponds* (1714) draws attention to the fishponds' more symbolic qualities, claiming that the supply of fish could help bind local society together: 'You may oblige your Friends and neighbours, by making presents of them, which from the countryman to the King is well taken.'[47] Much like kitchen gardens, the inclusion of fishponds in the garden could thus be an effective means of demonstrating an owner's active involvement in the husbandry of his estate.

Fishponds could also facilitate the important estate duty of entertaining family and guests through the leisured pastime of fishing. Again, this is evident from North's comments: 'there is advantage enough in the mastery of fish, from the diversion, not to speak of the employment that it brings to a family.'[48] Although the fishponds were later modified to form the large Basin we know today, they nonetheless remained a prized feature of the gardens at Wanstead. In 1755, Sir Horace Walpole, 4th Earl Orford (1717–97), wrote to Richard Bentley about his visit to Wanstead and referred to the fishponds: 'I could not help telling my Lord Tilney, that they could certainly burn the poor fish for the gold, like old lace.'[49]

Josiah's landscape improvements at Wanstead were well received by contemporaries, as illustrated by Harris's poem of 1702, which praised the gardens:

Say, ye Westphalian Wanstead's blooming Groves
And Chestnut Avenues, the verdant Loves
Once, Now the Heralds of Josiah's Name;
Ye's ever crescent Monuments of Fame![50]

Financing the landscape improvements at Wanstead

The purchase of a historic and illustrious estate was one achievement, but the funding of major improvements to it was quite another. Evelyn's description of the 'planting of avenues' and 'making' of fishponds in 1683 suggests that work on the gardens at Wanstead was underway around this time. Gibson's description of the avenues and fishponds indicate that the works were finished by 1691. We can therefore establish that Josiah's landscape scheme was implemented between 1683 and 1691. By this time, significant career and financial advancements had occurred.

After the death of his second wife, Josiah married Emma, widow of Sir Francis Willoughby of Wollaton, Nottinghamshire, and second daughter and co-heiress of Sir Henry Barnard, a Turkey merchant of Stoke and Bridgnorth in 1676.[51] The couple had two sons, Barnard (1677–98) and Richard (1680–1750). The marriage was advantageous for both parties. Josiah's wealth and recent acquisition of a landed estate made him a suitable candidate for marriage and ensured Emma's long-term financial and social security. Emma's first marriage to Willoughby had provided her with a generous dowry for widowhood and, crucially for Josiah, a substantial third portion.[52]

The East India Company

Josiah's career in the East India Company was arguably the most significant source of wealth behind the development of Wanstead's landscape. Although he had provisioned the East India Company ships early in his career, Josiah did not become a shareholder until 1671. When purchasing Wanstead in 1673, he owned only two per cent of stocks. Two years later, Josiah had become a leading shareholder, owning £12,000 worth of stock.[53]

Josiah sat on the General Court of the East India Company from 1674 until his death in 1699. In 1677, Josiah and Thomas Papillon were excluded from the directorate by King Charles II: 'they are persons that have behaved very ill towards his majesty, and that therefore his Majesty should take it very ill of the Company if they should choose them.'[54] The decision to prevent Josiah and Papillon from running for governor positions was likely due to their involvement in the attacks on the chief minister, Sir Thomas Osbourne, 1st Earl of Danby, in 1675. Josiah's temporary exclusion taught him an important lesson. In order to maintain control within the East India Company and obtain support from the king and Parliament, Josiah needed to secure a close alliance with the Crown. In 1678, he purchased a baronetcy for approximately £1,200. The title was symbolic of Josiah's newfound support and loyalty towards King Charles II and secured his position within the East India Company.

Meanwhile, Josiah's shares had increased to £23,000, the largest single block of shares, thereby giving him total control of the company.[55] Josiah's newfound loyalty to the Crown meant that, by October 1681, he was able to bribe Charles II successfully with 10,000 guineas, in the hope of obtaining a royal charter. The charter was confirmed in May 1682. Thereafter, 10,000 guineas became an annual bribe: 'by his great annual presents he could command both at court and in Westminster Hall what he pleased.'[56] Josiah's growing power and fortune is reflected in his holdings, which, in 1680, amounted to £17,000 and, by 1691, were recorded at £51,150.[57] He served as governor between 1681 and 1683, and as deputy governor from 1684 until 1686, and again between 1688 and 1690.

Aside from its financial contribution, it is difficult to determine precisely what effect the East India Company had upon Wanstead's appearance. Throughout the long 18th century, company profits provided merchants with generous funds for country house purchases, refurbishment and interior design.[58] East India Company director

Elihu Yale (1649–1721) displayed many exotic treasures at his London residence, including broadcloths, silks and muslins, as well as India Japan cabinets.[59] In 1751, naturalist George Edwards referred to a painting of Josiah's, 'little Indian buffalo', belonging to Sir Hans Sloane: 'his Picture was an Original from Nature, done by Order of the late Sir Josiah Child, of Wanstead in Essex, Bart. The Creature was a Present to Sir Josiah, from the East-Indies.'[60] Josiah's prominent position in the East India Company suggests he was likely to have been the recipient of exotic gifts on several occasions. Unfortunately, late 17th-century accounts of Wanstead do not describe the interior, nor do inventories or household accounts for Josiah's manor survive. It seems likely that in addition to exotic pets, domestic goods, such as those acquired by Yale, would have also been displayed at Wanstead.

Descriptions of Wanstead House during the early 18th century reveal that the furnishings were modern, designed in keeping with Colen Campbell's classical mansion and William Kent's baroque interior scheme. However, John Macky's 1722 account refers to chinoiserie wallpaper, silks and damask hangings on the ground floor.[61] In 1748, Pehr Kalm described Wanstead's furnishings as 'what varieties the East and West Indies can supply.'[62] Such furnishings by the mid-18th century were not unusual and, without the relevant evidence, it is difficult to determine confidently whether these were heirlooms or later acquisitions, deemed appropriate for display at an estate founded by one of the East India Company's most powerful merchants.

Landed investments

Josiah's will of 1696 lists several other properties belonging to the East India magnate: Cannons, Royden, Halstead, Bois Hall, Abells, Temple Hall and Parslowe.[63] Reference throughout the will to Wanstead as a 'mansion', while other properties are described as 'manors', indicates this was Josiah's most valuable asset. These landed estates, together with his properties in London and Jamaica, were a major source of wealth, providing an annual income of around £7,300.[64] Although the income generated from these properties did not necessarily contribute to the purchase of Wanstead or the landscape's initial development, they no doubt helped to maintain it. The ownership of other landed estates in the county helped to expand Josiah's influence in Essex, where he had held important political roles including commissioner for assessment between 1670 and 1680 and again in 1689–90, deputy lieutenant in 1688, and sheriff in 1688–9.

Significantly, several of these properties were purchased during the 1690s, when Josiah's position in the East India Company was weakening. The Glorious Revolution of 1688 terminated the short reign of Catholic King James II and established the Dutch Protestant King William III and Queen Mary II as England's new monarchy. Josiah's allegiance to the Tory party and his close association with the former Catholic court, had become unfavourable. Unlike his former associate, Thomas Papillon, Josiah resisted the enlargement and reconstruction of the company into the New East India Company (chiefly made up of Whigs). A long series of attacks, led by Papillon, were launched on Josiah, forcing him gradually to withdraw from the company. In 1698, he wrote to Papillon, 'now when I am going out of the world, I am neither concerned for the Old Company nor the New one.'[65] The investment in other landed properties during the 1690s therefore reflects a more cautious, older Josiah, making efforts to ensure that the family's wealth and the security of Wanstead did not rely entirely on the East India Company.

Josiah Child's legacy as founder of the Wanstead estate

The fortunes Josiah amassed through the East India Company, his marriage to Emma Willoughby, and landed investments not only contributed to the development of Wanstead, they elevated Josiah's social status above and beyond his mercantile peers. Crucially, Josiah's baronetcy and wealth provided his daughters with generous marriage settlements and dowries. In 1682, his daughter Rebecca married Charles Somerset, Lord Herbert of Raglan and heir to the 1st Duke of Beaufort, at the chapel at Wanstead, with a marriage portion of £25,000.[66] By marrying into landed gentry, the Child family had successfully penetrated the highest echelons of society.

The wedding was lavishly celebrated at Wanstead. Among guests in attendance were the ambassadors to the Sultan of Bantam, who had arrived in London two months earlier as the first diplomatic visitors to England from any Indonesian state.[67] Their visit attracted great attention. They received a gun salute at Tower Hill and were invited to several audiences with King Charles II at Windsor.[68] Their presence at Rebecca Child's wedding indicates that Wanstead was among the important receptions the ambassadors attended while touring the capital. Moreover, it highlights the role that ownership of a family seat like Wanstead could play in cementing advantageous relationships through acts of generous hospitality and entertainment.

Josiah died on 22 June 1699 and was buried at the parish church, St Mary the Virgin, north of Wanstead House and visible in Kip and Knyff's *View of Wanstead to the north (in two sections)* (*see* Fig 1.4). Josiah's fortune at the time of his death was estimated to be around £200,000, making Harris's romantic description of him as the 'Albion Croesus', the famously wealthy king of Lydia in 560–46 BC, most fitting.[69] His role as founder of the Wanstead estate was commemorated throughout the Georgian era. In 1724, Daniel Defoe commented

> Sir Josiah Child, as it were, prepar'd it in his life for the design of his son, tho' altogether unforeseen; by adding to the advantage of its situation innumerable rows of trees, planted in curious order for avenues and vistos, to the house, all leading up to the place where the old house stood, as to a center.[70]

In 1789, the *New London Magazine* praised Josiah's contribution by commenting: 'This noble seat was prepared by Sir Josiah Child, who added to the advantage of a fine situation a vast number of rows of trees, planted in avenues and vistas leading up to the spot of the ground where the old house stood.'[71]

Despite his high status and success, Josiah was widely unpopular and generally perceived as ruthless and manipulative. Correspondence written by Cassandra Willoughby, Duchess of Chandos (1670–1735), illustrates the fraught relationship he shared with his step-children and refers to several episodes when he attempted to manipulate their mother and take advantage of the family's financial assets:

> Sir Josia Child had hitherto received the produce of my brothers estate out of which he would allow my bro[r] such a proportion as he thought fit for him to spend, which was less than my bro[r] would now be contented with: and therefore in order to get possession of more he made complaint to the Lord Chancellor Jevffrys, and also brought into court and action against Sir Josia Child for cutting down timber and for other waists upon my mothers' jointure.[72]

Publicly, his reputation was equally poor. His conduct at court, Parliament, and in business affairs suggests he was fickle and principally concerned with his own self-interest and advancement. Evelyn described him as 'most sordidly avaricious.'[73] His aggressive foreign policy as governor of the East India Company came under fire during the Anglo-Mughal war of 1686–9. After the loss of Bantam to the Dutch in 1682, Josiah was eager to gain British trading privileges across the Mughal Empire. As deputy governor, Josiah arrogantly rejected new tax measures and commanded East India troops to engage in an attack against the Mughal Army in an attempt to seize control of several port cities on the western coast of India. The British faced a humiliating defeat against the Emperor Aurangzeb and the war cost the company dearly. Josiah's role in what came to be known as 'Child's War' demonstrates the degree to which he was willing to exploit power overseas to further his own interest, one of these, of course, being his personal estate at Wanstead.

When evaluating Josiah's legacy in the 21st century, one must consider his aggressive foreign policies as governor of the East India Company and as a founding member of the Royal Africa Company and owner of a Jamaican slave plantation. Goods imported to Great Britain by the East India Company were exported and exchanged for slaves on the West African coast. These slaves were then transported by the Royal African Company. Josiah's leading position in both the East India Company and Royal African Company thus places him at the centre of this booming, exploitative market. Furthermore, Josiah's ownership of a Jamaican plantation demands attention. Unfortunately, detailed evidence regarding the plantation has yet to come to light. His will of 1696 makes no reference to it and there is no evidence that connects the family with activity in Jamaica after his death.[74] Nonetheless, his active participation in the Atlantic slave trade undoubtedly advanced Josiah's wealth and the developments of Wanstead during the late 17th century.

Emerging scholarship has drawn attention to the relationships between the Atlantic slave trade and East India Company and the erection, acquisition, renovation and occupation of the English country house.[75] Wanstead was no exception. A lack of known archival sources means that this topic requires further investigation in order to fully assess its financial impact on Wanstead, but considering its establishment in this

Fig 1.6
Monument to Josiah
Child at the Church
of St Mary the Virgin
(c 1700), attributed to
John Nost.
[Wanstead Image
Archives]

light contributes to a wider understanding of how trade, exploitation and colonialism in the Caribbean and Asia shaped the English country house.

Contrary to public perceptions of Josiah both then and now, his descendants nonetheless saw fit to erect a somewhat ostentatious life-size marble monument in the parish church to commemorate his legacy (Fig 1.6).[76] The monument depicts Josiah standing on a pedestal, looking upwards, with his left hand on his side while the other points downwards. He is clothed in ancient Roman dress, a symbol of civic virtue, used in comparable monuments, such as Grinling Gibbons' monument to Viscount Campden and his family (1688) in Exton and Michael Rysbrack's monument to Thomas, 1st Baron Foley, and his family (c 1735–8) at Great Witley.[77] Josiah's coat of arms is displayed above his head and, at his feet, lies the reclining figure of his second son, Barnard, who had died from a bout of smallpox in 1698. Barnard's gaze is fixed with reverence towards his father. Flanking the figures on either side are putti (cherubs), one holding a human skull, a *memento mori*, the other with a torch in one hand and a trumpet in the other. On either side of the monument, two women mourn the loss of father and son.

Its location within the parish church made the monument accessible to a public as well as a private audience, manifesting continuity of name, title, and of ownership of the Wanstead estate on which the church stood. While access to Wanstead House was selective, few would have been turned away from the parish church. When the medieval church was rebuilt in the late 18th century, the monument was relocated into the new church where visitors, seated under the patriarchal gaze of Josiah's effigy, continue to be reminded of his once powerful hold over the land. Throughout his ownership, Josiah was eager to adopt the lifestyle of the landed elite, while maintaining links with his mercantile fortune; the monument in St Mary's Church commemorates his success in doing so in no uncertain terms. With the start of the new century, it was now the turn of his descendants to continue Josiah's legacy.

Notes

1   Latham 2003, 490.
2   ERO D/DGn 181, Conveyance, 5 December 1661.
3   Latham 2003, 490.
4   Previous scholars have maintained that Child's father was a London merchant who acquired considerable wealth, bought property in Bedfordshire, and was appointed sheriff of Bedfordshire in 1640. However, although Child was the son of *a* Richard Child, a merchant of Fleet Street, there is no evidence to suggest he was in fact the son of the sheriff, nor that he came from any substantial wealth. See Grassby, 'Child, Sir Josiah'. Letwin 1959, 12.
5   Beer 2000, 305.
6   Grassby, 'Child, Sir Josiah'.
7   Letwin 1959, 12; Hotson 2006, 138.
8   Grassby 2001, 146.
9   Grassby, 'Child, Sir Josiah'.
10   Ibid.
11   Ferris, 'Child, Josiah'.
12   Letwin 1959, 16.

13 Grassby, 'Child, Sir Josiah'; Ferris, 'Child, Josiah'; Sheridan 1994, 271.
14 Sheridan 1994, 271.
15 Zahedieh 2013, 72.
16 Zahedieh 2013, 71.
17 Zahedieh 2013, 72; Letwin 1959, 16.
18 Beer 2000, 305.
19 Hunt 1996, 3.
20 Harris 1702, 5.
21 Goldring 2014, 206.
22 Goldring 2016, 16.
23 Goldring 2016, 17.
24 Ibid; Hyrn 1823, 599–600.
25 Tallis 2018, 171.
26 Adams 1995.
27 Parsons 1973, 318.
28 Wrightson 2000, 303.
29 Beer 2000, 305.
30 Gibson 1796, XII, 186–7.
31 Harris 1702, 3.
32 Gibson 1796, XII, 186–7; Debois Landscape Survey 1990, Appendix B, F.1.01.
33 Harris 1702, 34.
34 Jeffery 2003, 12.
35 See Debois Landscape Survey Group 1990, Appendix B.
36 See Debois Landscape Survey Group 1990, Appendix B, A.10.02.
37 Anon, 'avenue, n'.
38 Couch 1992, 174.
39 Ibid.
40 Rapin 1672, 3; Mollet 1670, 2.
41 There are three unattributed views of Wanstead and its landscape that appear to have been produced around *c* 1730. The similarity in style suggests they are the work of one artist and intended as a series of views of the estate. The 1822 sale catalogue attributes two of these views to Charles Catton the Elder. See day 9, lot 136, 'A Bird's-Eye View of the Grounds and Country round Wanstead House' and day 9, lot 179, 'Gentlemen going out Hunting, with their Attendants and Dogs', now catalogued in the Parham House collection as 'A view of Wanstead House, Epping Forest.' A third view taken from the north-east, behind the greenhouse, is not recorded in the sales catalogue but seems to be by the same hand. This view features in J Harris 1979, *The Artist and the Country House*, and is attributed to Charles Catton the Elder or Samuel Scott. The appearance of the landscape suggests that these paintings were produced shortly after the formal gardens were removed in *c* 1730. The inclusion of wings in 'A view of Wanstead House, Epping Forest' at Parham House, suggests the view was produced around the same time as the Rocque plan, when this idea was still expected to be implemented. Charles Catton the Elder was born in 1728. It is therefore not possible that he produced these views. Harris's alternative attribution to the marine painter Samuel Scott seems unlikely as there are no contemporary references to his work at Wanstead, nor does he feature in the 1822 sale catalogue. The artist for these views therefore remains unidentified and will be referred to as anonymous throughout this study.
42 Mollet 1670, 1.
43 Dalton 2009, 3–37.
44 Adams 1995, 239.
45 Beer 2000, 306.
46 Gibson 1796, XII, 186–7.
47 Williamson 1995, 34.
48 North 1713, 73.

49   LWL Horace Walpole to Richard Bentley, the Earl of Strafford, 17 July 1755.
50   Beer 2000, 305.
51   Grassby, 'Child, Sir Josiah'.
52   Wood 1958, 124.
53   Grassby, 'Child, Sir Josiah'.
54   Letwin 1959, 17.
55   Grassby, 'Child, Sir Josiah'.
56   Ibid.
57   Ibid.
58   For further information about how empire in Asia shaped British country houses, their interiors and the lives of their residents, see Finn and Smith 2018.
59   Bingham 1939, 313.
60   Edwards 1751. Thanks to Richard Arnopp for providing this transcription.
61   Macky 1722, 21.
62   Lucas 1892, 176.
63   NA PROB 11/451/289, Will of Sir Josiah Child of Wanstead, Essex, 1696.
64   Grassby, 'Child, Sir Josiah'.
65   Papillon 1887, 88.
66   Roberts 2015, 10.
67   Stern 2001, 69.
68   Jones 1982, 9.
69   Harris 1702, 33.
70   Furbank and Owens 1991, 40.
71   'A Description of Wanstead House in Essex', *New London Magazine*, April 1789, 210.
72   Wood 1958, 119.
73   Beer 2000, 305.
74   [https://www.ucl.ac.uk/lbs/estates/, accessed 5 April 2021]. Thanks to Chris O'Donnell for sharing his research findings with me on the connections between Wanstead and the Atlantic slave trade.
75   See Wills and Dresser 2020; Brown 2010; Finn and Smith 2018.
76   The monument to Josiah Child has been attributed to John Nost (d 1729). According to local historian Winifred Eastment, the first attribution to Nost comes from H Kerr, 'East of Aldgate', *Country Life*, 22 October 1943, 728–31. However, there is no evidence as to how this attribution was made. Other sources which refer to Nost included Anon 1947, *Seven Centuries of Wanstead Church*; Eastment 1969; Craske 2007; and Pevsner 1969. Biographer Richard Grassby suggests the monument was 'probably by Nost'. The Oxford Dictionary of National Biography for Nost, however, does not refer to Josiah's monument. Records for Nost held in the Witt Library do not refer to the monument either. The attribution therefore remains speculative.
77   See Baker 2000; Baker 2014; Craske 2007; Eustace 1982.

Part 2

Richard Child, Viscount Castlemaine and 1st Earl Tylney, 1704–50

Fig 2.1
Sir Richard Child of Wanstead (c 1705) by Jonathan
Richardson, oil on canvas, 76.2 × 63.5 cm.
[Miles Barton]

2 Setting the stage: Richard Child and 'the noblest gardens now in the kingdom',[1] 1706–13

Richard Child's inheritance of the Wanstead estate

Towards the end of his life, Josiah was embroiled in a conflict over his eldest son and namesake's marriage to Elizabeth Cooke, daughter of the wealthy London merchant, Sir Thomas Cooke, in 1691. The dispute between father and son proved so troublesome that his will of 1696 instructed that Josiah the younger would receive no more than the £4,000 settled on him at the time of his marriage. His fortune and estates, including the mansion at Wanstead, were instead settled on his two youngest sons from his third marriage, Barnard (1677–98) and Richard (1680–1750). When Josiah died in 1699, Richard, the youngest of the three, became sole heir. Josiah's ownership of several landed estates in Essex, combined with his role as governor of the East India Company and his estimated wealth of £200,000, provided a substantial inheritance.

In 1703, Richard's wealth was advanced further when he married Dorothy Glynne (1682–1744), the daughter and heiress of judge John Glynne of Henley Park, Surrey, and his wife, Dorothy, the daughter of Francis Tylney of Rotherwick. The marriage was an advantageous match that enabled Richard eventually to make claim to Dorothy's family name in consequence of her inheritance of the Tylney estates in 1731, assuming the name of 1st Earl Tylney by an Act of Parliament in 1733. One year after Richard's marriage to Dorothy, Josiah the younger died from pleurisy and Richard succeeded as 3rd Baronet. In addition to his inheritance, Richard received the £4,000 settled on his step-brother, bringing his annual income to approximately £10,000.[2]

Richard's considerable wealth was such that he arguably felt little need to embark on a career in trade as his father had done. Aside from the ownership of shares, connections with the East India Company diminished shortly before Josiah's death in 1699. Richard did, however, profit from the growing slave trade by investing in the South Sea Company, founded in 1711 as a private-public partnership in the shipment of slaves to South America. Unlike many of his peers, who suffered tremendously from the company's financial crash of 1720, Richard managed to avoid financial oblivion. In 1722, Daniel Defoe commented:

> South Sea was a general possession, and if my Lord Castlemain was wounded by that arrow shot in the dark it was a misfortune. But it is so much a happiness that it was not a mortal wound, as it was to some men who once seemed as much out of the reach of it. And that blow, be it what it will, is not remembered for joy of the escape, for we see this noble family, by prudence and management, rise out of all that cloud, if it may

be allowed such a name, and shining in the same full lustre as before.
This cannot be said of some other families in this county, whose fine
parks and new-built palaces are fallen under forfeitures and alienations
by the misfortunes of the times and by the ruin of their masters' fortunes
in that South Sea deluge.[3]

To what extent the investment contributed to Wanstead remains unclear.
John Macky notably described Wanstead as one of the leading 'South
Seats', which now adorned the villages outside the capital.[4] Richard also
seems to have been familiar with Robert Knight, cashier of the South
Sea Company, with whom he attempted to orchestrate a marriage for
his daughter Lady Emma. There is, however, little to suggest that he was
actively involved in the company.[5] Regardless, Richard's investment in the
South Sea Company once again draws attention to the role that colonial
expansion and the Atlantic slave trade seem likely to have played in
Wanstead's early development.

During the early years of his inheritance, Richard demonstrated
a 'certain political flexibility' as he attempted to secure his status and
legitimacy among the landed elite.[6] Between 1708 and 1710 he served
as a Tory member of the Houses of Parliament, representing Maldon
in Essex. He was also a member of the October Club, a group of Tory
parliamentarians active between 1711 and 1714. Richard's association
with the Tory party during this period is likely to have been due to their
dominance during Queen Anne's reign. Their sympathy for her Anglican
religious views and their greater tolerance of a royal prerogative in
Parliament had won them favour with the Crown and thus were the better
party for the socially ambitious Richard to align himself with.

Richard's political allegiances, however, began to shift towards the Whig
party when the Hanoverian, George Ludwig, Elector of Hanover (1660–
1727) succeeded to the throne after Queen Anne's death in 1714. George's
succession was made possible by the 1701 Act of Settlement, which had been
designed to secure a Protestant monarch when the risk of a Catholic Stuart
uprising remained very real. The Act was strongly backed by a Protestant
Whig party, eager to restrain the power of the monarchy and protect the
partnership between Crown and Parliament that had been established
during William and Mary's reign in the late 17th century. Their support for
the new Hanoverian regime established the Whigs as the favoured party of
the new era and may account for Richard's political transition.

Richard's efforts to further his social status can also be seen in his
attempt to purchase a peerage from George I's mistress, the Duchess of
Munster, in 1715. On learning of his application for peerage, English
ministers wrote to chief minister, James Stanhope, 1st Earl Stanhope
(1673–1721), demanding that a decision be deferred until the next session
of Parliament. This was perhaps to test Richard's loyalties to the new
king as well as his obedience in the House of Commons. Consequently,
it was not until 1718 that Richard could claim his new title as Viscount
Castlemaine of County Kerry and Baron Newtown of County Donegal.[7]
The Child family had no known connection with Ireland and there is no
evidence to suggest he ever took up his seat in the Irish House of Lords.
His purchase of an Irish peerage may have been due to the simple fact
that it was cheaper than a British title. Alternatively, the granting of an

Irish title may have been perceived as a compromise by the ministers who opposed Richard's requests. Nonetheless, the purchase of peerage was significant, allowing Richard to consummate the process begun by his father in the late 17th century of entering the landed elite.

'A Design worthy of an English baronet, and equal to the greatest French Peer': the early Wanstead landscape (1706–c 1713)[8]

A young wealthy heir like Richard is likely to have sat for several portraits. Unfortunately, the 1822 sale catalogue does not identify any of the sitters in the portraits displayed at Wanstead. The scandal surrounding Wanstead and the family at the time of the sale may have given the sellers cause to believe that the collection would sell more easily without bearing any association to the Child/Tylney family. The plainly described portraits have since become dispersed, making it difficult to establish the identities of sitters and the whereabouts of these lost portraits.

A portrait attributed to Jonathan Richardson (1667–1745) and listed as lot 328 on day 10 of the sale, however, has recently been identified as one of the few known portraits of Richard (Fig 2.1). Richardson had trained under John Riley (1646–91), who painted Richard's father, Josiah in 1685 (see Fig 1.1). The success of his portraits established Richardson as one of the nation's most popular portrait painters and made him an obvious choice of artist for the young heir. The apparent age, style of wig and clothes worn by the sitter suggest it was painted around the time of his inheritance, and his confident gaze communicates a readiness to take on his role as custodian of Wanstead.

Ownership of a family seat was a key requirement of the landed elite. Richard's inheritance provided him with the necessary requisite, but further improvements were required if Wanstead was to compete with the nation's leading houses. The additional funds received by Richard when he inherited his half-brother's marriage settlement in 1704 set in motion the next phase of landscape improvements at Wanstead. These works were necessary to complete his father's late 17th-century landscape scheme but, most importantly, they provided the first opportunity for Richard to make his mark on the estate.[9]

Wanstead's proximity to London attracted many visitors and it was subject to great scrutiny. *Flora Triumphans*, an anonymous poem dedicated to Richard, highlights the public attention Wanstead was already receiving at the time of its publication in 1712: 'Hither all equal Homagers resort: CHILD to his Rural Bowrs ev'n calls a COURT.'[10] It was therefore necessary that the landscape complied with contemporary taste and impressed visitors with its modernity. In c 1706, Richard employed George London (1640–1714) of the acclaimed Brompton Park Nursery. London and his business partner Henry Wise (1653–1738) were in great demand, supplying garden designs, choice plants and specimen trees to wealthy and elite gentlemen including Lord Weymouth at Longleat, the Duke of Devonshire at Chatsworth, and the 3rd Earl of Carlisle at Castle Howard. London also served as royal gardener to Queen Anne at Hampton Court and Kensington Palace. London's popularity derived from his ability to give an English twist to the European baroque gardening style practised by André Le Nôtre, whose gardens at Versailles had considerable influence over the English gardener. London's association with the most elite landscapes of the period made him a fitting choice for employment at Wanstead.

The two sources that best illustrate the early 18th-century landscape at Wanstead are the anonymous poem published in 1712, *Flora Triumphans*, and the engravings by Kip and Knyff, produced in *c* 1708 and published in the 1728 publication, *Le Nouveau Theatre de Grande Bretagne* (*see* Figs 1.2–1.4). The publication of these views provided Richard with an opportunity for self-aggrandisement on a major scale. As discussed in the previous chapter, the publication of these views meant that they were subject to exaggeration. Like the study of Josiah's late 17th-century landscape, these views must be carefully considered. The process of cross examining the views with contemporary descriptions and archaeological evidence, however, reveals that the engravings provide a broadly accurate impression of the early 18th-century scheme.

Parterres

Let us begin our journey into the early 18th-century landscape by imagining we are a visitor to Wanstead in *c* 1708. Exiting Wanstead manor, we would descend the short flight of steps situated beneath the eastern front of the house and visible in the top left corner of Kip and Knyff's *View to the north* (*see* Fig 1.4) and enter into an elaborate arrangement of parterres. The parterres at Wanstead are a prominent feature in all three of Kip and Knyff's views (*see* Fig 1.2–1.4) and are described in *Flora Triumphans* as a 'fragrant field, each Rich/The Noblest Growth from Nature's tend'rest womb.'[11]

A parterre was an ornamental arrangement of flowerbeds, consisting of intricate, symmetrical patterns, commonly found in French and Dutch garden design during the 17th century and made popular in England by London's superb execution of them at Chatsworth House (1699), Longleat (1695) and Hampton Court (1702). Like the English Elizabethan knot garden, parterres were typically planted near the house and designed for viewing from an elevated perspective. Kip and Knyff's *View to the north* shows how Wanstead's long gallery looked directly onto the parterre garden, allowing this feature to be admired from inside the house. Alternatively, passers-by could appreciate the intricacy of their design from the elevated pathways running alongside the garden.

The style of parterre depicted at Wanstead is typical of those attributed to London and engraved by Kip and Knyff for their 1707 publication, *Britannia Illustrata*. It is possible that they were not an entirely new feature. Although late 17th-century accounts of Josiah's gardens provide no commentary on them, remnants of the Elizabethan knot garden commissioned by Leicester in 1584 may have existed when Josiah Child purchased Wanstead in 1673.[12] Their absence from visitor accounts of the period was perhaps due to their poor condition or old-fashioned appearance. The parterre gardens depicted by Kip and Knyff and described in *Flora Triumphans* may therefore have been a feature improved and expanded by London in order to modernise Wanstead.

The four parterres at Wanstead consisted of two different designs. The two closest to the house represent what was commonly known as a *plain parterre* or *parterre à l'angloise*. This design was recognised as English due to its simplistic use of large areas of turf with scrolled and embroidered designs and gravel. During the late 17th century, many English gardens abandoned such a design as they sought instead to mimic French landscape architect André Le Nôtre's landscape scheme for Louis XIV at the Palais de Versailles. Queen Anne's introduction of the *parterre à l'angloise* at Hampton Court and Kensington by London's associate, Henry Wise, had revived its popularity, causing English gardens to incorporate such features once again.[13] Its introduction at Wanstead was, therefore, very much on trend.

The design of the parterres situated towards the bowling green were more in line with those found in Franco-Dutch gardens, consisting of a more complex geometric design of hedges and topiary. These are likely to have been influenced by London's visits to Versailles, where he had met Le Nôtre. The creation of a more English-style parterre alongside the Franco-Dutch versions suggests that gardeners in this country were gradually returning to, and redeveloping, their own distinct national style.

Canals

Running through the centre of London's ornate parterre garden was a straight canal with an octagonal basin and fountain at its eastern end. In 1712, the author of *Flora Triumphans* praised this canal as 'the Garden's central monument' and celebrated its aesthetic qualities by describing its 'silver streams, Brighten'd like CYNTHIA by SOL'S borrowed Beams.'[14] This gives the reader an impression of the waterwork as dazzling, near mystical even. Its creation in conjunction with a second canal further east created a false perception of one continuous stretch of water running through the estate. Like the extensive network of avenues, the canals helped emphasise the extent of the family's land ownership. The inclusion of the lower canal in Kip and Knyff's *View to the east* marks the beginning of what was to become a 30-year project in creating an elaborate artificial lake system at Wanstead (*see* Fig 1.2). This canal remains *in situ* in what is now known as the Ornamental Waters (*see* Fig 0.9).

The introduction of the canals at Wanstead can be attributed to gardener Adam Holt (b 1691), who had supplied plants to Henry Compton, Bishop of London (d 1713), and set up a nursery business in nearby Leytonstone.[15] Evidence to support Holt's employment at Wanstead appears in a diary entry written by Smart Lethieullier, a neighbour of the estate, in 1713: 'Mr Adam Holt (Sir Richard Child's Gardiner) began June 3rd 1713 to put Gardiners & Labourers into my field and to make a Canal'. This suggests that work on the canal was in its early stages or expected when Kip and Knyff produced their view in *c* 1708.[16] Holt's introduction of canals at Wanstead was likely to have been inspired by Le Nôtre's gardens at Versailles, which featured an impressive network of canals and displayed highly skilful hydraulic engineering through the use of fountains. They were, therefore, in keeping with the introduction of avenues and parterre gardens.

Bowling green

Proceeding along the canal, we would arrive at the bowling green, situated at the end of the parterre garden and canal and depicted in detail in Kip and Knyff's *View to the north* (*see* Fig 1.4). When John Macky visited Wanstead in 1722, he commented:

> At the bottom of the Canal is a Bowling-green, incircled with Grotto's & seats, with antique statues between each seat: And this bowling green is separated by a balustrade of iron from another long green walk which leads you to another long Canal at nigh half a mile distance.[17]

The bowling green at Wanstead was intricately designed, furnished with classical sculpture, and surrounded by elegant wrought iron fencing by French ironworker Jean Tijou (1689–1712), who produced screens at Hampton Court, Kensington Palace and St Paul's Cathedral.[18] Its central positioning complied with recommendations outlined by John James' *Theory and Practice of Gardening* (1712), a translation of Dezallier d'Argenville's original 1709 publication, which described bowling greens as 'one of the most agreeable compartments of a Garden and, when tis rightly placed, nothing is more pleasant to the eye.'[19] Its design appeared much like those described by James as 'composed'.[20] James advised that a 'composed' bowling green should be 'placed at the End of a large parterre, or to fill up a great Space, that you would keep entirely open', again recalling the positioning of the bowling green at Wanstead.[21] Kip and Knyff's *View to the north* shows that the eastern end of the bowling green formed a raised terrace from which views of the Long Walk (the Glade), canal and wider landscape could be enjoyed (*see* Fig 1.4). This demonstrates how landscape features were designed to interact with one another.

The introduction of a bowling green at Wanstead was necessary to accommodate one of the many gentlemanly pursuits that Richard would have been keen to provide for guests. Indeed, Kip and Knyff took care to depict the bowling green at Wanstead in use by a group of gentlemen. The demonstration of virtuous activities such as exercise and sociable exchange in an estate landscape was a convenient means of justifying expense.[22] Although James' publication provides a range of design suggestions for bowling greens, a common feature to all was a surrounding walkway and the provision of seating from which spectators could view the game. Evidence of seating and a surrounding pathway can be seen in Kip and Knyff's *View to the north* (*see* Fig 1.4). These features allowed passers-by to witness the gentlemanly leisure activities taking place at Wanstead without interrupting the experience of the grounds for others.

Significantly, the bowling green was perhaps the only feature at Wanstead not to have been subject to European influences. London described it as a distinctly English phenomenon which, contrary to other landscape features, was 'a compartment of a Garden which the French learn'd of the English, & therefore have no other word to express it but Bowlingrin'.[23] Its inclusion in the Wanstead landscape was therefore perhaps something of a patriotic gesture.

Wilderness gardens, mazes and mounts

East of the bowling green ran the Long Walk (the Glade), introduced by Josiah Child in the late 17th century. Kip and Knyff's *View to the east* shows that a series of quincunx avenues had now been introduced on the north and south side of this avenue (*see* Fig 1.2). These smaller avenues cut through large areas of wildernesses and led to small clearings known as wilderness gardens. The earliest example of a wilderness garden had been designed by John Evelyn for the Earl of Essex at Cassiobury in Hertfordshire in 1668. London closely studied Evelyn's garden at Cassiobury and was inspired by it when creating gardens for the Earl of Rochester at New Park in Surrey in 1692 and Cholmondely Hall in *c* 1704. It is likely, therefore, that their inclusion at Wanstead was among the features designed by London.[24]

Kip and Knyff's *View to the east* records the introduction of two circular mazes on the north and south sides of the Long Walk (the Glade) (*see* Fig 1.2). Later views of the estate reveal that these were replaced with clearings after the rebuilding of the house in *c* 1713 (*see* Fig 5.1). East of the mazes are two mounts with ziggurat paths, from which a visitor could take in the impressive view of the landscape. These are referenced in *Flora Triumphans* as 'now raising' with an 'artful spiral Circle round.'[25] Evidence for the mounts survives in the landscape, albeit in poor condition, and they are visible in the 2012 Lidar scan of the park (*see* Fig 0.8).[26]

The greenhouse

The views by Kip and Knyff reveal that two landscape buildings had been erected at Wanstead by this time: a banqueting house to the north of the bowling green and a greenhouse, also to the north, overlooking London's ornate parterre garden and canal (*see* Fig 1.4). In 1712, the author of *Flora Triumphans* described the greenhouse at Wanstead as

> A stately PILE [which] oerlooks the Crystal Fount
> Views in the watry Glas its Towry Front:
> Not all for proud Magnificence; no less
> A Sanctuary too reliev'd distress.[27]

When Colen Campbell published an elevation and plan of the greenhouse in the first volume of *Vitruvius Britannicus* in 1715, he stated that the structure was 'designed by another hand' (Fig 2.2).[28] John Harris has attributed its design to the architect William Talman (1650–1719), whose greenhouses at Chatsworth, Dawley and Wimpole Hall closely resemble that at Wanstead.[29] Moreover, Talman was closely associated with London, designing buildings for several of his gardens, making Harris's attribution all the more convincing. Demolished at the end of the 18th century, evidence for the greenhouse exists in the views by Kip and Knyff, the elevation and plan in *Vitruvius*, several visitor accounts and a 1799 sale catalogue.

In 1724, Daniel Defoe described the greenhouse at Wanstead as 'an excellent building, fit to entertain a prince.'[30] Indeed, Kip and Knyff's *View to the north* depicts an attractive structure, two storeys high and eleven bays wide, with one-storey, gabled side pavilions at its eastern and western ends (*see* Fig 1.4). The building features a pitched roof and a panelled parapet above the central five bays. The elevation of

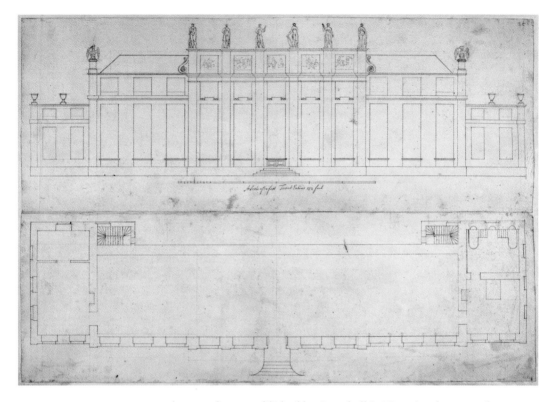

Fig 2.2
Design for Wanstead House,
London, for Sir Richard Child,
Viscount Castlemaine: plan
and elevation of a greenhouse
(c 1715) by Colen Campbell.
[RIBA Collections]

the greenhouse published by Campbell in *Vitruvius* shows an almost
identical structure, without the gables on the side pavilions (*see*
Fig 2.2). Although the *Vitruvius* elevation depicts the greenhouse as
rendered in stone, a description by French traveller Pierre Fougeroux in
1728 describes a brick façade.[31] Kip and Knyff's *View to the west* depicts
dormer windows behind the parapet (*see* Fig 1.3). These windows
are likely to have lit the three fruit rooms described in the 1799 sale
catalogue and accessed via the east and west staircases visible in the
Vitruvius plan (*see* Fig 2.2).[32]

Campbell's plan of the greenhouse shows that the building served
utilitarian and leisurely purposes, verifying Defoe's description of the
greenhouse as 'both useful and pleasant.'[33] The principle focus of the
greenhouse was to accommodate exotic plants and fruit trees during
the cold winter months. On his visit in 1728, Fougeroux described the
greenhouse as 'filled with trees inside and garnished with stands of
shrubs and plants of India palms, aloes etc.'[34] These were displayed in the
long greenhouse room which extended the entire width of the central
block and was lit from large south-facing sash windows. During the
winter, these plants were maintained by some form of indoor heating.
The poet of *Flora Triumphans* refers to 'winter urns', and Defoe similarly
described the greenhouse as being furnished with stoves.[35]

In spring, the doors to the greenhouse would be opened and the
vast collection of exotic plants poured out onto the surrounding lawn.
Flora Triumphans refers to such an event: 'See from those walls her
fair battalion pour/To their revisited dear Sun once more.'[36] One of the

anonymous views of Wanstead, formerly attributed to Charles Catton the Elder, records such an event by depicting a collection of orange trees in the foreground, on land close to where the greenhouse stood (*see* Fig 5.6). The emptying of the greenhouse freed up space for entertaining guests in the summer, perhaps imitating the summer supper parties hosted by Queen Anne at the Orangery at Kensington Palace.[37]

It is unclear when and how purchases for the greenhouse were made, but a significant amount was acquired from Bishop Compton's gardens at Fulham Palace after his death in 1713. In 1751, Sir William Watson provided an account of Compton's garden to the Royal Society, stating 'upon the death of bishop Compton, all the green-house plants and more tender exotic trees were, as I am informed by Sir Hans Sloane, given to the ancestor of the present Earl Tylney at Wanstead.'[38] The acquisition is likely to have come about via Adam Holt, who worked at Fulham around the same time he was employed at Wanstead. When the greenhouse and its contents were sold in 1799, the frontispiece for the sale catalogue boasted '100 orange and lemon trees, shrubs of various sorts, pine plants, melon frames.'[39] The sale of the greenhouse and its stock amounted to £671 7s 10d, suggesting that the building and its contents remained a prized feature of the landscape up until its dismantling in 1799.[40]

The plan of the greenhouse published in *Vitruvius Britannicus* shows that the building was designed to provide Wanstead's owners and their guests with a place of retreat (*see* Fig 2.2). At its western end was a chamber with two sunken baths on the north wall and a bed and a fireplace to the south. The pavilion at the opposite end of the greenhouse did not feature baths but does depict a fireplace. Fougeroux described a display of numerous prints, probably in this space, suggesting the room was intended for the comfort of Wanstead's owners and their guests.

The landscape improvements implemented by Josiah and Richard show little East Indian influence. However, the greenhouse is certainly representative of the types of goods made available by the expansion of trade with the east. Its construction can therefore be interpreted as a monument of sorts to the Childs' links with the East India trade and was thus most fitting for a landscape developed from a mercantile fortune.

*

Kip and Knyff's *c* 1708 views of Wanstead depict an impressive landscape that complied with contemporary tastes and imitated the gardens of the nation's royal palaces and leading country houses. The publication of *Flora Triumphans* in 1712 and the publication of views by Kip and Knyff (albeit not until 1728) represent how London's designs transformed the Wanstead landscape into 'a Design worthy of an English baronet, and equal to the greatest French Peer.'[41] Wanstead was one of London's last commissions prior to his death in 1711. According to Stephen Switzer, an employee of Brompton Park Nursery until about 1714, the designs London produced for Wanstead were equal in splendour to those featured at Blenheim and, furthermore, earned London the title of 'The English *Le Nôtre*.'[42] The successful completion of the landscape set the stage for the rebuilding of the old Elizabethan manor to commence.

Notes

1 Campbell 1715, I, 4.
2 Watson and Knights 2002.
3 Furbank and Owens 1991, 41.
4 Macky 1722, II, 5.
5 Thanks to discussion with Georgian Green.
6 Watson and Knights, 'CHILD, Sir Richard'.
7 Gibbs 1913.
8 Switzer 1718, 84.
9 Special thanks for a discussion with Richard Arnopp regarding Richard Child's inheritance.
10 Anon 1712, 3.
11 Anon 1712, 5.
12 Adams 1995, 178.
13 Jacques 2014, 206.
14 Anon 1712, 8.
15 Cowell 1998, 214–17; Jeffery 2003, 26.
16 ERO D/DK F1, Part of a Diary of a Wanstead Quaker, c 1707–15.
17 Macky 1722, 23.
18 Remnants of this fencing survives at the current Wanstead Bowling Club.
19 James 1712, 62.
20 Ibid.
21 Ibid.
22 Cabe Halpern 1992, 200–1.
23 London and Wise 1706, I, 430.
24 See J Harris 1986.
25 Anon 1712, 10.
26 Thanks to Richard Arnopp for a discussion of the Kip and Knyff views. See also discussion for view in Appendix II, Compass Archaeology 2013.
27 Anon 1712, 13.
28 Campbell 1715, 4.
29 Harris 1982, 43.
30 Defoe 1724 , I, 137.
31 NAL Fougeroux 1728, 103–6.
32 ERO SALE/B284.
33 Defoe 1724, I, 137.
34 NAL Fougeroux 1728, 103–6.
35 Anon 1712, 13; Defoe 1724, I, 137.
36 Anon 1712, 13.
37 Skelton 2010, 56.
38 Watson 1751–2, 243. Thanks to Richard Arnopp for providing a transcription of this source.
39 See ERO SALE/B284, frontispiece.
40 ERO SALE/B284.
41 Harris, 'London, George'.
42 Switzer 1718, I, 84.

3 Colen Campbell and the rebuilding of Wanstead House, 1713–17

U ntil the early 18th century, maintaining the old manor at Wanstead had served the Childs well, enabling the family to associate themselves with the estate's rich history and advance their social status. Prioritising landscape over architectural improvements had also been prudent and followed the principle stated in French landscape designer André Mollet's *Le Jardin de Plaisir* (1670), 'one ought to begin to plant even before the building of the House so that the Trees may become to half growth when the House shall be built.'[1]

The improvements carried out during the late 17th and early 18th centuries produced a setting suitable for an ambitious building scheme to flourish. In 1712, the author of *Flora Triumphans* described the house at the centre of the Wanstead landscape as a 'venerable pile.'[2] Nonetheless, it paled in comparison to the nation's great power houses of Chatsworth (1686–96) and Dryham Park (1698–1704) by William Talman (1650–1719) and Castle Howard (1699–1712) and Blenheim Palace (1705–24) by John Vanbrugh (1664–1726). The construction of a new mansion, equal in scale to England's leading country houses, would provide the socially ambitious Richard with the opportunity to display fully his wealth and strengthen his position among the landed elite.

Prior to the rebuilding of Wanstead House in *c* 1706, Richard had employed William Talman (1650–1719), one of the nation's most distinguished architects of the late 17th-century country house, to design a greenhouse for the formal gardens designed by George London. Talman's designs, however, displayed a mix of French and Italian baroque character, an increasingly unpopular style associated with French Absolutism, Catholicism and Papal Italy. Richard's decision to avoid a style that was rapidly falling out of favour may explain why Talman was overlooked in favour of the then aspiring architect Colen Campbell in *c* 1713.

Colen Campbell (1676–1729) was the eldest son of Donald Campbell, brother of Sir Hugh Campbell of Cawdor Castle in Nairn, Scotland. He likely graduated from the University of Edinburgh in 1695 and, having formally trained as a lawyer, was admitted to the Faculty of Advocates in 1702. Shortly afterwards, the young lawyer attempted to secure the office of Master of Works, a post previously held by Scottish architects William Bruce (1630–1710) and James Smith (*c* 1645–1731). Although unsuccessful, his attempt to secure this position marked the start of Campbell's transition into the architectural profession. It is unclear what inspired the career change, but the tight-knit circle of professionals in Edinburgh is sure to have exposed a young and ambitious Campbell to the city's leading architects.[3]

Details of Campbell's early architectural training are vague but, by 1712, he had received his first commission, Shawfield Mansion in Glasgow (demolished 1792), for banker and fellow clansman Daniel Campbell of Shawfield.[4] Campbell's design was a simple manor house in a Queen Anne style, seven bays wide and two storeys high with a central triangular pediment. Soon after its completion, Campbell migrated south. Like many Scottish professionals, he was eager to take advantage of the opportunities available in London after the Acts of Union between England and Scotland in 1706/7.

It is possible that Richard and Campbell met through London's elite social network. Like his father, Richard is likely to have resided at his London townhouse regularly on account of his positions in Parliament as MP for Maldon between 1708 and 1710 and then Essex between 1710 and 1734. Shortly after arriving in London, Campbell is known to have associated with the architect William Benson (1682–1754), who assisted Campbell in finding wealthy clients and with whom he later worked as Deputy Surveyor of Works.[5] Benson was well connected; his brother-in-law was Henry Hoare (1677–1725), a wealthy banker who is certain to have moved in the same social circles as Richard.[6] While we can only speculate on the circumstances behind their initial encounter, Richard's employment of Campbell provided him with an architect keen to undertake a major commission for a nouveau riche client.

Inspiring a classical design for Wanstead House

The first design for Wanstead is a pencil drawing dated 1713, shortly after Campbell's arrival in the capital (Fig 3.1). The design for the front elevation is a simple unbroken rectangle, 200 feet wide, with a rusticated ground floor and a raised *piano nobile* or Principal Grand Floor. The five central bays are fronted with a hexastyle Corinthian portico, 'the first yet practiced in this manner in the Kingdom'.[7] Adorning the balustraded parapet are classical statues and urns. Although the design looked back to Vanbrugh's baroque designs for Castle Howard and Blenheim Palace for inspiration, its façade was strikingly pure, emphasising the beauty of geometric balance and symmetry.[8] Campbell's proposal to rebuild the house in this manner was distinctly modern.

The ambiguity surrounding Campbell's early architectural training makes his use of the classical style intriguing. According to a petition submitted to King George I in 1715, he had 'studied Architecture here and abroad for several years.'[9] It is unclear, however, whether Campbell had undertaken a Grand Tour by this date. The decision to incorporate classical motifs into his design for Wanstead may instead have been linked to his association with the well-known Scottish architect James Smith (c 1655–1731).[10] Campbell appears to have been familiar with a collection of drawings belonging to Smith depicting Classical Italian architecture. Some of these drawings were by Smith himself; others were acquired in Rome during the 1660s or 1670s. Smith's designs were clearly influential and later used as a model

Fig 3.1
Unexecuted design for
Wanstead House, London, for
Sir Richard Child, Viscount
Castlemaine: elevation of the
west front (1713) by Colen
Campbell.
[RIBA Collections]

for Campbell later in his career. Campbell is likely to have purchased these drawings when Smith was facing financial difficulties after his governmental post ceased after the Act of Union with England was passed by the Scottish parliament in 1707.[11] It is Campbell's association with Smith and his familiarity with the architect's work that indicates his early exposure to the classical ideas incorporated into his designs for Wanstead.

Campbell's designs for Wanstead may also have been inspired by Benson's designs for Wilbury House in Wiltshire (1709). Wilbury House is widely credited as the first Palladian house in England. According to Campbell, its design was influenced by Inigo Jones (1573–1652), the 17th-century architect initially responsible for introducing the Palladian style to England through his designs for the Banqueting House in Whitehall (1619–22) and the Queen's House in Greenwich (1616–18).[12] The Palladian style championed by Jones derived from the buildings of Italian Renaissance architect Andrea Palladio (1508–80) and his renowned publication *Quattro Libri* (1570). Palladio's design principles were, in turn, inspired by the Classical forms, symmetry and proportions associated with the ancient Roman architect, Vitruvius (80–15 BC).

The Palladian movement under Jones was cut short by the onset of the Civil War in 1642. After the restoration of King Charles II in 1660, it was the grandiose European baroque style that dominated national architecture. By the early 18th century, the successes of the wars with France (1689–97), the War of the Spanish Succession (1702–14) and The Acts of Union between England and Scotland in 1707 gave rise to a renewed nationalistic sentiment. Many felt that the country needed a new style, divorced from any association with its former Catholic monarchs and Catholic Europe.

Poised to inherit the British throne under the terms of the Act of Settlement (1701), the House of Hanover recognised the need to adopt an aesthetic sympathetic to a new Protestant nation. The rational style of Palladianism that Jones had attempted to introduce a century earlier and which celebrated simplicity, form and order was well suited to Protestant philosophy. Moreover, its association with the ancient Roman architect Vitruvius made it highly appealing for members of the elite who perceived Augustan Rome as the golden age of enlightenment. It was therefore the style adopted for several court buildings in Hanover by the future king of Great Britain, George Ludwig, the Elector.

The anticipation of a Hanoverian succession brought ambitious British noblemen, merchants and politicians to Hanover, all with the hope of gaining favour with the expectant heir.[13] Benson was one of the many to make the journey and was inspired by the Hanoverian display of Palladianism. Returning to England in c 1707, it seemed logical and practical, even, that he adopted the Palladian style for his designs at Wilbury. Given his familiarity with the architect, it is perhaps unsurprising that Campbell applied some of the design motifs used by Benson when designing Wanstead.

The Wanstead commission was beneficial to both employer and employee. For Campbell, it provided him with the opportunity to demonstrate his ability to produce designs which incorporated the increasingly popular classical style. For Richard, the rebuilding of Wanstead was necessary for his own advancement, although it is unclear if he had any design input. There is no evidence to suggest he ever undertook a Grand Tour or that he possessed any rich architectural knowledge. Barbara Arciszewska states that the selection of an architectural model for the construction of a family seat was never guided by aesthetic concerns but instead was driven by the desire to conform with the tastes of the elite.[14] It is unlikely, therefore, that the design for Wanstead reflected any specific stylistic agenda on Richard's part. Fortunately, Richard's employment of Campbell and the designs produced for Wanstead House were soon made famous by their inclusion in *Vitruvius Britannicus*, an ambitious publication and the first of its kind to promote British architecture.

Colen Campbell and *Vitruvius Britannicus* (1715)

As work on Wanstead was underway, Campbell had become involved in *Vitruvius Britannicus*. The publication was a collaborative effort between London print dealers David Mortier, Peter Dunoyer, Joseph Smith and Andrew Johnston. All four had been involved in the publication of Kip and Knyff's *Britannia Illustrata* in 1707 and Captain John Slezer's *Theatrum Scotiae*, another collection of country house views, in 1693. The release of these publications had generated interest in topographical views of estates around the country and *Vitruvius Britannicus* was to provide a more detailed architectural survey of these sites.

In addition to providing a survey of existing architectural masterpieces, the first volume of *Vitruvius Britannicus*, published in 1715, featured designs by Campbell in the modern classical style. His designs for Wanstead featured early in the publication, just pages after views of Inigo Jones's Banqueting House and the Queen's House at Greenwich. The opportunity to publish designs for Wanstead in a new national style allowed Campbell to advertise himself to the notable list of peers who had subscribed to the publication in advance. His rather presumptuous decision to include proposals for the Duke of Argyle, the Earl of Llay (later 3rd Duke of Argyle) and Lord Percival show that Campbell was certainly not shy about making his ambitions for patronage known.

Vitruvius Britannicus has long been understood as a Palladian manifesto and Campbell's involvement as critical to its successful promotion.[15] This argument rests on the claim that Smith, Dunoyer, Mortimer and Johnston recruited Campbell as an architectural draughtsman to execute classical designs during the final stages of production in order to rival Giacomo Leoni's upcoming translation of Palladio's *Quattro Libri*.[16] It is speculated here that Leoni's project was viewed as a threat to *Vitruvius*, with both publications vying to be the first in England dedicated to Palladio's architectural treatise.[17]

Recent scholarship, however, has disputed the idea that the publication was intended as a Palladian manifesto.[18] The combination of Campbell's classical designs with those supplied by baroque architects Christopher Wren (1632–1723), Talman, Nicholas Hawksmoor (1661–1736) and Vanbrugh suggests that the publication was a more eclectic affair.[19] An investigation into the drawings for engraving for *Vitruvius Britannicus* has established that Campbell was responsible for producing almost all the drawings for engraving as well as the introductory material and description of plates, far too great a workload to have been produced at the final hour.[20] This instead suggests that Campbell was involved from an early stage and drawing on a variety of architectural influences when gathering material for the publication.[21] Furthermore, it is argued that Campbell's lack of professional experience at this time makes it less likely that he was specifically sought out to support a Palladian agenda.[22]

In line with this argument, interpreting *Vitruvius Britannicus* as a Palladian manifesto risks overestimating the intentions behind Campbell's early designs, particularly those for Wanstead. The classical façade of Wanstead House, described by one contemporary as 'a fine [a] piece of architecture as any in Italy', has long been taken as a key example of 18th-century English Palladianism.[23] Such a label is somewhat misleading. Certainly, the design was influenced by the classical Palladian ideas being reintroduced in Great Britain during the early 18th century; however, the variety of architectural details identified in Campbell's designs for Wanstead reveal that, in fact, he experimented with a range of ideas and influences for his first major commission.

Moreover, the Wanstead commission occurred at a time when few Palladian country houses had yet been built in England and so, aside from observations made from Smith's collection of drawings or Benson's designs for Wilbury, there was a limited amount in the way of classical architecture for Campbell to draw upon. It is thus too restrictive to identify Wanstead with one specific architectural style. The house should not be taken as representative of a single architectural movement, but rather as the product of a conjunction of idioms present in England at the turn of the century.

Wanstead is therefore best understood as a house that marked the onset of English Palladianism, rather than a Palladian building in its own right.[24] The Palladian movement did not fully take hold in England until Richard Boyle, 3rd Earl of Burlington (1694–1753), returned from his Grand Tour in 1719, and with buildings such as Burlington's Chiswick (1717), or Campbell's designs for Mereworth in Kent (*c* 1723), based on Palladio's Villa Rotunda, or Stourhead (1721–4), based on Palladio's Villa Emo in Fanzolo, that Palladian ideas truly came into play.

The publication of Campbell's designs for Richard in the first volume of *Vitruvius Britannicus* was a significant milestone in Wanstead's history. Their inclusion alongside images of England's existing architectural masterpieces positioned Wanstead as a national triumph before the house was even complete. The availability of these views helped spread the news – particularly among the elite – that Richard was engaged in a costly (and, as luck would have it, fashionable) transformation.

Colen Campbell's designs for Wanstead House in *Vitruvius Britannicus* (1715)

The designs published for the first volume of *Vitruvius Britannicus* in 1715 included an engraving of the 1713 elevation with an accompanying plan (commonly known as Wanstead I) as well as a revised elevation, plan and section of the Grand Hall and Saloon (Wanstead II). A third design for Wanstead's front elevation was published in the third volume of *Vitruvius Britannicus* in 1725. Eighteenth-century views of the estate and contemporary visitor accounts reveal that it was Campbell's second design that best represents what was eventually built.

Wanstead I
The first design for Wanstead is a more polished and complete version of the 1713 drawing (Fig 3.2). The front elevation is a 200ft long unbroken rectangular block, three storeys high, the Principal Grand Floor raised by a rusticated ground floor. A Corinthian hexastyle portico occupies the five central bays. Access to this portico is by double stairways to either side. At roof level, a balustraded parapet, adorned with urns and statues, extends across the width of the house. Campbell's accompanying text provides little comment on the design itself: 'I was a little confined to the Dress of the Windows, which are without Pediments, and Several other Conveniences being wanting, the following design [Wanstead II] was preferred.'[25]

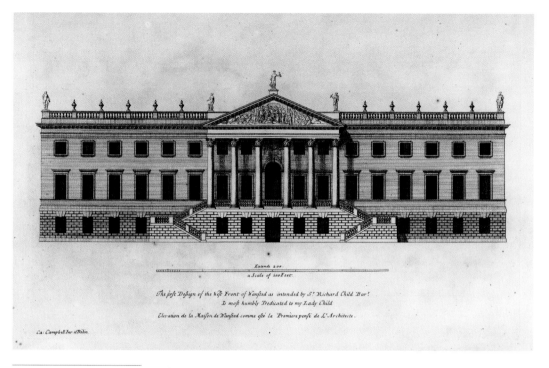

The first Design of the west Front of Wansted as intended by Sr Richard Child Bart
Is most humbly Dedicated to my Lady Child

Elevation de la Maison de Wansted comme este la Premiere pensé de L'Architecte.

Ca: Campbell Inv: etDelin.

Fig 3.2

Unexecuted design for Wanstead House, London, for Sir Richard Child, Viscount Castlemaine: elevation of the west front (1715) by Colen Campbell.

[RIBA Collections]

Wanstead II

Having decided that the original design was neither magnificent nor extensive enough, Campbell's second proposal for Wanstead extended the house by 60 feet and raised its centre from the adjoining wings, removing much of the first storey proposed in Wanstead I (Fig 3.3).[26] Campbell's description for the modified design reads as follows:

> extended 260 Foot, raised from the Court by a large Rustick Basement 15 Foot in Height: The Situation requiring this Height, to afford the State Apartments a Prospect to these excellent Gardens. You ascend from the Court by double Stairs of each side, which land in the Portico; and from thence into the Grand Hall, 51-Foot-long and 36 wide, and in Height the same.[27]

Extending its length and raising its centre transformed the earlier simplistic form into a considerably grander and more imposing façade. The portico to the improved façade was not just a decorative feature. The Corinthian order of Wanstead's hall was similar in size and nearly ranged with that of the portico, making Campbell's creation of a temple-like centre to the house 'pretty forcibly implanted'.[28] According to John Summerson, no previous English house had displayed such spectacular and rational loyalty to Rome.[29] The modified design also featured a cupola above its portico, closely imitating Vanbrugh's baroque country house at Castle Howard. The proposal for a cupola was never realised. Perhaps it seemed clumsy mounted upon Wanstead's elegant design or perhaps its association with the Catholic baroque edifice was considered inappropriate.

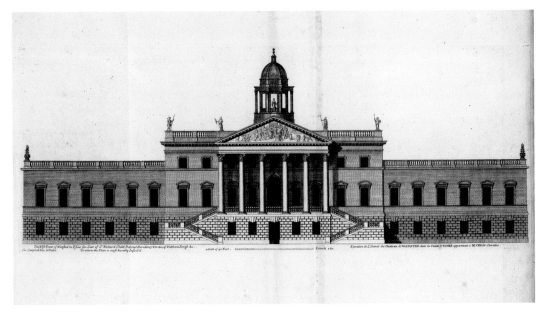

Fig 3.3
Design for Wanstead House,
London, for Sir Richard
Child, Viscount Castlemaine:
elevation of the west front
(second scheme) (1715) by
Colen Campbell.
[RIBA Collections]

Other modifications to the original design included the introduction of Venetian windows in an alternating sequence across the entire length of the *piano nobile*. These appear like those designed by Palladio for the Palazzo Thiene in Vicenza in 1546–58. Later views of the house would confirm that, unlike the cupola, this modification to Wanstead's original design was executed.

Wanstead III

The third elevation for Wanstead House was published in the 1725 edition of *Vitruvius Britannicus*, several years after building work was complete. This design featured two towers flanking the principal façade of Wanstead II. It is possible that the towers proposed were under consideration to provide additional space for Richard to entertain at Wanstead, now that he had been elevated to Viscount Castlemaine in 1718.

Visitors to the estate around this time anticipated such modifications albeit in a varied form. In 1722, John Macky described the 'spacious area' between the Basin lake and the house, 'on each side of which the offices are to be built; the foundations of them are not yet laid.'[30] This suggests that Macky had understood that wings, rather than towers were anticipated. Likewise, French traveller Pierre Fougeroux commented on the likely introduction of wings flanking the sides of the central court.[31] Cartographer John Rocque's 1735 map of Wanstead and an anonymous view once attributed to Charles Catton the Elder and produced in *c* 1730, also depicts these 'wings' (*see* Fig 5.1).

Later commentary and views of Wanstead reveal that, due to insufficient funds, or perhaps a practical realisation that the house was already of a sufficient size, no such additions were made; 'what a building this would be, were the wings added.'[32] Archaeological research such as the 2012 Lidar scan of Wanstead Park reveals the distinct footprint of Wanstead House but shows no evidence of the adjoining wings, confirming they were never constructed (*see* Fig 0.8). The publication of a third design for Wanstead, however, demonstrated further Campbell's architectural abilities and gave rise to ideas adopted for subsequent commissions.

Wanstead's internal layout

Accompanying the two elevations in the first volume of *Vitruvius Britannicus* (1715) were floor plans of the *piano nobile*, the Principal Grand Floor of the house. The first scheme corresponds with the Wanstead I elevation (Fig 3.4). Measuring 200 feet in length, it is comprised of four quarters, with three interlocking rooms positioned on the west- and east-facing fronts. To the north and south, the house is divided into smaller rooms. At the centre of the plan is the Grand Hall, which faced west and was the largest of Wanstead's state rooms, and the Saloon, where a terrace with double stairways led into the gardens to the east.

The *enfilade* passages are continuous throughout the plan and there are four internal staircases. The two staircases adjacent to the Grand Hall were intended for family and guests. Two spiral staircases appear hidden from view to the north and south; these were presumably designed for servants to move freely between floors without intruding on the family and their guests. The use of an *enfilade* floor plan indicates that, although Wanstead's façade was largely classical in its style, its layout was baroque in character and differed considerably from the villa-like arrangements of Palladio's Villa Rotunda that Campbell later imitated for Mereworth Hall in *c* 1720–5.[33]

Fig 3.4

Unexecuted design for Wanstead House, London, for Sir Richard Child, Viscount Castlemaine: plan of the principal floor (first scheme) (1715) by Colen Campbell. [RIBA Collections]

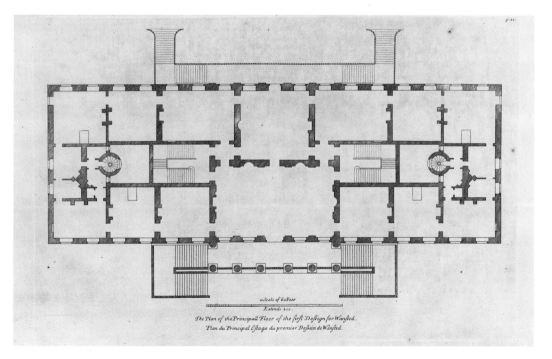

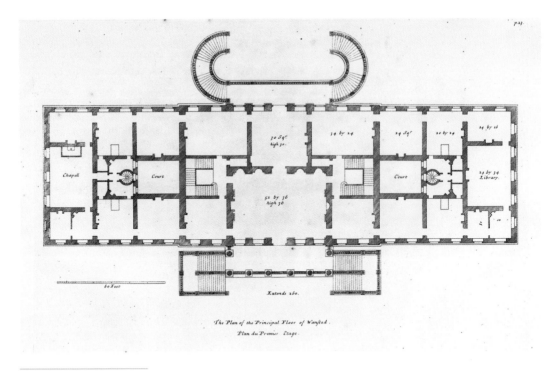

The Plan of the Principal Floor of Wansted.
Plan du Premier Étage.

Fig 3.5
Design for Wanstead House,
London, for Sir Richard Child,
Viscount Castlemaine: plan
of the principal floor (second
scheme) (1715) by Colen
Campbell.
[RIBA Collections]

The second plan presents the layout of the house once Campbell's original design was extended (Fig 3.5). Campbell described this plan, which now featured four apartments of four to five rooms each, as follows:

> the Salon, being an exact cube of 30 Foot, attended with two noble
> Apartments of State, all fronting the Gardens. To the great Court
> are excellent Apartments for Sir Richard and my Lady with great
> Conveniences: And the whole Plan is closed with a decent Chappel in one
> End, and a handsome Library in the other: The Offices are below, equal to
> the Court and the Mezonins above.[34]

The measurements provided for the rooms specify that the Grand Hall remained the largest space in the house, spanning 52 feet high and 36 feet wide; its towering proportions were well suited to the temple-front of the house. The adjoining Saloon measured 30 feet square, and all other rooms around 24 feet square.[35] The plan depicts a library occupying the south wing and measuring 34 feet in length. The proposal for a library here was never realised and instead modified to accommodate the Ballroom. Likewise, the proposed chapel in the north wing is not mentioned in later descriptions, suggesting that it too, was eventually omitted from the design.[36] The executed design for Wanstead established it as one of the largest houses of England. In 1768, Arthur Young compared the rooms of Wanstead with Holkham, Houghton, Blenheim and Wilton. From the number of rooms and size, Young identified Wanstead as second only to Holkham.[37]

Section of the Grand Hall and Saloon

Campbell's section of the Grand Hall and Saloon is the earliest representation of the Wanstead interior. It is one of the few sections to be published in the first volume of *Vitruvius Britannicus* and was by far the most elaborate (Fig 3.6).[38] Its inclusion alongside Campbell's proposed elevation and plan is testament to the Grand Hall's and Saloon's status as central features of the Principal Grand Floor and the formal entry and exit points of the house. Their significance as some of the most impressive rooms belonging to Wanstead House is evident by the numerous visitor descriptions made throughout the 18th century.

The inclusion of a section of the Grand Hall and Saloon suggests Campbell had some input into the interior design of Wanstead House prior to William Kent's (1685–1748) employment in *c* 1720. The section provides a view of the north wall featuring raised decorative moulding and panelling, doorframes and a fireplace. The section shows that, although Campbell placed great emphasis on producing a classical exterior, he was more flexible in his approach to the interior where he applied common characteristics of English baroque interiors of the late 17th century.[39]

Campbell's section hints at the types of decoration expected of a mansion of this kind by including what appears to be a large Classical painting hanging on the north wall of the Saloon. The plan for Campbell's

Fig 3.6
Design for Wanstead House, London, for Sir Richard Child, Viscount Castlemaine: section (second scheme) (1715) by Colen Campbell.
[RIBA Collections]

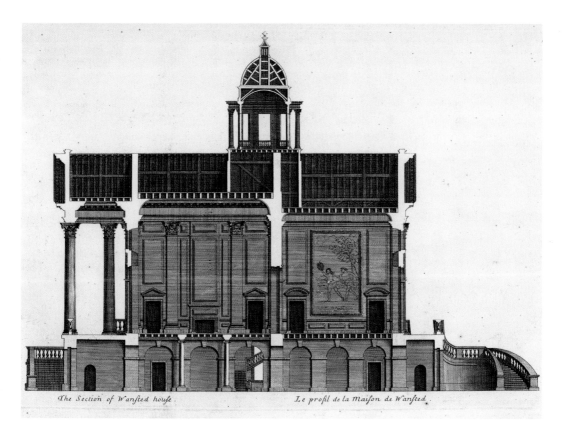

The Section of Wansted house.   Le profil de la Maison de Wansted.

second scheme features niches, presumably designed to accommodate the display of Classical statues. As the following chapter will demonstrate, these decorative schemes were realised during Wanstead's development. Although Campbell was soon to be replaced by Kent, the inclusion of a section in *Vitruvius* was no doubt an attempt to show his versatility and ability to design equally grand interiors for large country houses.

Wanstead House and its influence in English country house building

The earliest record of Wanstead's completion appears in an article for the *Weekly Journal or Saturday's Post* on 20 July 1717, which reported that the Prince of Wales had dined with Richard at the new house. We can therefore establish the period of construction to have occurred between 1713 and 1717.[40] This was comparatively quick when we consider the length of time taken for other houses of the period. Blenheim Palace, for example, was constructed between 1705 and 1722, work being on hold between 1712 and 1716. Castle Howard's central block and eastern wing took around nine years to complete.[41]

Wanstead House was faced in Portland stone and estimated by Horace Walpole as costing around £100,000.[42] Campbell's designs successfully created a classical mansion quite unlike anything seen before in England. The commission helped to establish him as one of the leading architects of his day and led to other important commissions, including the remodelling of Burlington House, London (1718–19), Mereworth Castle, Kent (1722–5), Houghton Hall, Norfolk (1721), and Compton Place, Eastbourne (1726–7). Of all his works, it was his first commission at Wanstead that was considered his finest. George Vertue identified Wanstead among Campbell's best work, while visitors to the house were equally complimentary: 'the stile of architecture ... striking; the whole is of Portland stone, and is esteemed, with justice, one of the most beautiful and magnificent private houses in Europe.'[43]

The publication of *Vitruvius Britannicus* between 1715 and 1725 distributed Campbell's designs for Wanstead in print shops across the country and, consequently, had a major influence upon country house building in the first half of the 18th century.[44] Wanstead's proximity to London also enabled many visitors to travel easily and see the house for themselves, encouraging widespread enthusiasm for Wanstead's architectural beauty. A printed view by George Robertson, published as late as 1781, depicts two male figures in discussion while drawing the house, suggesting that appreciation for Campbell's design continued long after the house was built (Fig 3.7).

The simplicity of the Wanstead design meant that much of the building's influence lay in the fact that such splendour 'required no inordinate skill to imitate', with many houses quickly adopting Wanstead's grand portico to adorn their façades.[45] In addition, the classical features which the house introduced coincided with ideas expressed in the 3rd Earl of Shaftesbury's widely read *Letter concerning the Art, or Science of Design* in 1712. In this, Shaftesbury criticises the state of architecture at the time:

Fig 3.7

A view of Wanstead in the county of Essex, the seat of the Rt. Honble. the Earl of Tylney (1781) by George Robertson, engraving, 29.05 × 44.29 cm. [The British Library]

'tis no wonder if so many noble Designs of this kind have miscarry'd amongst us; since the Genius of our nation has hitherto been so little turn'd this way, that thro' several Reigns we have patiently seen the noblest publick buildings Perish (if I may say so) under the hand of one single court architect.[46]

The 'one single court architect' to whom Shaftesbury refers was Sir Christopher Wren (1632–1723). The association of Wren's baroque style with the Stuart court had arguably helped it to fall out of favour due to the new political structure of early 18th-century Great Britain. Although Wanstead was not entirely a Palladian design, its classical façade appealed to those eager to adopt such ideals once the 3rd Earl of Burlington had promoted the Palladian movement.

The closest derivative of Wanstead House appeared in the reconstruction of the east front of Wentworth Woodhouse in Yorkshire by Thomas Watson-Wentworth, Lord Malton, in 1733 (Fig 3.8). Having approached Burlington for ideas for the design of his east front, the earl was introduced to pictures of Wanstead and he promptly decided to reproduce its façade. Unlike Wanstead, Wentworth introduced additional service wings, extending from the central block. Flanking these wings are the towers proposed in Wanstead III (1725).

Fig 3.8
Wentworth Woodhouse,
east front.
[Wentworth Woodhouse]

At Nostell Priory in West Yorkshire, architect James Paine (1717–89) based his design of a simple rectangular two-storey block over a rustic basement on Campbell's first design for Wanstead (Fig 3.9). Paine's design for a house 13 bays wide and the flattening of its portico, however, created a less imposing façade than that displayed at Wanstead. John Wood the Elder (1704–54) was similarly influenced by Campbell's 1713 design for Wanstead when designing Prior Park in Bath for Ralph Allen (1693–1764) in c 1735 (Fig 3.10). Its main body was designed as a rectangular classical form, two storeys high with a rusticated basement and 15 bays wide, with its central bays set beneath a hexastyle portico. Conscious of the similarity between the two, Allen demanded that the Corinthian columns fronting Prior Park exceeded those at Wanstead by one and a half inches.[47] Other examples of architectural features taken from the Wanstead designs are evident at Houghton Hall (1722), where the proposed towers Campbell designed for Wanstead III were constructed.

Wanstead's influence on country house building during the first half of the 18th century is undeniable, with few able to imitate fully its innovative architectural splendour. According to one contemporary, none of the houses that imitated Wanstead were quite as impressive: 'Mr Colin Campbell was the architect who, by the execution of this noble structure, has given hints to succeeding artists, but has never been rivalled by any imitations.'[48] Campbell's contribution to Wanstead was recognised by the inclusion of his portrait in the portico, now displayed at Compton Place in Eastbourne (Fig 3.11). The completion of the new family seat

Fig 3.9
Nostell Priory.
[National Trust Images/
Matthew Antrobus]

Fig 3.10
Prior Park.
[Picfair]

Fig 3.11
Stucco portrait in ceiling of
Colen Campbell (2011).
[Compton Place, Eastbourne/
Paul Carstairs/Alamy Stock
Photo]

was a pivotal moment in Wanstead's history. Richard had successfully transformed the Elizabethan manor into an architectural masterpiece. It was now time to create an interior that would amaze all who stepped inside Wanstead's classical shell.

Notes

1   Mollet 1670, 2.
2   Anon 1712, 15.
3   O'Hara 2010, 90–1.
4   Goodfellow 1964, 123.
5   Harris 1981, 60.
6   Sambrook, 'William Benson'; Weekes 2018, 18.
7   Campbell 1715, I, 4.
8   Colvin 2008, 214; Summerson 1977, 322.
9   Colvin 2008, 209.
10 For Smith, see Colvin 2008, 755–8; Macaulay, 'Smith, James'.
11 O'Hara 2010, 92.
12 Campbell 1715, I, 5.
13 See Fry 2003, 183.
14 Arciszewska 1992, 41.
15 Summerson 1993, 296; E Harris 1986, 342; Savage 1998, 52; Connor 1977, 14–30.
16 See E Harris 1986, 340–5; Harris and Savage 1990, 139–44.
17 E Harris 1986, 342.
18 Worsley 1995, 95–8; O'Hara 2010; Rumble 2001; Fry 2003, 180–92.
19 Worsley 1995, 98.
20 See O'Hara 2010.
21 O'Hara 2010, 158.
22 O'Hara 2010, 161.
23 See Harris 1981, 62–3. Harris describes Wanstead as a model not only for the 'great house' but in reduced form, for the Palladian villa with wings. Giles Worsley also frequently refers to Wanstead House as a Palladian house throughout *Classical Architecture in Britain: The Heroic Age* (New Haven and

London, 1995). Summerson describes the designs for Wanstead to have been treated in 'the Palladian manner' and states that Campbell must also be credited for inventing what is loosely termed the 'Palladian House'. See Summerson 1993, 200–1.

24 I am grateful to Steven Parissien for a discussion regarding the Palladian movement. Parissien suggests that the term 'Palladian' did not come into use until the 19th or even 20th century, and Burlington and his followers were keen to celebrate Inigo Jones rather than an Italian Catholic. It is therefore unlikely that the term 'Palladian' would have been in use in the first half of the 18th century.

25 Campbell 1715, I, 4.

26 Breman and Addis 1972, 24.

27 Campbell 1715, I, 4.

28 Summerson 1993, 322.

29 Summerson 1977, 322.

30 Macky 1722, 20.

31 NAL Fougeroux 1728, 105.

32 Muilman 1771, 130. Dr. Rob Wiseman's Lidar scan of Wanstead Park shows no evidence that any such additions to the house were made.

33 Campbell's interest in designing villas does not become prominent until volume 3 of *Vitruvius Britannicus* (London, 1725). For further discussion, see Worsley 1995, 106.

34 Campbell 1715, I, 4.

35 Campbell 1715, I, pl. 23.

36 John Macky's 1722 account does refer to a chapel, but it seems likely that his visit occurred while building was under way and the chapel was still anticipated.

37 Young 1768, 281.

38 O'Hara 2010, 117.

39 Worsley 1995, 198.

40 *Weekly Journal or Saturday's Post*, 20 July 1717, np; Thanks to Ray Weekes for sharing this article. See Weekes 2018, 19.

41 Green 2009 (private research).

42 LWL Horace Walpole to Richard Bentley, the Earl of Strafford, 17 July 1755.

43 Vertue 1798, III, 435; Muilman 1771, 228; Shaw 1788, 28.

44 Summerson 1993, 201; Harris 1981, 62.

45 Summerson 1977, 201.

46 Shaftsbury 1732, 400.

47 Peach 1885, 219.

48 Shaw 1788, 28.

Fig 4.1
A View of Wanstead House,
Epping Forest (c 1730)
Anonymous, oil on canvas,
104 × 127 cm.
[Parham House, West Sussex]

4 The interiors of Wanstead House, 1720–50

'Great Britain affords a much larger variety of Curiosities in the Seats, Parks, and Gardens … than any country upon the Face of the Earth.'[1] So wrote John Macky in the first volume to his 1722 work, *A Journey Through England*. Like Kip and Knyff's *Britannia Illustrata* (1707) and Colen Campbell's *Vitruvius Britannicus* (1715), *A Journey Through England* aimed to increase appreciation among the 'nobility and gentlemen of Great Britain' (to whom it was dedicated) of the nation's architectural triumphs and stunning landscapes at a time when many were venturing across the Continent in search of such delights as part of the Grand Tour. Many of the noblemen and gentlemen who read Macky's book will have done so out of inquisitiveness, for included within its pages is one of the earliest known descriptions of Wanstead House.

Macky's account sets the scene for the reader, describing Wanstead's setting as 'a spacious Forest very flat for many Miles, well planted with Trees and full of Deer.'[2] He praised the landscape attributed to George London as 'the finest Gardens in the World', and made his approach to the house by way of the central avenue planted by Josiah Child in the late 17th century (*see* Fig 1.3).[3] By now, the two semicircular ponds fronting Wanstead House had been united to form 'a Pond, or rather a Lake, being a Bason of Water of near half a Mile in Circumference' (Fig 4.1).[4] The section of the avenue which originally cut through the ponds remains submerged beneath the water's surface. In 1816, Humphry Repton commented that the union of these ponds was inspired by Le Nôtre's gardens at Versailles and Vaux la Vicomte:

> experience having pointed out the monotony of a long avenue, where the house is always seen in the same point of view, Le Nôtre boldly conceived an idea, which was realized at Woburn, at Wanstead, and in the front of some other palaces, viz. to obstruct its course by placing a large round basin, or pond, in the middle of the avenue, which not only obliged the road to pass round it, but, by acting as a mirror, shewed the house doubled in its reflection on the surface, and thus increased the importance of its architecture.[5]

The forecourt between the house and Basin was described by Macky as 'a spacious area.'[6] A printed view of the house from *c* 1725 depicts the forecourt as paved.[7] Later views show its north and south sides flanked with obelisks and statues, including two life-size marble statues of Hercules by Laurent Delvaux (1696–1778) and Omphale by Peter Scheemakers (1691–1781).[8]

Upon entering Wanstead House, Macky encountered an interior in its early stages of furnishing: 'when finished, [Wanstead House] will be inferior to few Royal Palaces of Europe.'[9] Such praise undoubtedly put pressure on Richard's ability to create an interior scheme equal to its strikingly modern façade. Furthermore, the success of Campbell's designs published in *Vitruvius Britannicus* had already made Wanstead a popular tourist destination. It was critical that Richard's choice of furnishings met, and even exceeded, public expectations. Although it was common for families in country houses to retain older furniture of lineage, Wanstead was a relatively recent acquisition and new and impressive pieces were required.

William Kent at Wanstead House: adopting a Kentissime scheme

The furnishing of Wanstead House was an ambitious project that occupied Richard until his death in 1750. Colen Campbell's section of the Grand Hall and Saloon at Wanstead, published in the first volume of *Vitruvius Britannicus* in 1715, is the earliest view of the interior and one of the few interior views produced by Campbell. The section suggests that the architect was involved in the initial interior planning of Wanstead House, providing designs for panelling, mouldings and chimneypieces. The door cases depicted in the section, for example, correspond with those painted by the artist Joseph Frans Nollekens (1702–48) in his portrait of Richard and his family in the Saloon in 1740 (*see* Figs 3.6 and 4.12). On his visit in 1771, Peter Muilman described the door cases in the Grand Hall as 'plain, but little carved, though in a good stile', much like those proposed by Campbell.[10] Arthur Marks attributes the doorways and putti depicted in Hogarth's portrait of the family in the Ballroom to Campbell, who executed similar doorways in the Saloon at Burlington House and the Stone Hall at Houghton. To what extent his designs were implemented elsewhere at Wanstead is unknown.[11]

Campbell's employment at Wanstead ceased shortly after building work was complete, when William Kent (1685–1748) replaced Campbell as Richard's key designer. This was possibly due to Campbell's removal from his post as deputy to the Surveyor of Works. In 1718, the architect William Benson had replaced Christopher Wren as Surveyor General, and appointed Campbell as his deputy. The post was, however, short lived. In 1719, the two men falsely claimed that the Palace of Westminster was in danger of collapsing, so that they might replace it with a new classical structure in their own design. Once the House of Lords uncovered the lie, Campbell and Benson were promptly dismissed.[12] Richard's views on the scandal are unknown, but it is likely that these events, which led to Campbell falling out of favour with King George I, meant he was no longer deemed appropriate for employment at Wanstead. The earliest evidence for Kent's employment at Wanstead appears shortly after Campbell's dismissal, in a letter to one of his patrons, Burrell Massingberd, on 3 June 1720: 'I am at present upon ye greatest works in England. Lord Burlington's Ld Duck Shandoe's & Lord Castellmaine's [Richard Child].'[13] The works Kent referred to at Wanstead were the painting of several ceilings on the principal floor, including the Grand Hall, Ballroom, Saloon and Dining Room.[14]

The commission probably came about thanks to Kent's key patron, Richard Boyle, 3rd Earl of Burlington (1694–1753), with whom he resided at Burlington House in Piccadilly after returning to London from his Grand Tour in 1719. At Burlington House, Kent painted several ceilings in the manner of Raphael, whose work he had studied intensively abroad. Burlington's patronage of the young artist led to connections with other supporters of the Whig party, probably including Richard. Richard's employment of Kent may alternatively have been due to a familial tie. Kent's letter to Massingberd in 1720 reveals that he was employed by the Duke of Chandos at Cannons in Middlesex at the same time as the Wanstead commission. James Brydges, the Duke of Chandos, was married to Richard's stepsister, Cassandra, and the connection may have underpinned Kent's employment at both houses.

In addition to Wanstead, Burlington secured Kent with major commissions, not least the patronage of the Crown. In 1722, he painted several ceiling paintings at Kensington Palace. Kent's credibility as a painter, however, was undermined by his weakness in figure drawing. Horace Walpole described Kent's paintings as 'below mediocrity', and his ceiling paintings as 'void of every merit.'[15] The ceiling painting at Wanstead was regarded by Walpole as 'proof of his incapacity.'[16]

It was not until Kent turned his attention to the decorative aspects of his paintings, that his strengths as a designer flourished.[17] At Kensington, his skills were perfected as he designed furniture for several of the palace's state rooms.[18] Over the course of the next two decades, Kent went on to design furniture, buildings and landscapes for numerous wealthy clients at notable country seats such as Sir Robert Walpole at Houghton (c 1725–33), Thomas Coke, 1st Earl of Leicester, at Holkham (c 1729–43), and Richard Temple, Viscount Cobham, at Stowe in Buckinghamshire (c 1728–33), as well as Burlington's own villa at Chiswick (1726–9). Walpole praised Kent's skills as a designer: 'To compensate for his bad paintings, he had an excellent taste for ornaments, and gave designs for most of the furniture at Houghton, as he did for several other persons.'[19]

Kent's progression from painter to designer is reflected in the range of works produced for Wanstead House from 1720. Portraits set in the Ballroom by William Hogarth (1697–1764) in 1728–30 and the Saloon by Nollekens in 1740 depict the family among an array of seating furniture and console tables designed by Kent. Their display in Wanstead's most notable rooms and their inclusion in these important painted commissions denote Kent's pieces as prized possessions.

Kent's long-term employment at Wanstead was typical. At Chicheley he was employed between 1717 and 1724 and at Easton Neston between 1718 and 1734. Clients employing Kent for a substantial period were investing in a major design scheme for their country seats. Such schemes were described by Walpole as 'Kentissime.'[20] Evidence obtained from Hogarth's and Nollekens's portraits, visitor accounts and the 1822 sale catalogue reveal that, like many of his peers, Richard employed a Kentissime scheme at Wanstead.

The success of Kent's designs for the nation's leading country seats and royal palaces established his reputation as the leading designer of the early Georgian period. Yet what appeal Kent held for wealthy clients like Richard remains somewhat of a mystery.[21] His association with

Burlington, who championed the new, fashionable, Palladian style, was certainly advantageous. However, Kent was notably apolitical and his skills as an artist were dubious. Julius Bryant has proposed that much of the appeal was constituted by what he describes as the 'Grand Tour Syndrome'.[22] Kent's ability to recreate environments reminiscent of those experienced in Italy reminded many of his clients of their happy and youthful sojourns abroad. The ambience of a Kentissime scheme was not only indicative of a highly educated gentleman, it evoked a nostalgia that many were eager to indulge in back home. There is no evidence that Richard undertook a Grand Tour, but these experiences were commonplace among the nation's elite and, understandably, an aesthetic he, too, was eager to adopt.

Wanstead was among Kent's earliest commissions and, although he was not the first, Richard was certainly one of Kent's important patrons. The commission provided Kent with the opportunity to demonstrate the full breadth of his artistic ability, from ceiling paintings to seating furniture, tables and chimneypieces. Kent described his ceiling paintings for Richard to be among the 'greatest works in England', a clear indication of the significance the commission held for the artist. For Richard, Kent's contribution was valued from the outset. In 1725, George Vertue described a full-length portrait of the artist by William Aikman, on display in Wanstead's Grand Hall (Fig 4.2): 'Mr. Kent his picture at length done by Mr Eckman & plac'd up in hall of my Lord Castlemaines in Essex, where he has painted much for his Lordship.'[23] Such a tribute was without precedent.

Walpole stated that '[Kent's] oracle was so much consulted by all effected by taste … nothing was thought complete without his assistance.'[24] This suggests that Kent not only designed furnishings for an interior, he also acted as an advisor. The display of tapestry hangings attributed to the Gobelins workshop in the Ballroom at Wanstead was typical of the furnishings Kent advised for his interior schemes.[25] Works that formed part of a Kentissime scheme were therefore not always by the designer's hand.

Visitors to Wanstead House during the second half of the 18th century often described Wanstead's furnishings as outdated. In 1781, Lybbe Powys described the Principal Grand Floor as 'fitted up in the ancient taste.'[26] When the exiled Louis Joseph, Prince de Condé, leased the estate in the early 19th century, he described the rooms at Wanstead as 'decorated in old-fashioned style, and … never used, even though they are richly furnished.'[27] This suggests that Richard's heirs made few changes to the early Georgian scheme.

Fig 4.2
William Kent (c 1723–5) by
William Aikman, oil on canvas,
197.1 × 103.9 cm.
[National Portrait Gallery,
London]

Establishing a Kent attribution

The 1822 sale catalogue does not refer to Kent when describing items of furniture associated with him and, beyond references to Kent's ceiling paintings, there is little evidence that directly supports his furniture designs at Wanstead. How is it possible then to establish a Kent attribution for the furnishings at Wanstead House? Susan Weber, curator of the 2013 exhibition *William Kent: Designing Georgian Britain*, describes Kent as infamous for his lack of documentation and that evidence for Kent's designs is often circumstantial. Fortunately, items associated with the designer are sufficient to identify the hallmarks of his style, such as the scallop shell, a major baroque motif adopted by Kent from Italian palaces.[28] Furniture described in the 1822 sale catalogue and depicted by Hogarth and Nollekens exemplify Kent's heavily baroque, gilded style. Several of these pieces were purchased from the Wanstead sale in 1822 by the 6th Duke of Devonshire for display at Chatsworth House and the Earl of Pembroke for Wilton, where they remain to this day. These items bear close resemblance to other pieces associated with Kent on display at Houghton and Holkham, thereby supporting a Kent attribution.

Publications made during Kent's lifetime also help to identify works by the designer. John Vardy's *Some Designs of Mr Inigo Jones and Mr. Wm. Kent* (1744), for example, displays the breadth of Kent's work and the design motifs he commonly deployed. Further evidence of his designs can be obtained from his decorative ceiling paintings, which often feature furniture designs like those he designed for the country houses where he was employed. His ceiling painting *Banquet of the Gods, of The Wedding Banquet of Cupid and Psyche*, painted for Burlington House in 1719–20, depicts the gods centred around a large gilded table, typical of the style with which he became associated.[29] Similar table designs appear in both the Hogarth and Nollekens portraits of the Child family. The vignettes he produced for Alexander Pope's translation of *The Odyssey* in 1724–5 and John Gay's *Fables* in 1727 also include examples of Kent's early designs, helping us to attribute items to the designer.[30]

The early Wanstead interior: a guided tour

The sale of Wanstead's contents in 1822 and the demolition of the house two years later has dispersed evidence far and wide. Cross-examining visitor accounts, pictorial sources and the 1822 sale catalogues, however, helps to reconstruct the lost interior. Crucially, visitor accounts of Wanstead House often focus on the state apartments belonging to the Principal Grand Floor. This suggests that visitors were granted access to this floor only, making it the most public space of the house. Before we follow in the footsteps of the 18th-century visitor and venture into Kent's opulently furnished state apartments, it is worth taking a moment to explore the lesser-known and more private areas of Wanstead House in order to obtain a more rounded understanding of the interior and how it functioned.

Campbell's second elevation of Wanstead House, published in the 1715 volume of *Vitruvius Britannicus*, depicts three floors: the rustic ground floor (named on account of its rusticated façade), the Principal Grand Floor (or *piano nobile*) and a second floor set above the central nine bays (*see* Fig 3.3). However, Wanstead was built to an even larger scale than views of the house would have us believe. The 1822 sale catalogue reveals that there were in fact two additional storeys, the basement and third floor (set behind the parapet). There is no known plan for the basement, but listings from the June 1822 sale catalogue record ten rooms at this level, including the Kitchen, Bakehouse, Confectioner's room, Dairy, Larder, Storeroom, Lamp room, Stewards' room and Servants' Hall. This is one of the few sources to draw attention to the extensive services and specialist staff required at a house of such grandeur.

Above the basement was the rustic ground floor. Macky's 1722 account is one of the few visitor accounts to describe the rustic ground floor and records a central lobby, from which four apartments of five rooms each were connected, two front-facing and two overlooking the gardens at the rear. If we are to imagine ourselves as a visitor such as Macky, then we are likely to have entered the rustic ground floor via the Stone Lobby, 'supported by fourteen pillars'.[31] The lobby, which appears in Campbell's section directly beneath Wanstead's Grand Hall, was later furnished with several mahogany shield-back hall chairs and pier tables with marble green tops and gilt frames, all of which have been attributed to Kent (Fig 4.3).[32] The north-west apartment, described by Macky as 'finished but not yet furnished', later accommodated Wanstead's chief managing staff including the butler, house steward, land steward and housekeeper. The 1822 June sale catalogue reveals that these rooms were comfortably furnished.[33]

Fig 4.3
Pair of George II hall chairs
(c 1730).
[Christie's Images/
Bridgeman Images]

The rest of the rustic ground floor was intended for family and friends, and furnished in a manner typical of the early Georgian period.[34] Macky's account records the apartment to the right of the Stone Lobby as 'my Lord's [Richard Child's] Apartment'.[35] Here, a number of impressive and costly furnishings were displayed. The Parlour, for example, was furnished with 'French prints, Marble Tables and a Marble Chimney Piece', and the Antechamber with 'Gold and Blue Brocade, Velvet brocaded Chairs and Marble-Tables and Chimney.'[36] Blue was a symbol of piety and sincerity, and a colour commonly found in the upholstery of everyday rooms of the period.[37] Its use in the Antechamber was appropriate and served as a contrasting prelude to the striking display of crimson damask (the principal colour of the early Georgian hierarchy of colours) in Richard's Bedchamber and Dressing Room.[38]

Adjoining Richard's apartment, overlooking the gardens to the rear, was Lady Castlemaine's (Dorothy Child's) apartment. Her Parlour, 'finely adorned with China paper, the figures of Men, Women, birds, Flowers, the liveliest I ever saw come from that country', was a strikingly feminine contrast to the blazing crimson of Richard's Bedchamber.[39] The Antechamber, Dressing room and Closet were furnished with China silk, as was typical of ladies' rooms of the early Georgian period.[40] Since the late 17th century, there had been a growing appetite for Asian goods, made attainable by growing trade. In addition, women were becoming increasingly influential over their domestic sphere and there was more opportunity to experiment with new fashions. Vast collections of Chinese porcelain, for example, were a prized feature of Queen Mary's furnishings at Kensington Palace, and Celia Fiennes described Lady Burghley's closet as 'very fine the wanscoate of the best Japan the cusions very rich work.'[41] As such, the use of Chinoiserie furnishings became associated with the private lives of ladies and the more comfortable and informal spaces of the home.[42] Its use in Lady Castlemaine's apartments was therefore typical for the period.

The other apartment that overlooked the rear gardens was, according to Macky, 'designed for the entertainment of friends', and included a Parlour where several family portraits were displayed, including one of Wanstead's founder, Josiah Child (*see* Fig 1.1), and 'my Lord's [Richard Child's] own picture at full length.'[43] The portrait of Josiah was produced *c* 1685 by John Riley, court painter to William and Mary. The other family portraits described may have been those attributed to royal court painter Godfrey Kneller (1646–1723), and recorded as hanging in the dining room upstairs when Lybbe Powys visited in 1781.[44] If this is so, then it is possible that Kneller's portraits hung in the furnished apartments of the ground floor prior to the completion of the state apartments upstairs.

Contemporary accounts of the house do not venture beyond the Grand Staircase adjoining the Grand Hall, suggesting that the first floor was intended for friends and family only. Here, the June 1822 sale catalogue records five Bedchambers, a Dressing Room and a Nursery with adjoining Sitting Room and Kitchen. The Bedchambers were elegantly furnished with items such as 'an excellent 6ft lofty double screwed four post bedstead, with handsome mahogany carved, and elegant white ground chints cotton furniture, lined green calico and japanned cornices', 'a bordered pier glass in a carved and gilt frame' and two 'handsome white ground chints cotton French rod window curtains.'[45] From the second floor were two service staircases leading to the comparatively demure third floor, where 14 bedrooms accommodated the lowest-ranking servants. No plans or descriptions of this floor are known, but the sheer quantity of rooms and the items recorded in the 1822 sale catalogue indicate that these rooms were cramped and comprised of the most basic furnishings.

The Principal Grand Floor

Having explored the lesser-known areas of Wanstead House, it is now time to explore the Principal Grand Floor. When Arthur Young (1741–1820) published a comparison of the nation's leading houses in 1768, he described the Grand Floor apartments belonging to this floor, as the 'best rooms', superior even to those at Holkham, Houghton, Wilton and Blenheim.[46] Indeed, the abundance of visitor accounts and the representations of the Ballroom and Saloon by leading portraitists Hogarth and Nollekens confirm that Wanstead's staterooms were widely admired throughout the 18th century.

Macky described the Principal Grand Floor as consisting of four apartments with 'five Rooms of state of each side … the whole twenty ending in a long Gallery on the South end, and a Chappel on the north end.'[47] This indicates that the Principal Grand Floor was built largely according to Campbell's second plan (Fig 4.4; see Fig 3.5).[48] The library depicted in Campbell's plan, however, was replaced by a Ballroom or 'long gallery', as described by Macky.[49] The chapel is not recorded in later accounts, suggesting that its brief mention by Macky was based on expectations rather than what had so far been built.

Fig 4.4
Marked-up plan of the Principal Grand Floor at Wanstead House, based on Colen Campbell, Design for Wanstead House plan of the principal floor, second scheme. [Plate 23 from **RIBA Collections** (2020) by Joseph Bacon]

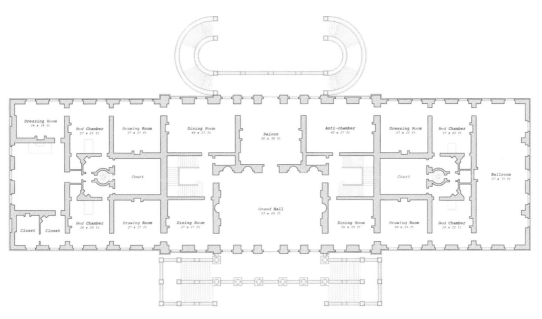

To best understand how Richard furnished Wanstead House, attention must be paid to three rooms, the Grand Hall, the Ballroom and the Saloon. This is because the best evidence survives for these spaces, as the most public and most elaborately designed and, therefore, the most commented upon.

The Grand Hall

The Grand Hall was the central feature of the Principal Grand Floor and the formal entry point for visitors arriving at Wanstead House. Access to the Grand Hall was via the external staircase beneath the portico or through the Stone Lobby on the ground floor where a 'backstairs of stone, balustrade with iron' led visitors into the Grand Hall above (*see* Fig 3.6).[50] When entering the Grand Hall, visitors would have been struck by its lofty height of 53 feet. Campbell's section shows its height was designed to exceed that of the adjoining Saloon and all other rooms belonging to the house. The Grand Hall was panelled throughout, with giant Corinthian pilasters and a plainly carved chimney piece on its north wall. The doorways were also plainly carved, with pointed pediments. It is unclear if the panelling featured here was stucco or oak. Walpole's description of 'finely carved Oak' at Wanstead suggests wainscoting was used at least for some of the state apartments.[51] The section by Campbell depicts only the north wall of the room and is the only visual evidence for the Grand Hall. However, standing in the Marble Saloon at Wentworth Woodhouse, built in 1733 and designed to resemble Wanstead's Grand Hall, gives some sense of how it must have felt for a visitor entering this impressively vast space (Fig 4.5).

Adorning the ceiling of the Hall was Kent's painting of *The Times of Day*, produced in *c* 1720.[52] No pictorial representations of the ceiling survive, but clues as to how it may have appeared can be obtained from Hogarth's 1728–30 conversation piece, *An Assembly at Wanstead House* (*see* Fig 4.8), which provides a glimpse of the ceiling Kent painted for the Ballroom. This depicts an Olympian scene set into a roundel gilt frame with decorative gold cornices and figures.[53] Given that Kent's ceiling paintings were executed according to hierarchy, it is probable that the ceiling painted to embellish the Grand Hall was of equal if not greater splendour to that illustrated by Hogarth.

Although some, including Walpole, criticised Kent's ceiling painting for the Grand Hall, contemporaries commented on it more than any other, suggesting that it was considered by many as his most impressive of the ceiling paintings at Wanstead.[54] The significance of Kent's painting of *The Times of Day* and his other works at Wanstead was celebrated in Aikman's portrait of the artist produced in *c* 1725 and displayed in the Grand Hall shortly after work on the ceiling was completed (*see* Fig 4.2). Kent is dressed as an artisan, holding thick paint brushes, presumably like those used to paint the ceiling above. The portrait not only served as a tribute; it prompted visitors to Wanstead to look up and admire Kent's highly decorative scene.

Catherine Tylney Long's restoration of the ceiling in 1810 reveals how Kent's work represented the original splendour of the house. Kent's decision to paint onto plaster proved fatal during the dismantling of the house in 1823–4: 'the historical paintings upon the ceilings so much

Fig 4.5
Wentworth Woodhouse,
Marble Saloon.
[Hannah Armstrong]

admired for their designs and the execution of them, being painted upon plaster, are rendered useless, as being irremovable; they must in the general wreck, return to the dust with that brittle composition which they now magnificently embellish.'[55]

Kent's ceiling painting was just the first of his designs for the Grand Hall. By the early 1730s, Kent had designed a selection of furniture including a large centre table with a carved and gilt frame, large side scallops and console legs on moulded plinths. Measuring 9 feet long, 6 feet wide and 3 feet high, its enormous scale was in keeping with the lofty hall in which it was displayed.[56] Kent designed similar side tables and console tables for Houghton Hall in 1725, Kensington Palace in 1724–5 and Ditchley in 1726. The tables he designed were inspired by those displayed in the Roman baroque palaces of the mid- to late 17th century that he is likely to have visited on his Grand Tour.[57] His design for the large centre table at Wanstead resembles that featured in an etching for 'The Pin and the Needle' in John Gay's *Fables* (1727). The scene depicts a large table in the centre of the room with a marble top on an ornately carved and gilt frame with large central scallops and console legs on moulded plinths. The table was purchased in the 1822 sale by the 6th Duke of Devonshire for Chatsworth House in Derbyshire, where it remains to this day.

Around this time Kent also designed a suite of wooden hall chairs. Specially designed hall furniture, in particular, chairs, only began to be introduced in the mid-1720s, making those at Wanstead an early example of this form of seating.[58] The earliest examples attributed to Kent were six mahogany settees designed for the Stone Hall at Houghton for Sir Robert Walpole in *c* 1728.[59] The Wanstead suite seems to have been produced shortly after. Providing this type of furniture emphasises the expansion of sociable activity, and the increasing need to facilitate visiting. Important visitors would not be kept waiting in the hall for long periods of time, so these items of furniture would have been largely used by servants and tradesmen.[60] Regardless, the seating in the Grand Hall would be among the first items that visitors encountered. It was imperative, therefore, that they were impressive and communicated the importance of the house through their design and the use of fashionable materials such as mahogany and walnut.[61] Kent's designs for hall chairs were intended to make a dramatic first impression and were made from fine, highly polished mahogany, a material imported from the colonies in North America and the West Indies, which enabled high-quality carving.[62]

The hall chairs were likely inspired by the Italian *sgabello* chairs, which were typically made from walnut and featured ornate carvings and the family coat of arms.[63] The June 1822 sale catalogue describes them as 'Four capital hollow shield-back wainscot-framed Hall Chairs, beautifully painted in flowers, and circular panel in front' and, most notably, 'painted with arms, &c.'[64] The painted arms described are likely to have displayed Richard's elevation to peerage in 1731 when he was made 1st Earl Tylney. The practice of adorning furniture with newly acquired arms was common practice among the nouveaux riches. Defoe's *The Complete English Tradesman* (1727) describes members of the newly moneyed elite, like Richard, visiting the Herald's Office, in search of the coat of arms of their ancestors 'to paint them upon their coaches & engrave them upon their plate, embroider them upon their furniture, or carve them upon their pediments of their new houses.'[65] Adorning the Grand Hall's furnishings with the coat of arms enabled Richard to communicate the family's newly acquired wealth and titles to visitors. Crucially, it was an effective means of leaving his mark on the fabric of Wanstead, demonstrating optimism for a lengthy future at the house, and providing future heirs with a sense of pride in family longevity.[66]

As a room designed to impress new arrivals, it was important that notable works of art were displayed here. In 1743, Richard commissioned the Italian artist Andrea Casali (1705–84) to paint several historical subjects for display at Wanstead House, three of which were hung in the Grand Hall.[67] Since his arrival in England three years earlier, Casali had been in demand by the likes of Thomas Coke, Earl of Leicester, and Alderman William Beckford, two notable Whigs who are likely to have been known to Richard. In 1743, Charlotte Fermour wrote to her mother, the Countess of Pomfret, giving a valuable account of her visit to Wanstead: 'after supper we all danced to our own singing, in order to teach Signor Casali (an Italian they have in the house) English country dances.'[68] Fermour's letter reveals that Casali was resident at Wanstead while employed by Richard, indicating that this was an important commission.

The three paintings Casali produced for the Grand Hall depicted scenes from ancient Roman military history, *Pompey Taking Leave of his*

Fig 4.6

Coriolanus Beseeched by his Wife and Mother to Spare the City of Rome (c 1743) by Andrea Casali, oil on canvas, 391.2 × 513 cm.

[Burton Constable Hall]

Family; *Cloelia before Porsenna*; and *Coriolanus Beseeched by His Wife and Mother to Spare the City of Rome* (Fig 4.6).[69] Several visitor accounts from the second half of the 18th century record their display in the Grand Hall, suggesting that these works were not replaced or relocated by subsequent owners.[70] The display of historical military subjects was typical in 18th-century country houses wishing to portray their owners as educated gentlemen. Furthermore, because the elite Whig circle promoted ancient Roman political, philosophical and architectural ideals as the model for Georgian society to follow, the most prestigious art was considered to be that which emphasised the virtues of the ancient hero.[71] The paintings'

Fig 4.7
Statue of Agrippina and her son, Chatsworth House.
[The Devonshire Collections, Chatsworth]

significance would therefore have resonated with his peers and the visiting public. Casali's *The Continence of Scipio*, also painted for Wanstead House, is currently displayed at Runcorn Town Hall, where it remains hung in a fine carved wood gilt frame by William Kent. This suggests that the designer produced frames for other paintings by Casali at Wanstead and further demonstrates Kent's extensive involvement in the furnishings of the house.

Besides the series by Casali and Aikman's portrait of William Kent, there is little evidence of artwork displayed in the Grand Hall until the second half of the 18th century, when visitor accounts describe a collection of Herculaneum sculpture.[72] These works are likely to have been acquired in Italy by Richard's son, John Child, 2nd Earl Tylney, and do not form part of the early Georgian scheme. The works described represented significant and influential political figures of ancient Rome such as Livia (the wife of the Roman Emperor Augustus), Domitian (emperor AD 81–96) and Agrippina (fourth wife and niece of the Emperor Claudius and the mother of the future Emperor Nero) (Fig 4.7). Their display alongside Casali's historical paintings added further grandeur to the room. Although Campbell was little involved in the furnishing of Wanstead, his section and floor plans give suggestions for the space by drawing several niches set into the walls (*see* Figs 3.5 and 3.6). The display of Herculaneum statues in these niches suggests that Campbell's implicit recommendations were eventually met. It was, however, Richard's employment of Kent to paint and furnish the Grand Hall that successfully introduced visitors to the magnificence that was about to unfold.

The Ballroom

Adjoining the Grand Hall were two apartments, consisting of four to five rooms each and accessed through an *enfilade* (*see* Fig 4.4). In 1781, Mrs Lybbe Powys described the experience of looking down the *enfilade* from Wanstead's Grand Hall: 'to look through the suite of apartments has a fine effect.'[73] Had Powys turned right into the *enfilade* described, she would have entered the dining room, where several portraits of Lady Castlemaine's family by the Dutch portrait artist Peter Lely (1618–80) were displayed alongside a painting of the Holy Family, three landscapes and two ruins. Here, Kent's ceiling painting represented the Four Seasons.[74] From the Dining Room, Powys would have passed through the Drawing Room where three flower paintings by the Flemish painter, Jan Baptist (1667–1746) were displayed beneath Kent's ceiling painting of Jupiter and Semele, an unusual subject which he also painted for King George I at Kensington Palace.[75] The chimney piece is described as elegant, with the family crest of an eagle taking up a snake at its centre. From the Drawing Room, Powys would have entered a bedchamber where mythological scenes of Apollo and Narcissus, satyrs and cupids were displayed alongside other iconographic works, before finally arriving at the Ballroom.[76]

The Ballroom at Wanstead House was among the first of its kind in England. It was an impressive space that connected the northern and southern suites of apartments and measured 75 feet long, the entire depth of the house.[77] In 1731, Richard reportedly hosted 'a grand Entertainment at his fine seat at Wanstead to his tenants and all the Parish of Wanstead, of both sexes, which were about 100 in number; and in the Evening was a Ball, which continued till Two the next Morning.'[78] Such an event was famously recorded by Hogarth in his 1728–31 conversation piece, *An Assembly at Wanstead House*, set in the Ballroom and likely commissioned to celebrate Richard's promotion in the Irish Peerage as Earl Tylney of Castlemaine around that time (Fig 4.8).[79]

The authenticity of Hogarth's scene has been challenged by art historians who propose that the work represents a false or exaggerated view.[80] Certainly, Richard's choice to employ Hogarth to paint the recently completed Kentissime interior was surprising given that Hogarth was well known to have held a deep dislike for Kent ever since the latter superseded Hogarth's father-in-law, James Thornhill (1675–1734), as royal painter in 1722. Furthermore, Hogarth opposed Kent's tendency to look towards foreign and, particularly, Italian influence for artistic inspiration and, following Kent's death in 1748, wrote 'never was there a more wretched dauber.'[81]

Hogarth also quite probably disliked Richard, his wealthy nouveau riche patron, who had a taste for the kind of luxury the artist was later to lampoon. The tapestry above Richard's head depicts a scene from *The Adventures of Telemachus*, in which the nymph Calypso is entertaining Telemachus, the son of Odysseus. This tapestry is a copy of a design

Fig 4.8

Assembly at Wanstead House (1728–31) by William Hogarth, oil on canvas, 64.8 × 76.2 cm. [Philadelphia Museum of Art/John Howard McFadden Collection]

by Bernard van Orley, a 16th-century Flemish painter and designer of tapestries and stained glass. In van Orley's design, a large silver urn can be seen in an upright position in the bottom left corner. However, in *An Assembly at Wanstead House*, this urn has been repositioned by Hogarth to appear that it is about to topple onto his patron's head.

Such detail may indeed have been in jest, but by and large Hogarth represented Kent's interior with a notable degree of veracity. As in the case of any commissioned artist at the beginning of their painting career, it surely would not have been in Hogarth's interest to produce an overtly satirical representation of the Wanstead interior and its sitters. Further evidence that Hogarth was not painting a work with more than perhaps a subtle dig or two is provided by Vertue's comments of January 1730: 'The daily success of Mr Hogarth in painting small family pieces & Conversations with so much Air and agreeableness Causes him to be much followd and esteemed.'[82] Moreover, this painting was a commission for a private client, and was never engraved, so any blatant satire would have lacked a public audience.[83] At most, this was a discreet critique for personal satisfaction. Instead, evidence obtained from visitor accounts, the 1822 sale catalogue and Wanstead's surviving, albeit dispersed, furniture reveals that Hogarth's painting in fact provides a detailed insight into how one of the most prized rooms of the house was furnished by 1728–30.

Like the Grand Hall, the earliest feature to be introduced into the Ballroom was probably Kent's ceiling painting. Hogarth's decision to include a view of the ceiling is significant as it is the only pictorial record of Kent's ceiling paintings at Wanstead. The evidence of such a painting in this space demonstrates continuity in Kent's interior design scheme. Like the ceiling Kent produced for the King's Drawing Room at Kensington Palace in 1722–3, that in the Ballroom is coved, with a heavy, gilded surround decorated with masks and festoons and figures with roundels in each corner.[84] The subject of the painting appears to be an Olympian scene, but the limited view in the Hogarth makes it difficult to establish specific details and visitor accounts provide little information.[85]

The next addition to the Ballroom is likely to have been a suite of seating furniture designed by Kent and intended to complement his earlier ceiling paintings.[86] These pieces were recorded in Hogarth's portrait of *c* 1728, suggesting that they were executed and put on display by this date. The settee on which Richard is seated to the right of the scene corresponds with lot 38 on day 13 of the 1822 sale, 'AN ELEGANT SQUARE SETTEE, in superb massive carved and gilt frame, with scroll elbows, the back stuffed in costly crimson Genoa velvet, and squab to correspond, on scroll legs, the frame ornamented with mermaids and festoons of flowers'.[87] Peter Brown, former director of Fairfax House in York, has linked this settee with that acquired in the June 1822 sale by the 11th Earl of Pembroke and his wife Catherine Woronzow for display at Wilton House, Wiltshire, where it remains.[88]

Similar gilded and crimson seating can be seen at the centre of the painting, where the card players are gathered. These are likely to have been those described in the catalogue as lots 39 to 45, 'A Ditto.' Lot 46 is similarly described as '*A ditto superb massive carved and gilt frame Conversation Stool*, to correspond (no back or elbows) with squab, in

Crimson Genoa velvet, *en suite*.'[89] This confirms that the chairs were designed by Kent as a suite, upholstered in luxurious crimson damask and designed to create a powerful, rich aesthetic for the Ballroom.[90] The descriptions from the sale catalogue correspond to the furnishings depicted by Hogarth and, while it has been proposed that the artist exaggerated their details, the objects prove themselves to be notably extravagant.

Another major feature introduced to the Ballroom around this time are the two tapestries depicted in Hogarth's *Assembly*. These correspond with descriptions in the June and September 1822 sale catalogues and the 1795 house inventory of tapestries depicting *Alexander the Great at the Battle of Granicus* and *Telemachus and Calypso*.[91] These hangings may have been supplied by Kent, who acquired tapestry hangings for his interiors at Chiswick and Houghton.[92] The tapestries measured 22½ by 11½ feet and, as Hogarth illustrates, fitted perfectly in the Ballroom,

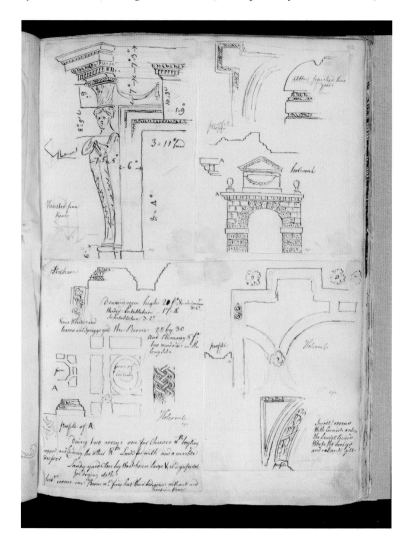

Fig 4.9
The Franco-Italian Album
(1749–55) by William
Chambers, pen and ink, 18.1 ×
12. 6 cm.
[Victoria and Albert Museum,
London]

suggesting that they were woven especially for Wanstead.[93] Although the 1822 sale catalogue lists the tapestries as having been produced by the Gobelins tapestry works established in the 17th century by Louis XIV, they were more likely to have been one of the many copies produced in Belgium, where weavers of the Gobelins workshop had relocated in the early 18th century.[94] Crucially, the tapestries displayed were similar to the Gobelin tapestries in Queen Anne's Gallery at Hampton Court that also depicted scenes from the life of Alexander the Great. Richard's ownership of tapestries like those designed by the Gobelins workshops reflects his eagerness to acquire and display commodities that conveyed European splendour and royal status.

Between the two tapestry hangings is a large marble chimneypiece flanked by two figures. The bust closest to the viewer represents an artisan wearing a turban much like that worn by Kent in Aikman's portrait on display in the Grand Hall. Is this another detail that Hogarth used to ridicule Kent? In 1749–55, architect William Chambers (1723–96) visited Wanstead and produced a sketch of a chimneypiece. The sketch is annotated as 'Wanstead Kent', and depicts a large female bust supporting a dentiled cornice and mantel (Fig 4.9). The similarity between Chambers' sketch and that depicted by Hogarth therefore supports a Kent attribution. The chimneypiece was one of two acquired by Lionel Rothschild for one of 19th-century London's most celebrated mansions, 148 Piccadilly, where they remained until the house was demolished after the Second World War. In 2013, the chimneypiece resurfaced in a London auctioneer's showroom, bearing striking resemblance to that which Chambers depicts (Fig 4.10). Above the marble fireplace, is Godfried Schalcken's (1643–1706) painting, *Portia Destroying Herself by Eating Fire*. The painting was recorded in several late 18th-century accounts and appears to be that which is listed in the

Fig 4.10
Marble chimneypiece (c 1730)
attributed to William Kent.
[Carlton Hobbs]

Fig 4.11
The Suicide of Portia by
Godfried Schalcken, oil on
canvas, 103 × 130.5 cm.
[Sotheby's, London]

Robins sale catalogue as lot 167 on day 9 (Fig 4.11).[95] A comparison between the existing painting and that depicted by Hogarth is further proof of the artist's accurate portrayal of the Ballroom.

If we situate ourselves in Hogarth's conversation piece, then exiting through the door on the immediate right of the canvas would lead us into the back suite of apartments overlooking the gardens. A visitor to the house in 1788 commented on the views from these apartments as 'very extensive and beautiful.'[96] Passing through a State Bedchamber, a Dressing room, and an Antechamber, we would eventually reach the Saloon.

The Saloon

Like the Ballroom, the Saloon was a relatively new concept in the early 18th century, present only in the most elite country houses such as Blenheim, Castle Howard and Cannons (demolished 1748). The earliest use of the term appears in Ephraim Chambers' 1728 publication, *Cyclopaedia*, which described the Saloon as 'a Grand Room, in the Middle of a Building, or at the Head of a Gallery ... a state room.'[97] Campbell's plan and section of the house confirms that the Saloon at Wanstead was designed as such (*see* Figs 3.5 and 3.6). Campbell's plan notably records the room as the 'Salon', suggesting its design was inspired by the *salons* of French royal palaces. These were spaces intended for the use of friends and family and positioned at the centre of a house. Access to a *salon* could be directly from outside (like an English hall) or preceded by a vestibule.[98] Campbell's plan and section shows an external staircase on the east elevation providing access from the grounds, directly into the Wanstead 'salon'. A frontispiece on the exterior of a building would indicate the salon's location within the interior by featuring pilasters, a pediment or separate roofs forming terminal pavilions. An anonymous view of the gardens shows that Campbell's salon was expressed as such (*see* Fig 5.6). Later accounts describe Campbell's 'salon' as a 'saloon' and so will be referred to as the latter henceforth.

In 1740, Richard commissioned the artist, Joseph Frans Nollekens, to paint another portrait of his family and friends, this time in the Saloon (Fig 4.12). The scene is set around a card table, where Richard's wife Dorothy holds her cards in her hand and leans back towards Richard, who is seated to the right and dressed in a striking blue suit, embellished with gold embroidery. The commission of a second conversation piece, ten years after Hogarth had completed his portrait of the family in the Ballroom, provided a record of another important room at Wanstead. It also demonstrated the continuity of family wealth and elite sociability under Richard's ownership.

The authenticity of Nollekens' portrait has been challenged, particularly because of what was thought to be a Venetian window depicted on the left. The 1984 exhibition catalogue for *Rococo: Art and Design in Hogarth's England* at the Victoria and Albert Museum stated that the room portrayed could not be at Wanstead, as 'Venetian windows only occurred in the unexecuted tower additions designed by Campbell in 1720.'[99] The exhibition catalogue for the 1987 exhibition *Manners and Morals* likewise argued that 'the problem is that room cannot be connected to Wanstead, which had no Venetian windows such as the one shown here.'[100] Peter Brown has pointed out that the views of Wanstead's east front show that what was mistaken for a Venetian window was, in fact, the arched door which led visitors from the Saloon onto the east terrace (*see* Fig 5.6). Further evidence for the arched doors appears in the 1822 sale catalogue which records lot 6 from the Saloon as a pair of crimson damask window curtains to the 'large arched folding doors.'[101]

Kate Retford has demonstrated that, contrary to many 18th-century conversation pieces that typically portray a group of sitters in fabricated or adjusted settings, Nollekens' portrait has proved itself an accurate representation and thus a relatively rare example within the conversation piece genre.[102] As Retford states, 'Child's lavish interiors and impressive possessions clearly attracted a level of public notice which must have encouraged their commemoration.'[103] In addition, Richard's employment of Nollekens was based on the close relationship he shared with the artist. George Vertue described Nollekens as being much employed by 'people of Fashion. Mostly & particularly by Lord Castlemaine [Richard Child].'[104] When its owners were forced to sell off the contents of the house in 1822, 17 works by the artist were listed in the sale catalogue, 2 of which were described as recording views of the Child family at Wanstead.[105] This suggests that Richard was one of Nollekens' greatest patrons and thus the ideal candidate to best

Fig 4.12

Lord Tylney and his Family and Friends at Wanstead House, Essex (1740) by Joseph Frans Nollekens, oil on canvas, 86.4 × 109.2 cm.

[Fairfax House, York]

represent the family in their home, a setting with which he would have been all too familiar.

Like Hogarth's *Assembly*, Nollekens' portrait of the Saloon provides several examples of the furnishings Kent produced for Richard. These include a suite of 'Mahogany Chairs covered in Crimson Velvet Brass Nail'd', recorded in an inventory made in 1795 and the 1822 sale catalogue.[106] Five of these chairs surround the card table positioned at the centre of the room and recorded in the sale catalogue as lot 20, '*A pair of Pier Card Tables*, to correspond, tops to turn on swivel and lined crimson Genoa velvet, 3 feet wide.'[107] Another of Kent's suite of eight chairs is positioned by the large arched door, where a nurse leans towards Richard's grandson, James. Kent's use of crimson was appropriate for the Saloon, which, like the Ballroom, was an important, sociable space, worthy of luxurious furnishings. This is further emphasised by the crimson carpet which sprawls beneath the sitters' feet towards the viewer.[108]

Further examples of Kent's furnishings for the Saloon appear to the right of the group, in the side table positioned beneath an empty arched niche and described in the 1822 sale catalogue as 'A GRAND SQUARE VERD ANTIQUE SIDE TABLE, on a superb massive carved and gilt frame, with Grecian scroll truss supports, tastefully decorated with festoons of oak leaves and acorns, shell and scroll ornaments in the centre, on deep moulded plinth, 5-feet-9 by 2-feet-5.'[109] This side table was probably one of a pair. Its companion is likely to have been positioned beneath a niche on the opposite side of the room and recorded in an undated sketch of the Saloon.[110] In 2011, one of these side tables sold at Christie's for £73,250 (Fig 4.13).[111] The table as sold differed slightly by featuring a shaped marble top rather than the rectangular top depicted by Nollekens. This was probably a later addition made to the table which otherwise can certainly be attributed to lot 27 on day 16 of the sale.

Central to the scene is a grand marble chimneypiece and an over mantel on the wall behind the sitters. This chimneypiece is considerably grander than that which Campbell designed for the Grand Hall (*see* Fig 3.6) and appears more in keeping with those attributed to Kent and depicted by Hogarth in the Ballroom (*see* Fig 4.8). The chimney piece and overmantel are among several pieces sold during the sale of Wanstead's building fabric between 1823 and 1824 and identified at a building on Hills Road in Cambridge, which houses the largest known collection of fabric from Wanstead (Fig 4.14).[112] The current whereabouts of Casali's *Pandora*, once framed by the overmantel, is unknown. While late 18th-century accounts attribute the painting to Nollekens, the sale catalogue records the work to be among several that Casali produced for Richard, three of which were displayed in the adjoining Grand Hall. Charlotte Fermour's 1743 account supports the display of Casali's work in the Saloon: 'He [Casali] is painting pictures for the salon, and I believed them well done.'[113] The high status of the Saloon is such that if the viewer of Nollekens' scene were able to step back to obtain a wider view, they may have glimpsed another ceiling painting by Kent.

The depiction of an empty niche to the right of the sitters suggests that the furnishing of the Saloon was in fact incomplete at the time of the painting's execution and further additions to the space were anticipated. In 1748, Swedish explorer Pehr Kalm described Wanstead as furnished in 'the most costly way', but noted that the interior remained unfinished 'because the owner's resources did not allow him to incur further expense.'[114] Kalm therefore draws our attention to the continuing

Fig 4.13
George II gilt wood side table (c 1730) by William Kent. [Christie's Images/Bridgeman Images]

Fig 4.14
Marble fireplace and
overmantel at Hills Road,
Cambridge.
[Hannah Armstrong]

and lengthy, not to mention costly, process of furnishing a house like
Wanstead.

If we are to imagine ourselves as a visitor in 1740, then the Saloon
is an appropriate end point to our tour of the house. Exiting through the
arched door depicted by Nollekens, we would descend into the gardens
below. Here we would have encountered a landscape, somewhat altered
from Richard's early 18th-century scheme, suggesting that further
modifications had occurred as Wanstead's magnificent interior had come
to fruition.

Notes

1 Macky 1722, I, iii.
2 Macky 1722, I, 20.
3 Macky 1722, I, 19.
4 Macky 1722, I, 20.
5 Repton 1816, 161.
6 Macky 1722, I, 20.
7 Tuffs 1988, 9.
8 Jeffery 2003, 16–17.
9 Macky 1722, II, 5.
10 Muilman 1771, 228.
11 Marks 1981, 8; Stutchbury 1967, 29.
12 Sambrook, 'William Benson'.
13 Blackett-Ord 2001, 109.

14 For references to these ceiling paintings, see *Wanstead House Sale*, day 10, lot 365; Shaw 1788, 29; Anon 1800, 126.
15 Walpole 1871, 383.
16 Vertue 1798, III, 383.
17 Brindle 2013, 144.
18 Weber 2013, 471. See also Brindle 2013, 271–301.
19 Vertue 1798, III, 383.
20 Byrant 2013, 184.
21 Ibid.
22 Byrant 2013, 186.
23 Finberg 1934, XVII, 24.
24 Vertue 1798, 384.
25 Weber 2013, 476.
26 Climenson 1899, 205.
27 Sevelinges 1820. Thanks to Richard Arnopp for a transcript of this correspondence.
28 Weber 2013, 452, 470.
29 Weber 2013, 470.
30 Ibid.
31 Macky 1722, I, 21.
32 Weber 2013, 484; *Wanstead House Sale*, day 14.
33 Macky 1722, I, 22.
34 Ibid.
35 Macky 1722, I, 21.
36 Ibid.
37 Cornforth 2004, 120.
38 Ibid.
39 Macky 1722, I, 21.
40 Ibid.
41 Cornforth 2004, 253.
42 Ibid.
43 To date, only one portrait of Richard Child, 1st Earl Tylney, has been identified by Miles Barton. This is the portrait attributed to Jonathan Richardson and sold in the Wanstead sale as day 10, lot 328. This portrait, however, is not full length. The description of a full-length portrait of Richard therefore implies that there is another portrait representing the earl that remains in a private collection and is yet to be uncovered. See Barton 2011.
44 Climenson 1899, 206.
45 *Wanstead House Sale*, day 13, lots 10, 14 and 20, 163.
46 Young 1768, 281.
47 Macky 1722, I, 23.
48 Figure 4.4 is a reproduction of Wanstead's floor plan based on a description and measurements published in Young 1768, 196–9.
49 Macky 1722, I, 23.
50 Macky 1722, I, 22.
51 LWL Horace Walpole to Richard Bentley, the Earl of Strafford, 17 July 1755.
52 Anon 1794, 288; Anon 1800, 126; Shaw 1788, 29; Climenson 1899, 205.
53 See Dorment 1986, 160.
54 LWL Horace Walpole to Thomas Bentley, 17 July 1755; Shaw 1788, 29.
55 Stead, 78.
56 *Wanstead House Sale*, day 12, lot 26.
57 Weber 2013, 490.
58 Cornforth 2004, 36.
59 Weber 2013, 483.
60 Ibid.
61 Weber 2013, 482–3.

62 Weber 2013, 471.

63 Weber 2013, 483.

64 *Wanstead House Sale*, day 12, lots 28–30.

65 Defoe 1727, 244.

66 Stobart 2013, 1–43.

67 Shaw 1788, 29; Muilman 1771, 228; Anon 1794, 288. Other views by Casali include *Pandora* in the Saloon and *Angelica and Medora* in the north-east Drawing Room on the Principal Grand Floor.

68 RHC, YW301, Charlotte Fermour to her mother, Countess of Pomfret, 13 October 1743.

69 The sale catalogue for June 1822 claims that Andrea Casali had been brought over to England by Richard Child. Casali's biographer, John Ingamells, however, argues that Casali did not arrive in England by way of Child's invitation, but in fact was encouraged to come by the 4th Earl of Carlisle and the director of the Royal Society of Antiquaries, Sir Charles Frederick, whose portrait he painted in Rome in 1738. George Vertue claimed that the artist had been invited to England by Carlisle 'promising his interest and promotion to business.' Coriolanus (believed to have lived during the 5th Century BC) and Pompey (106–48 BC) were Roman military figures and Porsena was an Etruscan king known for his war against the city of Rome *c* 508 BC.

70 Muilman 1771, 228; Shaw 1788, 29; Anon 1794, 288.

71 Myrone 2006, 73.

72 Muilman 1771, 228; Shaw 1788, 29; Anon 1794, 288.

73 Climenson 1899, 206.

74 Anon 1794, 289.

75 Ibid; Brindle 2013, 121.

76 Anon 1794, 289.

77 Ibid.

78 Atwell 1954, 71; Stead, 30.

79 See BL Add MS 27 995 f.1, Hogarth's *Account taken January first 1731 of all ye Pictures that Remain unfinish'd*. For discussions regarding the commissioning of the painting, see Dorment 1986 and Einberg 2017.

80 Marks 1981; Dorment 1986.

81 Dorment 1986, 159.

82 Finberg 1934, XXII, 40.

83 Dorment 1986, 159.

84 Brindle 2013, 117.

85 Dorment 1986, 160.

86 Weber 2013, 474.

87 *Wanstead House Sale*, day 13, lot 38.

88 Ibid; see Robinson 2009, 42–7.

89 *Wanstead House Sale*, day 13, lots 39–46.

90 *Wanstead House Sale*, day 13, lot 46.

91 NA C 111/215, LONG v PHIPPS: Inventories of household furniture, plate, linen, china, books, wines and effects of Sir James Tilney-Long, deceased, at Draycot House near Chippenham, Wilts, and Wanstead House, Essex. Hereafter NA. See *Wanstead House Sale*, day 10, lot 7; BNF CVE 39280 *Catalogue of superb Gobelin tapestry*, day 2, lot 64 and 65.

92 Weber 2013, 476.

93 Marks 1981, 11.

94 Marks 1981, 13.

95 Shaw 1788, 29; Anon 1794, 289; *Wanstead House Sale*, day 9, lot 167.

96 Shaw 1788, 31.

97 Chambers 1728, 12.

98 Girouard 1978, 128.

99 Snodin 1984, 35.

100 Einberg 1987, 122–3.
101 *Wanstead House Sale*, day 16, lot 6.
102 Retford 2013, 38–62.
103 Retford 2013, 44.
104 Finberg 1934, XXII, 137.
105 See lot 318, 21 June: Interior of the saloon of Wanstead House, with an Assemblage of Ladies and Gentleman – A Coversazione; and lot 311, 21 June, 'Females bathing in a landscape, with a distant view of Wanstead House.' A study of the latter reveals that this is not the setting of Wanstead, but the description in the catalogue is further evidence of the well-known relationship between artist and patron.
106 NA C 111/215, no. 40; *Wanstead House Sale*, day 16, lots 7–11. The chairs were purchased by the Earl of Pembroke at the Wanstead House sale in 1822 and have since remained at Wilton House.
107 *Wanstead House Sale*, day 16, lot 20.
108 The 1822 sale catalogue describes this as an Axminster carpet. However, the Axminster carpet company was founded by Thomas Witty in 1755, more than a decade after Nollekens painted his view of the Child family in the saloon. This suggests that the carpet was either incorrectly attributed to Axminster in the sale catalogue or that listed in the catalogue was a later addition. See *Wanstead House Sale*, day 16, lot 3.
109 *Wanstead House Sale*, day 16, lot 27.
110 ERO I/Mp 388/1/57, Rough plan of Saloon at Wanstead House.
111 Christie's, 'The Exceptional Sale', 7 July 2011, lot 10.
112 Baggs 1996, 131–3. Thanks to Rosie France of the Chard Robinson Group in Cambridge for allowing me to visit the office and photograph the architectural fragments of Wanstead at no. 2 Hills Road, Cambridge; Casali's painting is recorded in the sale catalogue as *Wanstead House Sale*, day 9, lot 194.
113 RHC YW301, Charlotte Fermour to her mother, Countess of Pomfret, 13 October 1743; The visitor account published in *The Ambulator* describes the painting as one of Nollekens' own works. Later accounts by William Tegg and George Atwell likewise refer to Nollekens as the creator of this picture. However, comparisons between *Pandora* and other works by Casali do seem to verify the 1822 attribution.
114 Lucas 1892, xi.

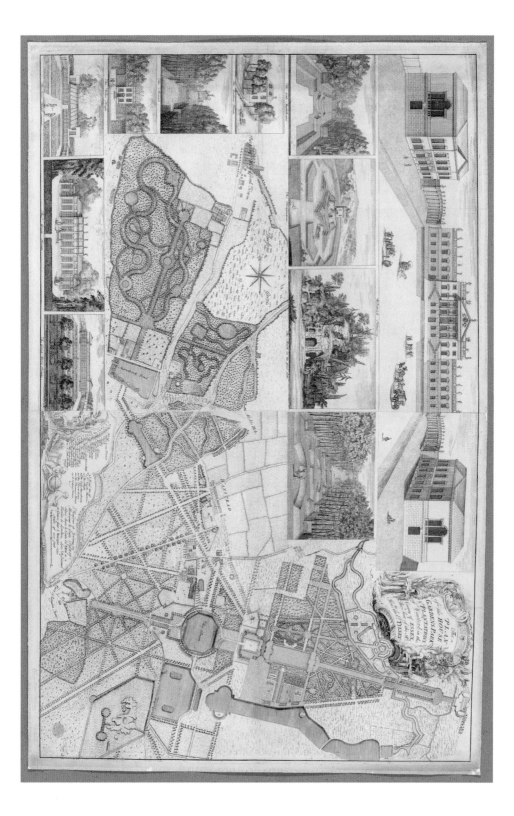

5 The artinatural landscape, 1725–50

I n May 1748, Pehr Kalm visited Wanstead with a Mr Warner and 'several of his Swedish friends.'[1] Recording his experiences of the house and grounds, Kalm described the landscape at Wanstead as 'all that can be required and produced by art in a garden.'[2] By this time, the rigid formality of the gardens introduced by George London in c 1706 had been replaced by a landscape considerably more natural in its appearance. The developments that had taken place since the rebuilding of the house were carried out in response to the declining popularity of the formal garden, which had been criticised as early as 1712 by essayist and politician Joseph Addison (1672–1719):

> Our Trees rise in Cones, Globes and Pyramids. We see the Marks of the Scissars upon every plant and bush. I do not know whether I am singular in my Opinion, but for my own part, I would rather look upon a Tree in all its Luxuriance and Diffusion of Boughs and Branches, than when it is thus cut and trimmed into a Mathematical Figure.[3]

In 1738, Batty Langley (1696–1751) similarly condemned the fashion, blaming London and Wise for its introduction in England:

> These regular gardens were first taken from the Dutch and introduced into England in the Time of the late Mr London and Mr Wise, who being then suppos'd to be the best gardn'rs in England {the Art being in its infancy to what it is now} were imployed by the Nobility and Gentry of England to lay out and Plant their gardens in that regular, stiff and stuft up manner in which many yet appear.[4]

The new style adopted to replace the early 18th-century formal gardens was described by Langley in his *Practical Geometry* (1726) and *New Principles of Gardening* (1728) as the 'Artinatural'. The artinatural was a reworking and loosening of formal landscape features through the adoption of asymmetrical elements such as serpentine paths.[5] The style, which emerged gradually, reflects the move towards the more natural landscapes that dominated English gardens under the influence of Lancelot 'Capability' Brown (1716–83) during the second half of the 18th century.[6] A more natural approach to gardening represented the tastes of the dominant Whig party, who had rejected the formality of royal European gardens. Richard's conversion from Tory to Whig at the time of the rebuilding of Wanstead House may therefore have played some part in spurring his decision to soften the formality of the early 18th-century gardens.

Fig 5.1
A Plan of the House, Gardens, Park and Plantations of Wanstead, the Seat of the Earl of Tylney (1735) by John Rocque, engraving, 69 × 106 cm.
[The British Library]

John Rocque's Plan of the House, Gardens, Park and Plantations of Wanstead

The second phase of Richard's landscape improvements is best represented in cartographer John Rocque's (1709–62) *Plan of the House, Gardens, Park, and Plantations of Wanstead* published in 1735. The plan featured an aerial perspective of the estate alongside vignettes of the latest landscape features (Fig 5.1). A front elevation depicting Wanstead House with the addition of wings flanking both sides of the forecourt was also included.

As with all pictorial evidence representing a lost landscape, the authenticity of Rocque's survey must be carefully considered. From 1734, Rocque had established himself as a 'dessinateur de jardins', producing elaborate plans of notable estates, many of which were based near London.[7] Much like the views produced by Kip and Knyff in the early 18th century, Rocque's plans were published and viewed by a wide audience. It is therefore possible that the views produced were exaggerated in order to flatter Rocque's client and impress the public. Moreover, the plan may have been produced while improvements were in process and thus presents features not yet completed.

Between 1741 and 1745, Rocque produced a comprehensive survey of London and its environs (Fig 5.2). Included in the top right corner of the map was a view of the Tylney estate, which Rocque had surveyed

Fig 5.2
Plan of London and its environs (1741–5) by John Rocque, engraving.
[London Metropolitan Archives, City of London]

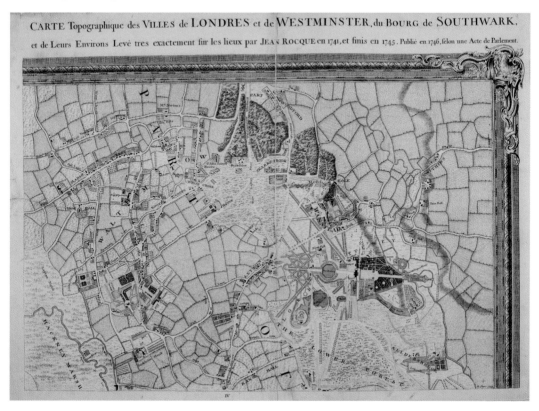

a decade earlier. A comparison between the two surveys reveals that Rocque's representation of the estate in 1735 was largely accurate. The omission of features such as the wings flanking the house and the island shaped like the British Isles to the south-west seems to have been due to a lack of funds rather than an intention to exaggerate 'the house and garden, which had not been fully completed, because owner's resources did not allow him to incur further expense.'[8] Several visitor accounts and archaeological evidence further confirm the accuracy of Rocque's representation of the landscape in 1735.

To date, there is no known documentation that establishes the landscape designer responsible for executing the second phase of improvements at Wanstead. John Harris has attributed Rocque's vignette of Wanstead's front elevation to William Kent, suggesting he remained associated with the estate up until 1735. Features recorded by Rocque's plan, such as the Grotto on the mount, bear the hallmarks of Kent's landscape style, raising the question of whether Kent contributed to the second phase of improvements at Wanstead.

Certainly, by the time Rocque produced his plan of Wanstead in 1735, Kent had famously 'leaped the fence and saw that all nature was a garden.'[9] He had designed garden buildings and improved the grounds for several notable clients including Richard Temple, 1st Viscount Cobham, at Stowe in 1729, Thomas Coke, Earl of Leicester, at Holkham in 1730 and Henry Pelham at Esher in 1733. Kent's commissions were often well documented in the form of the sketches which he would make. However, no such sketches exist for Wanstead. Moreover, some of the features introduced to Wanstead by 1735 predate Kent's entry into landscape design. Any contribution made by Kent would therefore have been among his earliest experiments in landscape design and thus remains speculative.

The second phase of improvements began around 1725, with the introduction of channels and islands to the north and south of the straight canal featured in Kip and Knyff's *View to the east* (*see* Fig 1.2). These alterations softened the formality of Holt's canal and were recorded on a survey produced by James Cradock in 1725 (Fig 5.3).[10] This modification marked the beginning of what was to become an extensive lake system at Wanstead. Rocque's 1735 plan shows a string of water introduced along the southern boundaries of the estate. In December 1735, *The General Evening Post* reported 'The Right Hon. The Earl of Tylney, having a grant from his majesty, is making a fine large pond, of about 10 Acres, on Epping Forest, fronting his house, which when finished will be exceedingly beautiful. There are near 100 Men now daily employ'd at work upon it.'[11] The report is likely to refer to the Great Lake recorded by Rocque, south-west of the house (*see* Figs 5.1 and 5.2). In 1748, Kalm described the effect of the new and extensive lake system at Wanstead:

> The difficulty met him [Richard] at the place where the house should
> be built, that there was no water; but money could cure all such things.
> Where, previous to that time there was scarcely anything but a ditch with
> a little water in it, we now saw a large flowing river, all made with art and

Fig 5.3

Map of Wanstead and Ilford
(1725) by James Cradock.
[Essex Record Office]

Fig 5.4

La maison de Wanstead
House à milord Castlemaine
(1728) by Pierre Fougeroux,
watercolour on paper.
[Victoria and Albert Museum,
London]

Fig 5.5

A Prospect of the Park and
House at Wanstead (c 1730),
Anonymous, oil on canvas,
145 × 233.5 cm.
[Mike Booth/Alamy Stock
Photo]

human labour. He had dug about the whole place many ponds, of which
one and another resembled a little lake.[12]

In 1788, Revd Stebbing Shaw described the landscape as 'adorned
with water', demonstrating the pleasing effect of the expansion of the
waterworks.[13]

In addition to the introduction of large pieces of water, Rocque's
plan shows that the ornate parterre gardens, canal and bowling green
introduced by London and recorded in Kip and Knyff's *View to the east*
and *View to the north* (*see* Figs 1.2 and 1.4), had been replaced by a
wide grassy avenue. This modification occurred shortly after the formal
gardens were recorded in a sketch by French traveller, Pierre Fougeroux
in 1728 (Fig 5.4). Significantly, Fougeroux's sketch of Wanstead and
the other major estates he visited that year, such as Wimpole, Boughton
and Blenheim, reveal that, despite the waning popularity of geometric
gardens, the display of parterres and canals remained common in the
gardens of the upper echelons of English society.[14] The eradication of such
features was therefore gradual and does not seem to have occurred at
Wanstead until the 1730s. An anonymous view taken from the east shows
the effect of the new grassy avenue (now known as the Glade) (Fig 5.5).
Another view, seemingly by the same hand, depicts the avenue beneath
the house in closer detail. Here figures engage in a game of bowling on
the lawn (Fig 5.6), suggesting that, although the bowling green had been
removed, such social pursuits continued.

From this avenue, Rocque introduces the viewer to the serpentine
pathways laid out to the north and south. These serpentines were

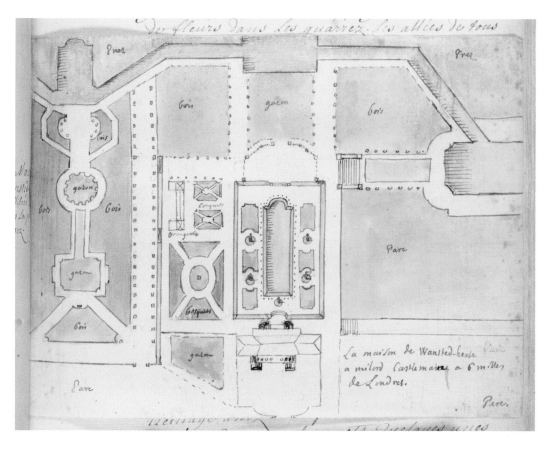

Fig 5.6
Wanstead House from the east
(c 1730), Anonymous, oil on
canvas, 99 × 124.5 cm.
[Digital image courtesy
of the Paul Mellon Centre
Photographic Archive]

designed to cut through areas of the wilderness and connect with the smaller avenues planted by London and recorded by Kip and Knyff in *c* 1708 (*see* Figs 1.2 and 1.3). Similar designs were implemented by Kent at Esher in 1731–7 and their introduction here has been associated with the designer.[15] The use of serpentines softened the original geometric form implemented by London in *c* 1706. The earliest representations of such gardens were published in the third volume of *Vitruvius Britannicus* in 1725, which featured a view of the formal garden at Castle Howard, with meandering serpentines cut into the formal box work. In 1722–24, similar gardens were introduced at Sir Robert Walpole's residence at Houghton. Architectural historian John Harris states that their introduction at Wanstead provides one of the best examples of the artinatural gardening style during this period.[16]

Rocque's 1735 plan illustrates how the meandering serpentine paths guided visitors towards a variety of landscape features: the Amphitheatre, Grotto and Fortification Island. The insertion of architectural structures into a garden was in response to the poet Alexander Pope's (1688–1744) influential ideas on the picturesque that advocated for landscapes to be perceived as 'topographical paintings' and the scene for an event in which visitors could partake.[17] The erection of a Grotto, Fortification and Amphitheatre at Wanstead created several such settings and were presumably intended to facilitate quiet contemplation while also providing a setting for social interaction and intellectual discussion.

The introduction of landscape architecture in the artinatural gardens at Wanstead created variety and surprise. Pope's well-known couplet in his *Epistle to Burlington* (1731) describes the benefits of such an experience: 'He gains all points, who pleasingly confounds/Surprises, varies and conceals the bounds.'[18] The variety of the improved landscape reflects Richard's sensitivity to the perceived disadvantages of the earlier geometric style and demonstrates his efforts to ensure that the gardens continued to comply with new gardening trends. The importance of these structures at Wanstead is emphasised by Rocque's representation of them in vignettes surrounding the 1735 plan.

The Amphitheatre

Estate views and plans produced during this period show that several amphitheatre structures were proposed for the gardens at Wanstead. Crucially, not all of those depicted were implemented. When James Cradock made his survey of the estate in 1725, he recorded an amphitheatre overlooking the straight canal, where the Grotto Boathouse was later constructed in *c* 1760 (*see* Fig 5.3). The anonymous view from the east also records this amphitheatre, but there is no archaeological evidence for the structure. The views may therefore have been depicting an unexecuted proposal. The anonymous view does, however, depict a second amphitheatre overlooking the Fortification Island (*see* Fig 5.5). Rocque records this amphitheatre in both his 1735 and 1741–5 plans (*see* Figs 5.1 and 5.2).

Access to this Amphitheatre was via a series of walks and serpentine pathways to the north of the central avenue. Archaeological remains and Rob Wiseman's 2012 Lidar scan of Wanstead Park reveal that it remains *in situ*, albeit buried beneath undergrowth (*see* Fig 0.8).[19] To date, it has not been possible to attribute the structure to a specific landscape designer. Although its construction and design are similar to designs by Charles Bridgeman (1690–1738) for Claremont, Eastbury, in Dorset (1723), and at Stowe (1729), there is no direct evidence to support a Bridgeman attribution at Wanstead. Viewers of Rocque's plans will notice a second amphitheatre, south of the central avenue (*see* Figs 5.1 and 5.2). Its omission from later views, however, suggests that this amphitheatre was not constructed.

Like many features at Wanstead, the Amphitheatre was designed for social interaction. The 1735 plan provides two vignettes of the Amphitheatres, denoting their importance in the landscape (*see* Fig 5.1). One view shows a male and female in conversation in the foreground, and, in the background, a gentleman walks away. Landscape painters commonly deployed figures to illustrate that a landscape could serve as a site for the interactions between people, and between people and nature.[20] The depiction of such populated sites by Rocque was a deliberate effort to establish Richard's reputation as a good host who accommodated these experiences.

The Amphitheatre's inclusion in the landscape drew Classical associations into Wanstead's garden. The climate of Italy had encouraged outdoor performances in that country since the Roman period, and Italian gardens had thus long included amphitheatres among their various architectural features.[21] Despite the difference in climate, an amphitheatre at Wanstead was a feature which would invite association with the Classical world. The positioning of the Amphitheatre opposite the Fortification Island at Wanstead suggests that it was also a venue from which to view the battle re-enactments that took place there. The proximity between these two features emphasises how such features in the landscape were conceived to work together. Moreover, evidence of a play performed in the gardens for Queen Elizabeth I suggests that the Amphitheatre was built to provide the kinds of entertainment historically associated with Wanstead.[22]

The Fortification Island

The earliest record of the Fortification Island at Wanstead appears in Cradock's 1725 survey, which depicts a star-shaped island positioned within the recently canalised waterworks (*see* Fig 5.3). Its design mirrored that of Tilbury Fort in Essex, built for King Henry VIII by Bernard de Gomme and later used by Elizabeth I to defend London against the Spanish Armada and during the Anglo-Dutch wars. Its introduction into the Wanstead landscape was somewhat unusual and perhaps among the earliest of such structures to be created in Georgian England.[23] Later examples include the fortification at Newstead Abbey, built in 1749 (described by Walpole as 'two silly forts'), and that at West Wycombe, constructed in 1754. Evidence of the Fortification is today obscured by undergrowth, but the Lidar archaeological survey of the park shows the distinct star-shaped outline of the island recorded by Cradock and Rocque (*see* Fig 0.8).[24]

The view from the east depicts the Fortification Island with a brick-built fort tower and bastion at its centre (*see* Fig 5.5). Crucially, the Fortification was by no means built for defensive purposes. Instead, it was a folly designed to evoke historical associations. Ancient Romans employed such features for water-based performances known as *naumachia*, in which naval battles were recreated for large-scale entertainment. Such pursuits were popular during the Tudor and Elizabethan periods and may have occurred at Wanstead under the Earl of Leicester's ownership.[25] The island's resemblance to Tilbury Fort was perhaps intended to celebrate British history, and to recall the royal connections once enjoyed by Wanstead prior to Josiah Child's acquisition in the late 17th century. No contemporary descriptions of the Fortification exist, but the family's ties with the East India Company may well have meant that re-enactments of pirates attacking East India ships were performed for the entertainment of guests seated in the Amphitheatre opposite.[26]

Rocque's vignette of the structure shows a boat carrying passengers towards the island (*see* Fig 5.1). There are numerous references to boats being used for leisurely purposes on the estate. In 1722, Macky commented on a large gondola kept on the Basin, which Pehr Kalm later described as so large 'that they can sail to and fro on it with large boats'.[27] The 1822 sale catalogue lists a number of boats presumably used for leisure rather than utilitarian purposes. Such evidence indicates that water-based entertainments were frequent occurrences at Wanstead, the Fortification Island no doubt being a highlight of such events.

The early Wanstead Grotto

Another notable feature of Rocque's 1735 plan is the Grotto depicted on one of Wanstead's Mounts (*see* Fig 5.1). Evidence of a Grotto at Wanstead significantly predates Rocque's view. In January 1720, the *Daily Post* reported on a theft at the parish church, the summerhouse and a Grotto: 'about ten days ago the summer house in Lord Castlemain's [Richard Child] Gardens at Wanstead was also broke open, and there was stolen from thence a large Pannels of glass door, as also several glass pilasters out of the Grotto.'[28] This description provides us with an insight into the decoration used in the Grotto at Wanstead. Visual evidence of the structure, however, does not appear until *c* 1730, when a faint record of a grotto-like structure is depicted on the lake south of the house in the anonymous view from the east (*see* Fig 5.5), its location roughly corresponding with that recorded 'on the great lake' by Rocque in 1735.[29]

As the Grotto depicted by Rocque and included in the anonymous view of Wanstead cannot be seen in the views by Kip and Knyff, the structure must have been created between *c* 1708 and 1720, when the *Daily Post* published its report. The design depicted by Rocque bears close resemblance to other landscape structures designed by William Kent, such as Queen Caroline's Hermitage in Richmond Gardens (*c* 1730) and the Grotto at Esher (*c* 1733). However, evidence for a Grotto at Wanstead predates his experimentation with landscape design, weakening the case for a Kent attribution. When the 2nd Earl Tylney embarked on a series of landscape improvements in 1760, the materials from this Grotto were used to build a Grotto Boathouse in a new location, overlooking the Ornamental Waters, where it remains as one of the few extant features of the estate.

A working landscape

The improvements to the landscape carried out after the construction of Wanstead House reflect the changing tastes from the early 18th-century formal landscape to the looser artinatural style. The views of Wanstead produced during the early 18th century present an immaculate and completed landscape. However, the differences observed between these views suggests that Wanstead was in a continuous state of development. Moreover, such a vast and ornate landscape required considerable maintenance. In the anonymous view taken from the east, the artist has painted workers in the foreground, ploughing the land surrounding the canal (*see* Fig 5.5). Their inclusion in the portrait represents Wanstead in all its glory, as an effective, working estate, providing labour and benefiting all who interact with the land.

In addition to the novel features of the landscape, Rocque's 1735 plan illustrates the utilitarian features of the estate such as the kitchen gardens and vineyards. These appear in a similar location as to where Kip and Knyff illustrated them in *c* 1708 (*see* Fig 1.3). The scale and proximity of these features to the house suggest that they continued to assist with the daily running of the estate. The vineyards, however, appear to have been relocated to the eastern part of the Plain, where they are recorded in the anonymous view from the east (*see* Fig 5.5). Rocque's map also reveals that the kitchen gardener, steward and gardener resided on the estate grounds by this date. The 1822 sale catalogue includes items sold from the gardener's cottage, which comprised two parlours, a kitchen and three bedrooms, indicating that workers resided on site until the final breaking up of the estate.[30]

No further views or surveys of Wanstead were produced until the late 18th century. Rocque's surveys of the landscape are therefore a fitting conclusion, reflecting Richard's transformation of Wanstead into an estate designed to rival England's leading country seats. Like the furnishing of its interior, the development of Wanstead's landscape was a time-consuming, piecemeal process, which remained a constant preoccupation. In 1747, just three years before Richard's death, Smart Lethieullier, a neighbour in Aldersbrook, wrote that 'Ld: Tylney having this Summer made Considerable Alteration in his Park.'[31] Richard's creation of an impressive landscape, alongside the construction and fitting out of its new palace, is testament to his dedication towards the family seat and his role as custodian.

By the time Richard died in 1750, Wanstead's reputation as one of England's leading estates was well and truly established. He was buried in the family vault at the parish church, as requested in his will of 1746: 'My Body when it shall please God I shall dye I desire may be decently interred in the vault of my Family in the Parish Church of Wanstead in the County of Essex.'[32] But, as Richard was laid to rest, the legacy he left behind became vulnerable in the hands of his second surviving son.

Notes

1   Lucas 1892, 175.
2   Ibid.
3   Addison 1753, VIII, 74.
4   Langley 1728, xi.
5   Williamson 1995, 36.
6   Willis comments on a collection of drawings now held in the Bodleian Library which reflect the formal, transitional and progressive characteristics of Bridgeman's designs such as lawns, mounts, amphitheatres, ha-has, as well as rides and walks to provide key vantage points. Willis, 'Bridgeman, Charles'. John Harris credits many of the landscape features to William Kent.
7   Varley 1948, 83; See his first work, *Plan of the House, Gardens and Hermitage of Their Majesties at Richmond* (1734).
8   Lucas 1892, 176.
9   Dixon Hunt 1995, 43.
10 ERO D/DCW P7, J Cradock, Plan of Wanstead Park, 1725.
11 *General Evening Post*, 2–4 December 1735, np.
12 Lucas 1892, 175.
13 Shaw 1788, 31.
14 NAL Fougeroux, 1728, 105–7.
15 J Harris 1986.
16 J Harris 1986, 18.

17 For a discussion on landscape buildings and the picturesque, see Dixon Hunt 2013, 365–92.
18 Cabe Halpern 1992, 188.
19 This evidence is visible in Dr Rob Wiseman's Lidar scans of Wanstead Park. Thanks to Dr Wiseman for a discussion of these scans. See also Debois Landscape Survey Group 1990, Appendix 2.
20 For further discussion of figures in topographical paintings of country houses, Laurence 2003, 81–94.
21 Dixon Hunt 1987, 32; Mowl 2000, 74.
22 Hyrn 1823, 599–600.
23 Jeffery 2003, 55.
24 See Dr Rob Wiseman's Lidar scans of Wanstead Park for evidence of the fortification and Debois survey.
25 Adams 1995; Jeffery 2003, 29.
26 Jeffery 2003, 56.
27 Lucas 1892, 175.
28 *Daily Post*, 18 January 1720, np. Thanks to Richard Arnopp and Tim Couzens for pointing me in the direction of this evidence.
29 Jeffery and Arnopp note that there is no primary evidence that confirms that the Grotto was situated on the mount illustrated by Rocque in 1735 and caution that it may not have been located exactly as illustrated. Considering there is only the anonymous view taken from the River Roding, which also depicts the Grotto, this cannot be treated as an entirely accurate representation of the Grotto's location.
30 *Wanstead House Sale*, day 29.
31 Lethieullier 1779, 73–4.
32 Thanks to Tim Couzens for sharing a transcript of Richard Child's will of 1746.

Part 3

John Child, 2nd Earl Tylney, 1750–85

Fig 6.1
British Gentlemen at Horace Mann's Home in Florence (1763–5) by Thomas Patch, oil on canvas, 96.4 × 124.3 cm. [Yale Centre for British Art, Paul Mellon Collection]

6 John Child and the late 18th-century landscape

After Richard Child's death in March 1750, John Child (b 1712), his eldest surviving son, succeeded as 4th Baronet and 2nd Earl Tylney and inherited the family fortune and estates. Titles of nobility secured social status, fortunes and the family seat, making them welcome acquisitions. Becoming custodian of the family seat, however, came with significant responsibility. Owners were expected to demonstrate an active involvement in the estate by carrying out improvements that complied with modern tastes, providing employment and ensuring the house and grounds could support various forms of sociability. Wanstead's high status meant that many are likely to have watched John's inheritance with bated breath, eager to see how he would carry Wanstead into the second half of the 18th century.

Within just a year of his inheritance, John departed from Wanstead and set off for the Continent. Smart Lethieullier, a neighbour at Aldersbrook, commented, 'The social amuzements of this Neighbourhood are much Chang'd, for instead of being the Gayest & most Cheerful spot perhaps to be found in any Country, we are become as retired as if we were in Yorkshire. Tylney you know is gon abroad.'[1] John's departure was the first of many trips that the new earl would take to Italy during his ownership of Wanstead House. Correspondence between John and his brother-in-law, Sir Robert Long (1704–67), reveals that John was residing in Florence in 1752, where his wealth and status quickly made him a leading member of the Anglo-Florentine community. In December that year, he wrote to Robert of the good company he kept abroad: 'I had the very good fortune to be very intimate with the Prince and Princess of Naples, they show me on all occasions the greatest attention and I must say the same of all nobility here.'[2]

In his absence, John left matters of estate in the hands of relatives and trusted associates. His letters to Robert suggest he was content to temporarily relieve himself of the burden: 'I am sure there is nothing that Wanstead can afford, but what is entirely at your command as if it were your own.'[3] In 1754, he thanked Robert for informing him of business back in England: 'it is impossible for me to express thanks for the great care you have taken of my affairs in my absence.'[4] As heir to the Tylney fortune and the family seat, it was not possible, nor was it ideal, for John to remain abroad for significant periods of time. The demands of custodianship may therefore explain why John returned home to Wanstead the following year.

On 17 July 1755, Sir Horace Walpole wrote to Richard Bentley, 'I dined yesterday at Wanstead, many years have passed since I saw it. The disposition of the house and the prospect are better than I expected the garden, which they tell you cost as much as the house, that is £100,000 (don't tell Mr Muntz) is wretched.' The letter to Bentley demonstrates John's eagerness to impress visitors through the display of generous hospitality and wealth:

> The present Earl is the most generous creature in the world: in the first
> chamber I entered he offered me four marble tables that lay in cases
> about the room: I compounded, after forty refusals of everything I
> commended, to bring away only a haunch of venison, I believe he has not
> had so cheap a visit a good while.[5]

Walpole's visit must have been one of several occasions whereby
John received members of elite society at Wanstead. In June 1760,
for example, he hosted a supper and ball for the Duke of York at
the estate.[6] Such events reflect John's efforts to play the part of the
rightful heir and ensure Wanstead maintained its reputation under his
ownership.

'The furniture fine, but totally without taste': John Child's contribution to the Wanstead interior[7]

Despite John's best efforts to impress his guest, Walpole described the
furniture at Wanstead as 'fine, but totally without taste', and lambasted
the historic paintings by Andrea Casali that Richard Child had hung
with pride in the Grand Hall: 'such continence and incontinences of
Scipio and Alexander by I don't know whom!'[8] Kent's ceiling paintings
were described as featuring 'flame-coloured gods and goddesses, by
Kent', and the family portraits were ridiculed: 'Such family-pieces,
by – I believe the late Earl [Richard Child] himself, for they are as
ugly as the children that he really begot!'[9] Walpole's scathing remarks
reveal that Wanstead's ostentatious furnishings seemed in poor taste
and suggest that the Tylney family remained parvenus to some. Their
display of luxurious furnishings and recently purchased artworks
would have been perceived in a different light from those inherited by
the landed gentry.

Scathing as Walpole's remarks are, his letter to Bentley does
provide insight into how the house appeared in 1755, referring to the
whole great apartment as 'of oak, finely carved, unpainted and has
a charming effect.'[10] He also referred to 'twenty ebony chairs, and a
couch, and a table and a glass, that would have tried the virtue of a
philosopher of double my size!'[11] Significantly, Walpole's letter hints
at new acquisitions made by John, referring to 'four marble tables
that lay about in cases' in the Grand Hall. These may have been a
reference to the popular *pietra dura* table tops, an Italian speciality
much loved by Grand Tourists. Indeed, John was purchasing items
for Wanstead shortly after his inheritance. In 1752 he wrote to Robert
Long about a number of cases he had sent from Italy, 'amongst which
is a little Antique Boy which I had a good Bargain.'[12] Evidence of other
sculptures sent back to Wanstead appear in several visitor accounts
of the period which refer to statues representing poetry, painting,
music and architecture on display in the Grand Hall.[13] In 1787,
Hungarian politician Count Ferenc Széchényi of Sárvár-Felsővidék
referred to 'statues between the windows of which some are of
marble, and some plaster.'[14] Herculaneum sculptures of Livia and
Domitian and Agrippina were also displayed here (*see* Fig 4.7).[15] The

display of these powerful figures among Casali's historical paintings (*see* Fig 4.6) was fitting and reinforced the decorative scheme of the Grand Hall while highlighting the continuity of the Tylney family line and custodianship of Wanstead.

In the Saloon stood Apollo, Flora and a statue of Bacchus by the English sculptor, Joseph Wilton (1722–1803). Wilton lived locally (probably at Snaresbrook House) and it is certain they were familiar neighbours. This may account for John's commissioning of the sculptor. Wilton also resided at Horace Mann's guesthouse in Florence between 1751 and 1755. Through Mann, he gained several important English patrons including Lord Rockingham, Lord Charlemont and Lord Huntingdon.[16] As a member of the Anglo-Florentine elite, John too was a frequent guest to Mann's residence at Casa Manetti in Florence. A caricature portrait painted by Thomas Patch (1725–82) in 1761–3, shows John, dressed in red, seated in the centre of a group of gentlemen dining at Mann's residence (Fig 6.1). The commission may therefore have come about due to John's and Wilton's mutual friendship with Mann in Florence. On 9 November 1753, Mann described Wilton's most recent works in a letter to Walpole, referring to 'A Bacchus for Lord Tylney [John Child], far advanced.'[17]

The display of Classical sculpture at an English country house was the mark of an educated and cultured Georgian gentleman and gave John the opportunity to display his knowledge of Classical art and, to some extent, justify his sojourns abroad. Furthermore, it reveals John's efforts to contribute to the Wanstead interior. Aside from the collection of antique sculpture and improvements to the forecourt, there is little to suggest that John made substantial improvements to the house itself. A description of the house by an anonymous author in 1776 reveals that John reconsidered William Kent's proposal to add wings to the house, but that the idea was soon dropped once a 'most experienced builder' advised him to 'leave it like that.'[18]

Making his mark: John Child's improvements to the gardens at Wanstead

As earlier chapters have demonstrated, Wanstead's early owners went to great lengths to improve the landscape according to the latest trends in English garden design. Josiah Child's 'prodigious planting of avenues' imitated the landscapes belonging to the upper echelons of late 17th-century society and set the scene for the grand estate to flourish.[19] George London's formal gardens commissioned by Richard Child in *c* 1706 established Wanstead's reputation as the 'English Versailles', and John Rocque's 1735 survey illustrates the second phase of landscape improvements, where the artinatural style was successfully adopted.

By 1750, the growing popularity of natural landscapes led by Lancelot 'Capability' Brown (1716–83), then head gardener of Stowe, had taken hold of the nation. Brown's championing of the natural style was achieved by techniques such as replacing formal gardens fronting the house with wide lawns and introducing a sunken fence or a ha-ha to give the effect of making the different components of a landscape appear as one. Brown's designs were so well received that he undertook 40 major commissions between 1750 and 1760, including Croome Court, Packington Hall, Petworth, Wakefield Lodge and Wotton.[20] John's tendency to reside between Wanstead and Italy during this period meant that Wanstead was not, perhaps surprisingly for a house of such stature, among Brown's commissions.

Nonetheless, when John was home, residing at the Wanstead estate, improvements were made to the gardens. The earliest record for landscaping during his ownership appears in a letter written by Smart Lethieullier in 1759: 'He has executed the Grand Project of emptying the Great Bason before the house, it was judiciously executed by the help of a Syphon, without cutting the Bank, or doing any other damage.'[21] Lethieullier's letter reveals that the work on the Basin was one of several improvements implemented during this period: 'there are still considerable improvements made since I saw you there last Christmas & I hope that innocent pleasure will steal more & more upon him.'[22] One year later, Richard Pococke, then Bishop of Ossory, stated, 'Wanstead, Ld Tilney's, who is making some improvements in his park and garden, in a very good taste.'[23] Although it is unclear exactly what these improvements were, French astronomer Jerome Lalande's diary entry for 1763 reveals that the kitchen gardens had been relocated and a complex of hot houses and farm buildings had been erected north-east of the house by this date.[24]

In 1779, Leonard Searles, a member of a well-known family of surveyors and architects, who lived in the nearby village of Leytonstone, produced a plan of the Wanstead estate (Fig 6.2). A comparison between Searles' plan and those produced by Rocque in 1735 and 1745 reveals modifications made to Wanstead's lake system, with a mount and several small islands introduced along the south bank of the Heronry Pond.[25]

In the Ornamental Waters, the islands surrounding the Fortification Island had their early 18th-century geometric form softened. The view from the east depicts the two islands closest to the straight canal as simply turfed over (see Fig 5.5). On Searles' plan, they are recorded as having been united to form what is today known as Rook Island. In 1813, landscape designer Humphry Repton referred to these islands as 'beautifully clothed', suggesting they may have been deliberately planted during this period to create a more natural appearance from how they originally appeared in Cradock's map of 1725 (see Fig 5.3).[26]

Searles' map shows that the wilderness gardens flanking the central avenue in Kip and Knyff's c 1708 views were removed (see Fig 1.2). John Doyley's map of 1815–16 shows that these had been replaced with solid blocks of woodland (see Fig 9.9). Further improvements recorded by Searles include an orangery, north-east of the early 18th-century greenhouse. This presumably served as a standing ground for orange trees from the nearby greenhouse in the summer months.

Unfortunately, the improvements to the landscape recorded on Searles' map are largely undocumented. This makes it difficult to establish precisely when these changes were made and by whom. John was most active in landscaping during the 1750s and early 1760s, when he was intermittently at Wanstead, but it is possible that some of the

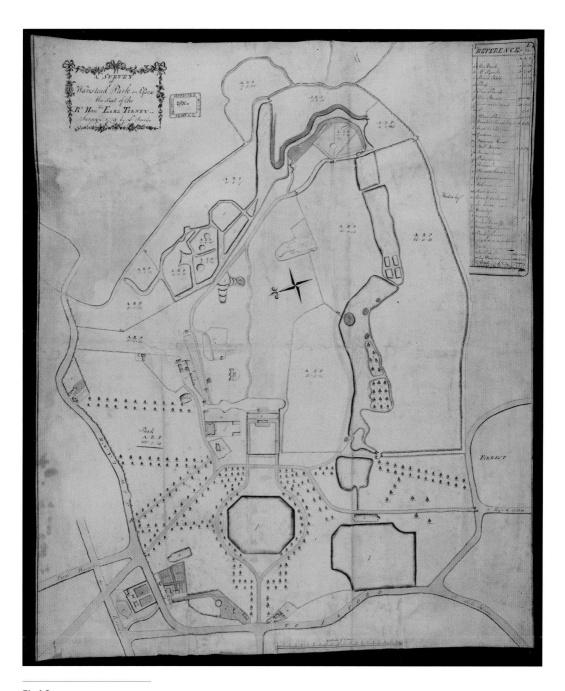

Fig 6.2
Survey of Wanstead Park
(1779) by L Searles.
[Essex Record Office]

works recorded by Searles were commissioned from afar and entrusted to Sir Robert Long. In addition, features recorded by Searles, such as the modifications to the north mount and the creation of a decoy pond on what is now Lincoln Island, do not seem to have been carried out. John's most significant contribution to the landscape, however, was the introduction of two landscape buildings, recorded on Searles' map and which remain *in situ* in Wanstead Park, the Grotto Boathouse and the Temple menagerie.[27]

The Grotto Boathouse

The grotto was an element commonly found in ancient Roman and Greek gardens. Generally defined as an artificial cavern, a grotto usually included fountains or other waterworks, and was decorated with rocks, shell-work, crystals, sculpture and ceramic reliefs.[28] The revival of the grotto during the Renaissance period, most notably by the architect and theatre designer Bernardo Buontalenti (1531–1608) at the Boboli Gardens in Florence, had considerable influence upon the 18th-century English gentlemen who visited these gardens on their Grand Tours and attempted to recreate them back home. The construction of a Grotto Boathouse at Wanstead was undoubtedly influenced by John's long sojourns in Italy.

The Grotto Boathouse was built overlooking the Ornamental Waters, just south of the straight canal. Construction began during the early 1760s on the site of the large Amphitheatre recorded by Cradock in 1725 (*see* Fig 5.3). A set of accounts made in 1761 and 1762 records 'sending rocks for the grotto', suggesting that some of the materials used to construct the Grotto Boathouse may have come from the original Grotto depicted by Rocque in 1735 (*see* Fig 5.1).[29] A letter to John, dated 25 February 1764, suggests its completion: 'I went to the grotto and it was very neat about it.'[30] The earliest visual evidence for the Grotto Boathouse, however, does not appear until Searles' plan of 1779 (*see* Fig 6.2).

The existing remains and an 1822 sketch by Charles Heathcote Tatham reveal that it was built on two levels and designed as a multipurpose structure (Fig 6.3–6.5). The lower level, designed for the storage and repair of boats, was accessed through an opening on the water, in the centre of its front elevation. The 'judiciously adorned' main chamber was accessed via a flight of steps from the waterfront elevation or through an opening to the rear.[31] Incorporating a Boathouse within such a wondrous and curious landscape feature obscured the more utilitarian aspects of estate life from the garden visitor.

There is little evidence to establish the architect responsible, but its design was broadly in line with contemporary methods in grotto construction, such as that by landscape designer Thomas Wright (1711–86) in his 1758 publication, *Universal Architecture*.[32] Wright's advice for a grotto 'of the Rustic kind', in particular, was distinctly similar to that at Wanstead:

be form'd out of the solid Rock, and may with the greatest propriety be ornamented with Ore, Fossils, Coralines and Moss … the situation is supposed to be low, must be refined, and will have a most agreeable Effect, if by the side of a River or Lake. As an Object it will best appear at a proper Distance within the powers of reflection from the water before it.[33]

Fig 6.3

Grotto Boathouse front elevation.

[Wanstead Image Archives]

Fig 6.4

Grotto Boathouse rear elevation.

[Wanstead Image Archives]

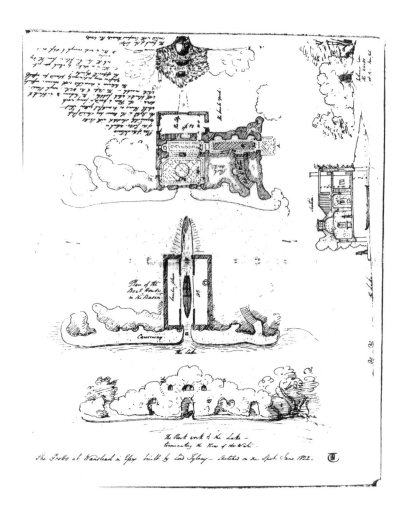

Fig 6.5
Sketch of the Grotto
Boathouse (1822) by Charles
Heathcote Tatham.
[Private Collection]

The use of such materials gave what was in fact a man-made structure the appearance of having risen from the earth, achieving a desired balance between man-made art and nature.[34] The grotto's relationship between art and nature was an ancient concept. Ovid's *Metamorphoses*, a copy of which was held in Wanstead's library, explores the intentions behind the grotto's design as a 'natural' structure: 'in a most secret nook, there was a well shaded grotto, wrought by no artist's hand. But Nature by her own cunning hand imitated art.'[35] Ovid's text notes how the grotto could closely imitate the natural world, placing the beauty of nature and art in parallel. In the grounds of country houses, which rigidly followed Classical architectural principles, the construction of such an intermediary structure was particularly important.

In addition to rough natural materials, statues, broken urns and crumbling columns were commonly used to adorn the exteriors of grottos to evoke Classical antiquity. The display of Greek mythological statues on the Wanstead Grotto, such as Andromeda, was an attempt to recreate a sense of the ancient in the grounds of a recently established landscape.[36] In the late 1990s, an archaeological dig around the Grotto Boathouse uncovered a sculpture of an eagle and snake, derived from the Tylney coat of arms.[37] This was presumably the one that once surmounted the structure. Much like the use of the coat of arms to adorn furniture in the interior of the house, such deployment here helped to emphasise the status of the Tylney title and estate.

Inside, the Grotto was richly decorated with 'every variety of shells, fossils, petrifactions, &c.'[38] It featured a concave roof and a 'balcony of

Fig 6.6
View of the Grotto chamber
before the fire of 1884.
[Redbridge Museums and
Heritage Centre]

glass windows forming a skylight.'[39] The floor was made from 'small pebbles not bigger than the top of one's thumb of a variety of colours and figures.'[40] In 1788, the Revd Stebbing Shaw claimed that its 'very valuable materials' had cost £2,000.[41] Descriptions of the main chamber's interior reveal that the Grotto served as a space 'large enough to entertain a company of twenty' during the warm summer months.[42] The 1822 sale catalogues list items such as a '3-feet mahogany Card Table, top lined green cloth', and 'two bamboo Chinese-frame Elbow Chairs with cane seats', presumably intended for the comfort of guests.[43] Evidence of other grottos possessing similar spaces appear in Joseph and Josiah Lane's Grotto at Oatlands, Weybridge, which included a gaming room furnished with card tables and Chinese furniture.[44]

Admiration for the Grotto-Boathouse continued long after John's death in 1785. In 1813, landscape designer Humphry Repton (1752–1818) described it as a 'sumptuous specimen' and admired it as a feature of a 'various' landscape: 'at such a distance as makes it an object to which the Walks may lead; since Walks in pleasure grounds although beautiful in themselves, must have some interest beyond the mere serpentine lines, however graceful.'[45]

While a considerable amount of its contents and decoration was sold off during the 1822 sales, photographs taken in the late 19th century shows its interior largely intact with glittering stalactites, shells and fossils adorning its cavern-like structure (Fig 6.6). Tragically, a disastrous fire in November 1884 destroyed much of the Grotto Boathouse. *The Morning Post* reported 'its destruction removes the only remaining monument of what was once one of the finest estates in the Eastern Counties.'[46] Although the fire caused considerable damage, the remains of some of its original façade and brick structure gives us an idea of the Grotto's appearance, size, layout and use (*see* Figs 6.3 and 6.4). Its crumbling ruin is an important landmark, igniting curiosity among many visitors to Wanstead Park.

The Temple Menagerie

As work on the Grotto Boathouse was being carried out, the building of a nearby structure, now known as the Temple, was also underway. Like the Grotto, the Temple is a rare survivor of the former estate (Fig 6.7). Representations of the structure do not appear until Searles' 1779 plan (*see* Fig 6.2), but proposals for a garden temple at Wanstead were under consideration from as early as 1759, when the architect William Chambers (1723–96) dedicated a design to Lord Tylney (John Child) in his *Treatise on the Decorative Part of Civil Architecture* (Fig 6.8).[47] Indeed, as Chambers and John had both been in Florence in 1753, it is likely that they had discussed designs for the structure then.[48] Chambers' description reads, 'designed by me some years ago … and proposed to be erected at Wanstead.'[49] It is unclear where Chambers intended his garden temple to be built, but certainly it would have been designed as an eye catcher to terminate one of Wanstead's many vistas.

The building, as erected, differed substantially from that illustrated by Chambers. Perhaps the design was unsolicited or, perhaps, too costly and not in keeping with John's taste. Instead of featuring the cupola shown in the plate, the building was given a Doric portico.[50] Fronting

Fig 6.7

The Temple.

[Wanstead Image Archives]

the structure with a portico evoked Classical associations akin to those of Wanstead House itself, reminding visitors who had wandered this far that they remained on the Tylney estate. The earliest record for the structure dates from 1762, suggesting it was a contemporary of the Grotto Boathouse.[51] The design can possibly be attributed to John Vardy (1718–65), the architect of Spencer House (1756) and close associate of William Kent, on account of a payment of £25 made on 11 March 1762, to a 'Mr Vardy'.[52]

The principal function of the structure seems to have been as a menagerie. The earliest record of a menagerie at Wanstead appears in naturalist George Edwards' (1694–1773) *Gleanings of Natural History* (1764), in which he published a sketch made two years earlier of a pigeon from the Isle of Nicobar, 'now living in the menagerie of the Right Hon. Earl Tilney at his house in Essex.'[53] Also included in Edwards' publication were sketches of a Lesser White Cockatoo: 'This bird I drew at Lord Tilney's hse in Essex'; and a 'very active, lively, diverting' monkey: 'I was obliged to part with him for want of convenient room; for which reason I presented him to a right honourable Lord Tilney in Essex, who has a convenient menagerie at a distance from his mansion-house to receive such animals.'[54] In 1763, Jerome Lalande (1732–1807) referred to a menagerie at Wanstead, but, like Edwards, did not specify its location.[55] A visitor account of 1789, however, describes the entrance to a menagerie, which 'takes the form of a Doric portico.' The visitor proceeds, describing its presence in the landscape: 'it forms an agreeable object ... admirably adapted for rearing every species of fowl.'[56] Searles' 1779 map records the Temple as a 'Poultry House', but an inventory made that year records it as a menagerie. Such evidence confirms that the menagerie referred to in visitor accounts was indeed the structure that we now know today as the Temple.

Searles' 1779 map of Wanstead shows the building north-east of the Heronry Pond, with wings flanking the central bay. Construction work to the building in 1997 revealed that these wings were added shortly after the building's initial construction, possibly built open to the roof to accommodate full-height cages and allow the exotic birds to fly freely.[57]

Searles also records a pond and outhouses behind the structure (*see* Fig 6.2).[58] This was perhaps intended for the display of hardier birds who could live outside in the summer months. John Doyley's 1815–16 map identifies the building as the 'Keepers Lodge and Pheasantry', suggesting it provided accommodation by the early 19th century.[59]

The erection of a menagerie at Wanstead introduced a fashionable feature to the landscape. Similar examples existed at banker and East India merchant Sir Charles Raymond's (1713–88) menagerie at Valentines Mansion in Ilford, also visited by Edwards and described by the naturalist as featuring 'some curious birds and other animals from the East Indies.'[60] Raymond's business partner, Francis Child (*c* 1735–63), kept a menagerie at his family seat at Osterley Park, which famously contained over 97 species of bird and had some similarities to that at Wanstead. Although it is unclear how John acquired birds for the menagerie at Wanstead, his collection is certain to have been facilitated by the return of East India ships. The display of such exotic commodities at Wanstead was fitting for an estate developed from an East India fortune.

*

The construction of the Grotto Boathouse and Temple Menagerie at Wanstead were the last improvements made to the Wanstead landscape prior to John's final departure to the Continent in 1763. Their survival in Wanstead Park provides significant examples of Georgian garden buildings and are among the few tangible features of the lost estate. It was not until Humphry Repton's employment in the early 19th century that the Wanstead landscape underwent any further improvements.

Notes

1   BL MS 752, f.54v, Smart Lethieullier to Dr Charles Lyttelton, 20 August 1751.
2   WSHC 947/2114, John Child to Sir Robert Long, 29 December 1752.
3   WSHC 947/2114, John Child to Sir Robert Long, 20 September 1752.
4   WSHC 947/2114, John Child to Sir Robert Long, 29 December 1752.
5   LWL Horace Walpole to Richard Bentley, the Earl of Strafford, 17 July 1755.
6   RHC, Letter from Lord Tylney to his brother, Sir Robert Long, 11 June 1760.
7   LWL Horace Walpole to Richard Bentley, the Earl of Strafford, 17 July 1755.
8   LWL Horace Walpole to Richard Bentley, the Earl of Strafford, 17 July 1755.
9   Ibid.
10 Ibid.
11 Ibid.
12 WSHC 947/2114, John Child to Sir Robert Long, 20 September 1752.
13 Serres de Latour 1788, 242.
14 Unpublished transcription of Sárvár-Felsővidék's visitor account provided by Richard Arnopp.
15 Muilman 1771, IV, 228.
16 Coutu, 'Joseph Wilton'.
17 LWL Horace Mann to Horace Walpole, 9 November 1753.
18 Volkmann 1788, *Nueste Reisen durch England: Vorzüglich in Absicht auf die Kunstsammlungen, Naturgeschichte* ... [extract]. This description appears to be closely based on 'A New Display of the Beauties of England' by an anonymous author (1776). Many thanks to Richard Arnopp for providing me with a transcription of this account.
19 Beer 2000, 305.
20 Phibbs, 'Lancelot Capability Brown'.
21 BL Stowe MS 752, f.102v., Smart Lethieullier to Dr. Charles Lyttleton, 25 September 1759.
22 Ibid.
23 Cartwright 1888, 80.
24 Special thanks to Richard Arnopp for providing me with a transcript of this material of Lalande's account.
25 See John Chapman and Peter André map of Essex, 1777.
26 ERO D/DCW P7, J Cradock, Plan of Wanstead Park, 1725.
27 Since the City of London purchased the grounds in 1882, this building has been referred to as 'the temple' due to its portico façade.
28 Fleming, Honour and Pevsner 1998, 243.
29 ERO D/DU 546/2. For a brief discussion of this Grotto, see Chapter 3.
30 RHC, Letter to Earl Tylney dated 25 February 1764 from Draycot.
31 Shaw 1788, 31.
32 Some local historians suggest that the site could be attributed to Joseph Lane and his son Josiah, responsible for the construction of Charles Hamilton's Grotto at

Painshill, Cobham (*c* 1740) (figs 120 and 121), as well as those at Oatlands Park, Weybridge (1747) and Fonthill in Wiltshire (*c* 1750), but there is no firm evidence to support such an attribution. For literature on Josiah and Joseph Lane, see Thacker 1976; E Harris 1979.

33 E Harris 1979, plate H.

34 Balmori 1991, 38; Harris 1991, 62.

35 *Wanstead House Sale*, day 31, lot 53. The sale catalogue notes that this was a 1742 publication suggesting Richard Child, 1st Earl Tylney or John Child, 2nd Earl Tylney could have bought it. Nonetheless it is a text which John Child would have been undoubtedly familiar with; Ovid, *Metamorphoses*, III, 157–61 as quoted in Balmori 1991, 44.

36 The sculpture of Andromeda is currently on display at the visitor's centre in the Temple at Wanstead Park.

37 Jeffery 2003, 33.

38 Shaw 1788, 31.

39 Harris 1991, 62. No reference regarding Curwen's description is provided in this article. Many thanks to John Harris for a discussion regarding this reference, obtained from the back of C H Tatham's sketch of the Grotto (1822), now in a private collection.

40 Harris 1991, 60–1.

41 Shaw 1788, 31.

42 Shaw 1788, 32.

43 *Wanstead House Sale*, day 31, lot 51 and lot 53; BNF CVE 39280, *A Catalogue of the superb Gobelin tapestry*, day 3, lot 126.

44 Thacker 1976, 19.

45 PGL Repton 1813. Thanks to Bryan Maggs for allowing me access to this material.

46 *The Morning Post*, Saturday 22 November 1884, 5.

47 *Wanstead House Sale*, day 23, lot 449; Chambers 1791, 136; The 2nd Earl Tylney was a subscriber to this volume, and a copy was recorded in the Wanstead House library at the time of the 1822 sale.

48 Ingamells 1997, 194–5.

49 Chambers 1791, 136.

50 Searles' 1779 map of Wanstead shows the building with wings flanking the central bay (ERO D/DCw P59). However, repair work undertaken in 1997 uncovered evidence of penny-struck pointing on the walls of this central section. This is a building technique used for the construction of outer walls, therefore indicating that the wings were an extension made after the Temple's initial construction. The addition to the south-facing side of the Temple first appears on the 1863 Ordnance Survey map, and therefore postdates the period under consideration here. There is no evidence in the 1822 sale catalogue of a building called the Temple.

51 Edwards 1764, 272.

52 HBA, Ledger 54/440, John Child 2nd Earl Tylney, February 1757–December 1793; Jeffery 2003, 32.

53 Edwards 1764, 272.

54 Edwards 1764, 231, 221–2.

55 Watkins 2002, 66. Transcript kindly provided by Richard Arnopp.

56 Fores 1789. Transcript kindly provided by Richard Arnopp.

57 Jeffery 2003, 32.

58 ERO D/DCw P59.

59 ERO D/DCY P2A.

60 Denford 2015.

7 'A bird of passage': John Child's sojourns in Italy[1]

On 1 July 1763, *Lloyds Evening Post* reported that 'Their Graces the Duke and Duchess of Richmond, the Earl of Tylney, Lord and Lady Spencer and other noble personages embarked last week at Dover for France.'[2] One year later, Sir Robert Long wrote to John in Florence, confirming that the earl was residing in Italy once again, and that he, Robert, was overseeing affairs at Wanstead: 'I dare say everything on this side of the water will be made easy by Xmas and I hope you have nothing to molest you where you are ... I will take care of you, as well as of Every concern also of yours that shall come to any change as far as I am able.'[3]

That year Robert wrote to his son, James Tylney Long, while he was staying with John in Florence, 'If my Lord thinks of staying abroad longer than this summer, twill be proposed ... that we may let his house [Wanstead], or do other things that may be necessary.'[4] This was not an unusual proposal; the leasing of a property while the owner was abroad was a common and effective means of keeping an estate financially secure. One year later, John wrote to Robert about the Whig prime minister, Charles Watson-Wentworth, 2nd Marquis of Rockingham's (1730–1782) desire to 'hire or borrow Wanstead for this season.'[5] John comments on his inability to say no to such requests indicates that applications like Rockingham's were common: 'you may very well imagine that I said it was at his service.'[6]

On 30 July 1764, *The New Daily Advertiser* reported 'their majesties [George III and Queen Charlotte] went to see the fine house of the Earl of Tylney on Epping Forest, and staid above two hours in the house and gardens.'[7] One month later, Robert wrote to John about the recent royal visit and a rumour 'which is spread that the King was about to buy it.'[8] The accuracy of this gossip is unclear, but it does indicate that John's absence from Wanstead was becoming common knowledge, and requiring action. Further evidence to suggest that John had yet to return to Wanstead is confirmed in Rockingham's list of 1766 and the 1st Duke of Newcastle's list of March 1767, both of which classed him as absent from Parliament, where he had stood as MP for Malmesbury since 1761. He did not stand again as MP in 1768.

Meanwhile, John spent excessively in Italy. In a letter to Robert in November 1765, he writes 'I am afraid I shall exceed the bounds that I had set myself', and raises concerns about whether he would be able to pay the £2,000 due to Mr Hoare of Hoare's Bank in the City of London by Christmas.[9] Crucially, he expresses little desire to spend on Wanstead: 'I would have no more expenses made at Wanstead but what is really necessary.'[10] John's instructions to reduce expenditure, however, do not seem to have been intended to protect the family seat but, rather, to allow himself to continue partaking in the extravagant lifestyle adopted by the

Anglo-Florentine elite; 'the arrival here [Florence] of a young court makes some additional expenses unavoidable.'[11]

Contemporary visitor accounts hint at the luxury with which John surrounded himself. Fellow Englishman and politician William Beckford of Fonthill (1709–70) described John's residence in Florence as 'a fine house all over blue and silver, with stuffed birds, alabaster Cupids, and a thousand prettinesses more.'[12] A house adorned so splendidly was, of course, designed to impress, and evidence suggests that John frequently entertained. Horace Mann recorded a dinner with three courses of 40 dishes, 'the best and most magnificent I ever saw, and so said those of the Court who were there. He dressed all his upper servants in new laced clothes.'[13] John also kept a 'most spacious and fine house' in Naples where he 'contributed much to the diversion of that City … he is even to give a public ball tomorrow evening, the only day in Lent that is permitted.'[14] In 1777, Lord Swinburne wrote, 'Lord Tilney has soirees every week which are very agreeable.'[15]

Back in England, attitudes towards the earl were growing hostile. Such expenditure abroad was condemned, especially by one who owned – but neglected – such a 'magnificent home' in England. In 1770, *Town and Country Magazine* expressed bewilderment, castigating John's preference for a life in Italy:

> I could not help be surprised that that nobleman should desert his native country, and such a magnificent home, to dwell among foreigners; where his dignity cannot be supported, and where the appellation of *Milord* affords so extensive a field for that fortune being exhausted among strangers by imposition. Which might with noble liberality be spent among his countrymen, to the advancement of the arts, the honour of himself and the support of many industrious individuals who virtually suffer much from the sums squandered abroad by English noblemen and gentlemen, who seldom are so well accommodated as they might be in their native country.[16]

The writer warns of the large amounts of money being spent abroad, demanding an explanation for John's behaviour:

> To what then are we to attribute his absence? I wish for the instruction of myself, and many others, you would … informe the public what are the reasons that incite his lordship's stay from England, to the diminution of his now buried rank, and the almost total deprivation of the benefit the neighbouring poor would receive from his estate. I beg this favour only with generous hope, that if it reaches his lordship's inspection, it may induce him to return to the deserted mansion of his pensive park.[17]

In 1772, *The General Post* complained of John's expenditure in Florence: 'were the owner as attentive to his affairs as he ought to be, much more would accrue to him from his valuable estate.'[18] That year *The Oxford Magazine* similarly commented on the impact of John's absence: 'The Present Earl residing abroad … this beautiful Seat is now running to ruin.'[19] These criticisms were not unusual during a period that witnessed growing concern about absentee landowners. In 1771, a correspondent to

Town and Country Magazine complained:

> When I look over Vitruvius Britannicus and see the numerous beautiful
> edifices in this island, I am animated with an unconquerable curiosity
> to visit every one … and am in hopes to find, that an hospitality reigns
> within the walls proportionable to the beauty of the architecture
> without; but how greatly I am mortified to find that scarce one in twenty
> is inhabited! 'Does my lord reside here constantly?' 'No Sir, he has not
> been here these four years.' Such is the customary answer.[20]

'He smells so sweet and talks like a waiting gentlewoman'[21]

Absence from the estate while a landowner resided in London was one
matter, and common, but to leave the country entirely was considered
unpatriotic and undeserving of high status and wealth. Of course, by
the second half of the 18th century, it was increasingly common for
Englishmen to spend time abroad. The Grand Tour had reached its peak
in popularity, and many young English gentlemen travelled through Italy.
John is first recorded in Italy aged 40, too old to be classed among those
youthful members of the elite completing their education on the Tour.[22]
He also stayed in Italy for much longer than was normal, associating
closely with Sir Thomas Mann, the artist Thomas Patch, and George
Clavering-Cowper, 3rd Earl Cowper, all of whom were living a life of
self-exile in Italy, their lifestyle contributing to widespread rumours about
their sexuality (*see* Fig 6.1).

John's sexuality had been the subject of gossip since he was a young
man. In 1738, Elizabeth Montagu described a curious incident whereby
John and his younger brother Josiah (1718–59) 'took their horses, and
went out of a frolic, and robbed a taylor who had just received a large
sum of Lord Tylney.' After recounting these events, Montagu concluded,
'I must say, I was much surprised to hear Lord Castlemain was concerned
in so manly an exploit; he smells so sweet, and talks so like a waiting
gentlewoman, I should never have suspected him to be able to put even
a taylor in fear of his life.'[23] When social reformer Jeremy Bentham
published his essay on paederasty in 1785, he proposed that John was
the model for the fictitious homosexual character, Lord Strutwell, in
Tobias Smollet's *Roderick Random* (1748).[24] Whether Smollet did base this
character on the 2nd Earl is unclear, but it is reasonable to assume that,
in a country where homosexual acts were strictly prohibited, John felt it
prudent to exile himself. While homosexuality was criminalised in Italy,
it was not quite perceived with the same degree of hysterical abhorrence,
and prosecutions were rare. Moreover, a wealthy foreigner from a more
powerful country was given some degree of impunity, so long as they
behaved discreetly.[25] In Italy, John could avoid the public scrutiny to
which he would have been subject in England and live contentedly among
like-minded members of the Anglo-Florentine elite. An anonymous
satirical poem, 'Sodom and Onan' (1776), captures this in somewhat
sanctimonious tones:

> For Safety flown to soft Italia's shore
> Where Tilney, Bristol, Jones and many more
> Of Britain's cast outs, revel uncontrol'd
> Who for their Beastial lust their country sold.[26]

John remained in Italy until his death in 1784. He was buried in the English cemetery in Leghorn (Livorno), an Italian port city in Tuscany, but his heart was returned to the family seat at Wanstead and buried alongside his forebears in the family crypt at St Mary's church.

John's role as custodian of Wanstead is a complex one. The improvements carried out to the landscape, particularly the construction of the Grotto Boathouse and Temple menagerie, as well as his acquisition of sculptures for Wanstead House, represent his efforts to demonstrate his involvement in the family estate despite his preference for a life overseas. Yet speculation surrounding his personal life is likely to have given him cause to prioritise his own needs over those of the family seat, putting the financial well-being of the estate under strain. General consensus lays blame on Wanstead's later owners for running the estate into the ground; however, a significant amount of scholarship on 18th-century estates reveals that it was not uncommon for landowners to be heavily burdened with financial debt for several generations.[27] John's accounts with Hoare's Bank in the City of London show signs of mounting debt. In 1779, Hoare's Bank wrote to John in Florence, 'your Lordship's account is at present overdrawn above Eleven Hundred Pounds. We are therefore to request the favor of you not to draw at so long a date, and should esteem your not overdrawing in these times as a particular favor conferr'd on us.'[28] John's lifestyle may therefore have played some part in initiating the financial disaster that later engulfed the family seat.

Even after his death in 1784, contemporaries remained critical, perceiving the 2nd Earl's behaviour as a far cry from the ideal image of a reputable estate owner:

> The crime of Pederasty is more in vogue at Naples than in any other city of Italy. … Lord Tylney, a great pederast, who died a few years ago, made Naples his residence during five and twenty years, on purpose to glut the better his bestial appetite. In order to avoid some criminal proceedings which threatened him in England, on account of the same darling passion, which no nation abhors more than the English, he bade an everlasting farewell to his country, and lived here in princely splendour upon an income of eighteen thousand pounds. He spent usually the summer in Florence, and in winter returned to Naples, where he gave the most brilliant feasts, and indulged his passion till he died.[29]

Without children of his own, John bequeathed Wanstead House to his nephew, James Tylney Long.[30] Although he had taken great care in helping his uncle with his affairs at Wanstead, James did not aspire towards the grand lifestyle associated with that estate. The obituary published in *The Gentleman's Magazine* in 1794 describes him as a man who 'felt very little relish for the gay and splendid scenes of what is called high life.'[31] Indeed, upon his inheritance, he remained at the more humble family residence, Draycot Cerne in Wiltshire. In addition, James would have been nearly 50 years of age when he inherited Wanstead, 'his great accession of fortune a few years before his death … certainly made no addition to his happiness'[32] When James Tylney Long died in 1794, the estate passed to his only son and namesake. The younger James sadly died in 1805, aged just 11. Without any other male heirs, Catherine, the eldest of James' three daughters, was next in line to inherit the family fortune and estates. In the hands of a young heiress, it was ripe for rejuvenation.

Notes

1   LWL Horace Mann to Horace Walpole, 28 June 1777.
2   *Lloyds Evening Post*, 1 July 1763, np.
3   WSHC 947/2114, Sir Robert Long to Lord Tylney, 20 August 1764.
4   WSHC 947/2116 Letter to James Tylney Long, 25 June 1764.
5   WSHC 947/2114, John Child to Sir Robert Long, 20 August 1765.
6   Ibid.
7   *Gazetteer and New Daily Advertiser*, 30 July 1764, np.
8   Stead, 19; WSHC 927/2114 Sir Robert Long to Lord Tylney, 20 August 1764.
9   WSHC 947/2114 John Child to Sir Robert Long, 20 November 1765.
10 Ibid.
11 Ibid.
12 Chapman 1928, 164.
13 LWL Horace Mann to Horace Walpole, 25 October 1768.
14 LWL Horace Mann to Horace Walpole, 15 February 1777.
15 Ibid.
16 'To the printer of Town and Country Magazine', *Town and Country Magazine*, np.
17 Ibid.
18 *General Post*, 27–9 August 1772, np.
19 'Description of TILNEY HOUSE', *The Oxford Magazine or Universal Museum*, 8, 1772, 242–43.
20 Anon 1771, III, 429.
21 Montagu 1825, 26.
22 Ingamells 1997, 960.
23 Montagu 1825, 26.
24 Bentham 1785.
25 Thanks to Richard Arnopp for a discussion regarding this subject.
26 Jackson 1776.
27 Habakkuk 1994; Clemenson 1982, 17; Mackley and Wilson 2000, 25–6.
28 HBA, Hoares & Co to Lord Tylney, 14 November 1779.
29 Trapp 1791, 307.
30 ERO D/DQs/12, Will of John 2nd Earl Tylney.
31 *The Gentleman's Magazine,* 28 November 1794, np.
32 Ibid. James Tylney Long carried out no improvements to the house or grounds but is credited with George Bowles of Wanstead Grove with commissioning architect Thomas Hardwick to rebuild the parish church in 1787–90.

Part 4

Catherine Tylney Long, 1805–25

(No. 834)   LADY CATHERINE LONG
ENGRAVING, AFTER MINIATURE BY CHALON

Fig 8.1
Catherine Tylney Long (c 1810), E Churton
after A Chalon.
[Geraldine Roberts/Stratfield Saye
Preservation Trust]

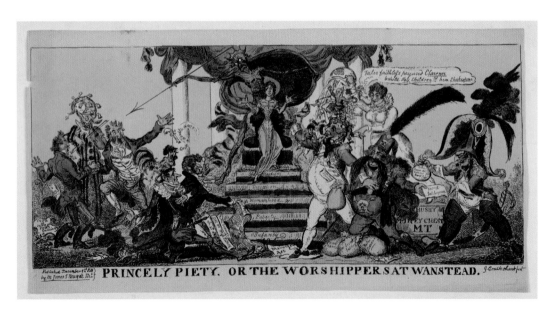

PRINCELY PIETY, OR THE WORSHIPPERS AT WANSTEAD.

Fig 8.2
Princely piety, or the worshippers at
Wanstead (1811) by George Cruickshank,
hand-coloured etching, 19.3 × 40.5 cm.
[The British Museum]

8 'The richest heiress of the British dominions'[1]

Catherine Tylney Long's inheritance of the Tylney fortune and estates made her one of England's wealthiest, most sought-after heiresses of the early 19th century (Fig 8.1). Competition among suitors was fierce. In 1810 Lady Harriet Leveson-Gower (later Lady Granville) wrote to her sister, Lady Georgina Morpeth, about her sighting of Catherine on a drive in Hyde Park: 'it was a droll to see Miss Long's admirers riding about her carriage as the guards do about the King's.'[2] Meanwhile, novelist Lady Charlotte Bury bemoaned the intense rivalry among the suitors: 'all this pother gives on a disgusting picture of human nature. Avarice in children is shocking, yet the united schools of Eton and Westminster are gaping after this girl as if she were fairer than a myriad of Venuses.'[3]

Satirical cartoonists enthusiastically took pen to paper to illustrate the public frenzy surrounding Wanstead's heiress. George Cruickshank's *Princely piety, or the worshippers at Wanstead*, published in 1811 for *The Scourge*, depicts Catherine, so rich that she appears golden, seated on a throne while a rabble of grotesque-looking suitors clamber at her feet below (Fig 8.2). Included among them are the actor Robert 'Romeo' Coates, the playwright Sir Lumley Skeffington, the Anglo-Irish aristocrat Lord Kilworth, Baron Ferdinand de Geramb, a French aristocrat of dubious lineage, and, most notably, the Duke of Clarence and William Wellesley Pole.

When Cruickshank's cartoon was published, Catherine had come of age and, by law, was free to marry whom she wished. Her loyalty to her mother, Lady Catherine, however, meant that the decision ultimately depended on her mother's approval. For the Tylney Long family, there was a lot at stake. Catherine's inheritance encompassed 23,000 acres of land spread across no fewer than six counties, an annual income of around £40,000 and several stately homes, including Wanstead House, the jewel in the family crown.[4] Her inheritance from her uncle, Mr Long, worth more than £200,000, made her the 'richest heiress in the British dominions.'[5] Catherine's choice of husband was therefore fundamental to the future well-being and security of the Tylney fortune and estates.

Aware of her responsibility to make a sensible match, Catherine was nonetheless a young romantic whose affections had become centred on William Wellesley Pole (1788–1857), son of William Wellesley Pole, later 3rd Earl of Mornington (1763–1845) and nephew to Arthur Wellesley, later 1st Duke of Wellington (1769–1852) (Fig 8.3).[6] From the age of 16, William had been sent on military services abroad and had fought in the Peninsular Wars under the command of his renowned uncle. He also worked at the British embassies in Constantinople, Vienna, Copenhagen, Lisbon and Cadiz. Since the Napoleonic Wars had put a stop to the English gentlemen's Grand Tour, William's sojourns abroad set him apart from his peers.

Fig 8.3
Miniature of William Pole
Tylney Long Wellesley (1804).
[Stratfield Saye Preservation
Trust]

William was undeniably handsome and stylish. He embraced the
life of the London dandy, a new breed of fashionable gentlemen, well
known for frequenting the clubs of St James'. Albeit worldly, fashionable
and well-connected, William's reputation was poor, he was a renowned
Lothario and he held little substantial wealth. William's apparent
worldliness no doubt impressed Catherine, but the positions he undertook
were arranged by his father to protect him from being sent to prison for
debts run up while living as a reckless young man in the capital.

Such a reputation led Catherine's family and her trustees to fear
that William's interest in the young heiress was purely a mercenary one.[7]
Their disapproval was worsened by the events of August 1811, when
a dispute broke out between William and Lord Kilworth over verses
published in *The Morning Chronicle*, which lampooned William's courtship
of Catherine. *The Examiner* reported that 'a more wretched set certainly
never appeared in print.'[8] William accused Kilworth of writing the verses
and the dispute soon led to a duel at Wimbledon, by now an illegal
custom that held a death penalty. Fortunately, William's right-hand man,
Colonel Merrick Shawe, settled the duel before any shots were fired, but
the conflict soon flared up again and a second duel was arranged for the
following week. This time, the duel took place and shots were exchanged,
but Kilworth missed and William soon showed mercy by firing his shot
in the air. Cruickshank's cartoon alludes to these events, depicting the
pair engaged in a foolish dance with pistols flying from their hands while
the figure of Death points towards them from behind Catherine's throne.
Such behaviour was unacceptable. Embarrassed about becoming central
to such a scandal, Catherine left London to join her mother and her aunt,
Lady Sarah de Crespigny, in Broadstairs, Kent.

For Lady Catherine and Lady de Crespigny, this was an opportunity to steer the young heiress's affections towards their preferred choice of suitor, William, Duke of Clarence (1765–1837), the third son of King George III and Queen Charlotte, and Admiral of the Royal Navy. Twenty-four years her senior and infamous for his 20-year relationship with Irish actress Dorothea Jordan, with whom he lived at Bushy Park with their ten illegitimate children, the duke was a far cry from the romantic ideal Catherine sought.

Cruickshank's *Princely piety* depicts the duke standing to the right of the throne, dressed in naval uniform (*see* Fig 8.2). He raises one arm towards Catherine, while the other assuredly holds back the French aristocrat, Baron de Geramb, who is kneeling on bags of golden coins, pleading for her attention.[9] Behind the duke stands Dorothea Jordan, who is emptying their brood over his head from a chamber pot (Jordan commonly meaning chamber pot in slang parlance).[10] Satirists often portrayed Dorothea as enraged about the duke's decision to abandon her for Catherine, but her correspondence reveals that she was, in fact, accepting of the duke's need to make a financially advantageous match and resolve his personal debts.[11] This was to become particularly important in February 1811, when the duke's father, King George III, was declared insane and unfit to rule and his older brother, George, was created Prince Regent. The duke was now second in line to the throne and so the importance of making an advantageous marital match and producing a legitimate male heir was potentially of the utmost importance.

For Catherine's family, the duke's improved royal status made him a far preferable candidate than William Wellesley Pole. Correspondence between Lady de Crespigny and the duke suggests that he was aware of his advantage over William and, that autumn, he moved to Ramsgate, Kent, to be closer to the heiress. Many of his letters from this period badgered Lady de Crespigny to influence Catherine. Unfortunately for the duke, William had also followed Catherine to Kent, where he was quickly forgiven for his part in the scandalous events of the summer. On 19 October 1811, the duke complained to Lady de Crespigny that William was 'always at her [Catherine's] elbow' and begged, 'Do try to persuade this dear and lovely angel to think more favourably of me. I really deserve her. I wish and cannot fail of making her happy.'[12]

William Heath's 1812 satirical cartoon, *The r----l lover, or, the admiral on a lee shore*, shows the duke pleading for Catherine's hand (Fig 8.4). The Kentian pier table and map of the Tylney estates, which hangs directly above, suggests that the scene is set at Wanstead House. Catherine stands at the doorway, extending her arm to mark her distance from her determined suitor. Catherine never accepted the Duke of Clarence, despite his best efforts. Charles Williams' cartoon, *The Disconsolate Sailor Miss Long ing for a Pole. Vide, the Waterman*, published that December, shows Catherine standing between her two most competitive suitors on the banks of the River Thames, her dress looped up to contain a heap of guineas and holding a document inscribed as 'rent roll' (Fig 8.5). Her other arm extends out towards William as she says to the duke, 'I am very sorry Mr Tugg, that I can't be yours for indeed I find it impossible to resist such a Pole.'

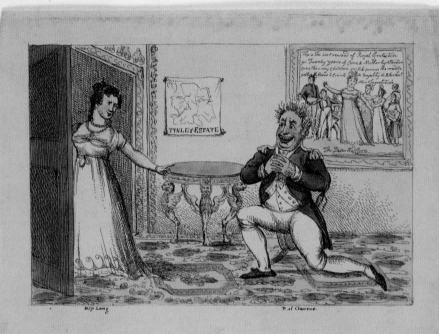

THE R----L LOVER,

OR,

THE ADMIRAL ON A LEE SHORE.

WHAT! leave a woman to her tears?
Your faithful friend for twenty years ;
One who gave up her youthful charms,
The fond companion of your arms !

Brought you ten smiling girls and boys,
Sweet pledges of connubial joys ;
As much your wife in honor's eye,
As if fast bound in wedlock's tie.

Your G——ce, no doubt, has often read,
When love gets in an old man's head,
So sharp he feels the madd'ning pain,
It makes him quite a child again.

Such was, I hear, the hapless case
That recently befel your G——ce ;
The passion thro' your blood ran strong,
Inspir'd by Wealth and T——y L——g.

But first, perhaps, when drinking deep,
You saw the maiden in your sleep ;
Her glittering wealth, the darling prize,
Dazzled your aged, love-sick eyes.

Have you not given the strongest proof
Of honor, honesty, and truth?
Who dare your constancy deride?
Has it not twenty years been try'd?

Thus he resolv'd without delay,
To see the maid that very day ;
Soon the disorder of his soul,
And cut out Mister W——ly Pole.

Arriv'd, and fill'd his R——l G——ts,
Crack'd all his jokes, and all his nuts,
He ask'd to be allow'd the bliss
To speak a private word to Miss.

The happy moment now arrived
By ingenuity contrived ;
He calls up flattery to his aid,
And thus address'd the list'ning maid :

Not Kilworth's Lord nor W——ly Pole
Love half so well, upon my soul ;
With either, or with both I'll fight,
And send 'em challenges to night.

Then tell me, dearest girl, I pray,
Can you to R——ly say Nay,
Will you deny my fond request,
And plunge a dagger in my breast?

The maiden heard him with a sigh,
And this her modest just reply ;—
Sir, if your passion is sincere,
I feel for one that is not here ;

One who has been for years your pride,
And is or ought to be your bride ;
Shar'd with you all your cares and joys,
The mother of your girls and boys.

'Tis cruelty the most refin'd,
And shews a mean ungenerous mind,
To take advantage of your power,
And leave her like a blighted flower.

Return to Mistress J——'s arms,
Soothe her, and quiet her alarms ;
Your present differences o'er,
Be wise, and play the fool no more.

Not more surpris'd did Romeo Coates
Hear the loud laugh from noisy throats ;
When to amuse John Bull, he play'd
Lothario, that gay faithless blade.

Not with more horror, Plomer's Knight
Receiv'd the news of Walsh's flight ;
Not more did Walsh with terror stare,
When A——ns caught him in the snare.

Ah! what avails my hopes and fears,
My sighs, my pleadings, and my tears,
Treats to the ball, the park, and play,
All time and money thrown away.

Ah! had I fram'd a billet doux,
As ancient lovers us'd to do,
Or got my brother Y——k to write
Something of darling and delight.

Such language might have charm'd her mind,
And made the stubborn fair one kind.
The damsel then with all her charms,
Had blest these now forsaken arms.

Oh! Peggy, once my care and pride,
Alas! too rashly thrown aside ;
Now you may smile with scornful face,
And triumph in a D——ke's disgrace !

The above is from an excellent Poem, called THE R——L LOVER, *by* P. PINDAR, Jun.

Etched and Published by S. W. FORES, Corner of Sackville-street, Piccadilly.

Dec 14 1811 1812

Upon the death of his older brother, King George IV, in 1830, the Duke of Clarence himself succeeded to the throne, becoming King William IV of Great Britain and Ireland. Had Catherine, 19 years previously, been able to 'resist such a pole', her future children would have become heirs to the throne, and Wanstead House a royal residence. Sir Josiah Child, founder of the Wanstead estate, could only have dreamed of such a prosperous future for his descendants.

Catherine's determination to marry William (above a prince no less) was plain for all to see. The family eventually gave in to her wishes and the couple became engaged in November 1811. The announcement received many letters of congratulations from members of William's family and close associates.[13] On 24 November, William's aunt wrote to Catherine, 'I know him to have the best of dispositions and an excellent heart and I most sincerely hope and believe that he will make you happy and prove himself worthy of the honour you have conferred upon him.'[14] William's father, the 3rd Earl of Mornington, wrote to his son:

> I most sincerely rejoice at your happiness and I trust in God you may continue to deserve the outstanding good fortune you have met with. I approve most highly of every sentiment you have expressed and in one word, can only say that if you will act up to the determinations you have formed, you will be all that your mother and I can wish you to be, and you cannot fail of making Miss Long happy.[15]

The letter adopts a different tone, however, when addressing concerns about the upcoming marriage settlement:

> I always have been very much averse to tying people up by settlement … I would thoroughly recommend that Miss Long should keep as much as she possibly can in your joint powers – I do not know anything about the property. If her estates are curtailed, of course no settlement of them be necessary. If they are not, I would advise their being kept open, and that in the fullest sense, leaving only a life interest to you in case of her receivership – If there is money, I would leave it all free to be used as you both choose. I would not settle anything on younger children, or at least, not much … my feeling is that you ought not to agree to Miss Long's property being tied up.[16]

Perhaps the 3rd Earl of Mornington's concerns were influenced by William's already vulnerable financial status due to the debts he had run up as a young man prior to his postings abroad. The impending wedding required these debts to be settled urgently: 'Trebeck [the family's solicitor] … will arrange everything respecting your debts and he will explain to you my ideas about getting rid of the annuity you hold.'[17] These comments regarding William's debts justify the concerns held by Catherine's family and trustees, who were anxiously making arrangements to ensure the protection of the Tylney fortune and estates. One newspaper account reported that 'The rolls of parchment employed in preparing the marriage articles conveyances, and other deeds, in preparation for the expected union of Miss Tilney Long and Mr. Wellesley Pole, are sufficiently numerous and bulk to load a cart.'[18]

Fig 8.4
The r----l lover, or, the admiral on a lee shore (1812) by William Heath, hand-coloured etching, 17.9 × 25.5 cm. [The British Museum]

THE DISCONSOLATE SAILOR or Miss LONG ING for a POLE. *Vide, the Waterman.*

Fig 8.5

The Disconsolate Sailor Miss Long ing for a Pole. Vide, the Waterman (1811) by Charles Williams, hand-coloured etching, 24 × 9.7 cm.

[The British Museum]

Although William was marrying Catherine, the settlement drawn up ensured his role was limited to life tenancy of only half of the Tylney estates. Therefore, while entitled to the rents and income from the estates based in Essex and Hampshire, he would never have the right to claim the Tylney estates as his own, nor did he have the power to sell. Instead, the estates would pass to any children the couple had.[19] Had Wanstead survived, Catherine's first son, William Richard Arthur Pole-Tylney-Long-Wellesley, would have been able to take up his rightful inheritance.

The marriage settlement also noted that Catherine was entitled to two sums of £5,000 from her father's will and her marriage portion, in addition to £7,700 per quarter as pin money for her independent income. This was intended for 'the separate use and benefit of Catherine Tylney Long, independently and exclusively of William Wellesley Pole and without being in anywise subject to his debts, control, interference or engagement and the same to be at the absolute disposal of Catherine Tylney Long.'[20]

A further condition of the marriage contract determined that William adopted the Tylney family arms and 'Tylney Long' as an additional surname. This ensured that future heirs or heiresses would continue to carry the family name and maintain the original Tylney ties to Wanstead. Aside from his father's estates in Ballyfin, Ireland, and the family mansions in Savile Row and Blackheath, William had comparatively little to offer and was eager for the settlement to be finalised.

On Saturday 14 March 1812, crowds of spectators and journalists gathered outside St James' Church in Piccadilly, eager to witness William and Catherine's marriage. Catherine's jewels, dress and veil of Brussels point lace was reported as so costly that 'if put up at auction, would have produced a sum of money equal to a year's maintenance of at least 500 poor families!'[21] The ceremony came to a halt, however, when it was realised that William had not thought to purchase a wedding ring for his bride. It is tempting to wonder whether this moment might have given Catherine a convenient pause for reflection. Fortunately, or rather, unfortunately, as history would have it, a ring was quickly sought from a nearby jeweller's shop and the ceremony completed. Making their escape from the crowds on Piccadilly, the couple exited the church through the side door onto Jermyn Street, reportedly spending the night at the Wellesleys' family chateau in Blackheath before proceeding to Wanstead the following day.[22]

Notes

1   Stead, 61.
2   Winter 1905, 214.
3   Winter 1905, 215.
4   Roberts 2015, 66–7.
5   Stead, 61.
6   William was the fourth and only son of William Wellesley Pole, 3rd Earl of Mornington, and his wife Katherine Elizabeth (1760–1851), daughter and co-heir of Admiral John Forbes (1714–96). William Wellesley acquired the additional surname of Pole when inheriting the estates of his cousin William Pole of Ballyfin, Queen's County, Ireland in 1778. See Norgate, 'Pole, William Wellesley'; Gash, 'Wellesley'.
7   ERO T/B 39 W.H.L; Stead, 25.
8   'Mr Wellesley Pole and Lord Kilworth', *The Examiner*, 18 August 1811, 536–7.
9   The duke had been appointed by his brother, the Prince Regent as Admiral of the Navy earlier that year.
10 The couple had resided at Bushy House in Teddington since the duke's post as Ranger to Bushy Park in 1797.
11 See Aspinall 1951.
12 WSHC, 2246, The Duke of Clarence to Lady de Crespigny, 19 October 1811.
13 RHC Box 4, Vol. 1, Letter Nos. 1–13.
14 ERO TA/404, Letter to Miss Catherine, from Oatlands, 24 November 1811.
15 RHC, William Wellesley Pole to William Wellesley, 19 November 1811, Vol, 1, Letter 8.
16 Ibid.
17 Ibid.
18 Stead, 64.
19 WSHC 2062/4 Settlement giving Miss Catherine Tylney Long an independent income after marriage.
20 Ibid.
21 *Liverpool Press*, 24 April 1812.
22 'INCIDENT'S OCCURRING IN AND NEAR LONDON, INTERESTING MARRIAGES, &c.', *La Belle Assemblée: or Court and fashionable magazine*, March 1812, 164–6.

Fig 9.1
Louis XIV Ormolu and Boulle
marquetry bibliothèque basse
(c 1705).
[Christie's Images/Bridgeman
Images]

9 The Pole-Tylney-Long-Wellesleys at Wanstead: a Regency revival, 1812–22

Reviving the Wanstead interior

As the newly married couple arrived at Wanstead House, Catherine is certain to have felt proud to welcome her husband into the ancestral home where she had recently commissioned extensive restoration work. Her father, James Tylney Long's will instructed that the estates and fortune were to be tied up and under the control of her trustees, Thomas Phipps and William Bullock, until she had come of age in 1810.[1] That year, Wanstead's exiled royal tenant, Louis Joseph de Bourbon, 8th Prince of Condé (1736–1818), who had leased the house since 1802 to escape the political tumult in France, departed Wanstead and relocated to Wimbledon.[2] After Condé's departure, Catherine secured an advance from her trustees to refurbish the house, which had been described by Condé as 'decorated in old-fashioned style, and … never used, even though [it is] richly furnished.'[3] The underuse by former owners, Sir John Child, 2nd Earl Tylney, and her father, Sir James Tylney Long, meant that Wanstead's interior was, for the most part, stylistically frozen in the early Georgian period. The former splendour of Wanstead House was thus in desperate need of reviving.

Especially important were William Kent's ceiling paintings, now a prized feature of Richard Child, 1st Earl Tylney's early 18th-century scheme. The groined ceilings, pilasters and cornices were also regilded.[4] In a letter dated 18 October 1810, Bullock wrote to Catherine at length about the progress of the restoration work being undertaken:

> The workmen here are going on with the Painting and other Works, as well as we could expect. They have nearly finished what was to be done upstairs, and as I think, in a Workman like manner: and they will proceed with the Ground Floor as fast as possible … the upper storey has been much the most troublesome and tedious – on account of the Ceiling and other carved work – I have not suffered them to do anything to the Grand Hall, upstairs, until you see it again, as I think more must be done to it than we talked of – and it will be as well to leave it till the last.[5]

In February 1811, Bullock updated the heiress on the work's progress, assuring her that 'no time will be lost in getting it completed.'[6] Catherine's status as a highly eligible heiress, and her much anticipated marriage, meant that finishing the project was urgent. Moreover, Catherine required an appropriate setting in which to display her status and to provide extravagant entertainments expected of a wealthy heiress such as the 'splendid déjeune', which she held on 10 July 1811.[7]

In addition to extensive restoration work, the newly married couple wasted no time in modernising Wanstead's interior. A plan of the Principal Grand Floor made by John Buckler in 1822 records a Billiard Room, Library and China Room, suggesting some of the state rooms were repurposed by William and Catherine.[8] Furniture from the Principal Grand Floor was reupholstered in a crimson and gold scheme, new silks and curtains were hung and Axminster carpets bearing the Long Wellesley crest were introduced throughout the state apartments.[9] Within the first year of their marriage, William and Catherine purchased several luxury goods from Vulliamy & Sons, whose shop was situated in Pall Mall and who famously served as clockmakers to the Prince Regent. Items acquired from Vulliamy's included mounted oriental porcelain, black marble pedestals and a Boulle clock by French clockmaker, Claude Raillard.[10]

The couple also commissioned Vulliamy & Sons to produce two large bronze chandeliers in an early 18th-century French style, similar to those that hung above the staircase at the Prince Regent's Carlton House and at Sir Harry Fetherstonhaugh's Saloon at Uppark House (*see* Fig 10.1).[11] Vulliamy's design for William and Catherine incorporated the family coat of arms, signifying the ongoing success of Wanstead under its newest owners. The June 1822 sale catalogue, which verifies the Vulliamy attribution, records the chandeliers hanging in the Grand Hall, where they made a notably grand addition beneath Kent's ceiling painting and alongside Casali's historical scenes and the 2nd Earl's collection of antique Italian marble sculpture.[12]

In 1814, William and Catherine's appetite for luxurious furnishings took them across the Channel to France. The significant amount of art and furniture released onto the market by the recent economic and social upheaval of the French Revolution had become comparatively accessible and affordable for English collectors such as the Prince Regent, Sir Harry Fetherstonhaugh and John Russell, 6th Duke of Bedford.[13] Items listed in the 1822 sale catalogue reveal that William and Catherine acquired a number of masterpieces during their visits to France in April and August 1814 and again in 1815, including ten items attributed to André-Charles Boulle (1642–1732), master cabinet-maker to Louis XIV, whose work was highly sought-after among Regency collectors (Fig 9.1).[14] Contrary to the *ancient regime* practice of displaying Boulle furniture in the picture gallery or cabinet only, the English collector took to displaying these luxurious pieces boastfully throughout the home.[15] At Wanstead, Boulle furniture was displayed in the Grand Hall, Drawing Room, Ballroom and the Blue Damask State Bedchamber, visible for all to admire.[16]

Other luxury items acquired by William and Catherine during their visits to France included a 'Very valuable tulip-wood oriental square jewel casket … with thirteen beautiful specimens of the rare Sèvres China exquisitely painted with flowers, Green and Gold enamelled borders' displayed in the Grand Drawing Room and attributed to the Parisian cabinet-maker and master of the French neoclassical style, Martin Carlin (*c* 1730–85).[17] The casket is one of three produced by Carlin, whose furnishings were highly popular among France's main dealers, Charles Dauguerre and Simon-Philippe Poririer, who had supplied Madame du Barry and Marie-Antoinette. Although the provenance of the Wanstead casket is unclear, it may have come from the home of the Comtesse de Provence, Marie Antoinette, or the Duchesse de Bourbon, where identical pieces were recorded.[18]

The acquisition and display of furniture that had once adorned the homes of French aristocracy was significant and re-established Wanstead's reputation as a fashionable residence. It was now on a par with the homes of England's leading tastemakers, including the Prince Regent, who had lavishly furnished Carlton House with costly Boulle items, and the 6th Duke of Bedford, whose apartments at Woburn Abbey were described in 1804 as 'newly furnished', with 'many very expensive articles, clocks etc. from Paris.'[19] Contemporary responses to the furnishings introduced by William and Catherine were positive. *The Morning Post* reported that William's furnishing scheme at Wanstead was 'in all the splendour of the modern taste' and *The New Monthly Magazine* claimed that its magnificence exceeded Carlton House.[20]

The extortionate cost of the new furnishings was likely justified by the desire to revive Wanstead's interior. Certainly, when William was called to the King's Bench in 1827 to defend himself against squandering Catherine's fortune, it was argued that the great expenses incurred were unavoidable:

> In order to maintain the rank in society which his wife held, it was necessary to form suitable establishments for his family, and incur great expense, which he did in the purchase of horses, carriages, jewellery and plate. He stated that at the time of his entering into the mansion of Wanstead House, it was not only necessary to repair, but to furnish it with suitable furniture, and so to lay out large sums of money in improving the grounds, and rebuilding farmhouses on the estate.[21]

William and Catherine's celebrity status once again cemented Wanstead's reputation as a popular tourist destination. The decision to embark on an extensive refurnishing scheme so soon after their marriage demonstrates their eagerness to create a setting suitable for hosting large-scale entertainments expected of an estate situated so close to the capital. In February 1814, *The New Monthly Magazine* reported that the alterations carried out by William were 'preparatory to the baptism of his infant son, William Richard Arthur (1813–63), and also in expectation of the return of his uncle, Lord Wellington, in the Spring.'[22] The baptism was a major event attended by the Duke of Wellington, the guest of honour, for whom a triumphal arch was erected at the entrance to the village of Wanstead. Other notable guests included the Prince Regent, the princes of Prussia, cabinet ministers, the dukes of Richmond, Newcastle and Devonshire, as well as 300 guests from 'neighbouring families of distinction.'[23] *The Morning Post* reported that 'no situation could be better calculated for the purpose than the celebrated chateau [Wanstead House].'

Contemporary accounts hint at the costs of the extravaganza. One paper reported that the Corinthian columns of Wanstead's famous portico were 'illuminated in the form of wreaths' and that guests were provided with 'a most sumptuous banquet, set out in the great hall; the whole was served on massive plate'. From midnight, guests danced in the recently restored Ballroom until two o'clock when the music ceased and an 'excellent supper … with covers for 500 persons' was served in the Saloon. After supper, dancing recommenced and continued until five o'clock in the morning. In the surrounding grounds, a military band performed throughout the night and barrels of ale and porter were in place for 'the comfort of all comers', suggesting that locals were invited to partake in the celebrations.[24]

In August 1816, an equally extravagant celebration was held for the baptism of William and Catherine's second son, James Fitzroy Henry (1815–51). The Duke and Duchess of Wellington, Dowager Duchess of Leeds, Marquis and Marchioness of Worcester, Marquis of Downshire and Lady Amherst were among the first guests to arrive, followed by the Austrian ambassador, Prince Paul Esterhazy and his princess, the French ambassador, the Marquis d'Osmond and his Lady, Count Núñez, the Spanish ambassador, and other members of the foreign corps diplomatique. On this occasion, flowering shrubs entwined the columns of the Grand Hall and the balustrades of the staircases, where a military band from the Royal Artillery at Woolwich performed. In the Grand Hall and Saloon, a banquet for which 'every cover was of massive silver', was served to over 400 guests, the wines 'most costly and abundant.'[25] Throughout the night, guests delighted in dancing to a band of musicians in the Ballroom and Saloon. *The Morning Post*'s account of the celebrations praised the recent improvements.[26] Wanstead House was now suitably restored and fitted out to accommodate magnificent entertainments.

Many contemporary accounts attributed Wanstead's new furnishings to William.[27] If so, we can perhaps interpret William's furnishing scheme as his attempt to leave his mark on the magnificent mansion to which he could claim life tenancy only.[28] Further evidence of this can be found in the restoration of Wanstead's pediment above the portico, which now incorporated the Wellesley coat of arms.[29] For Catherine, the restoration and improvement of Wanstead House was an opportunity to demonstrate her dedication to the role of custodian. Indeed, John Child, 2nd Earl Tylney's will of 1785 instructed his successors to re-evaluate Wanstead's interior as and when they saw fit, but noted that furniture should be replaced with goods 'of an equal or greater value.'[30]

The improvements carried out prior to and after William and Catherine's wedding reflect an unwavering optimism for a lengthy and prosperous future at Wanstead House. The costs of restoring and furnishing Wanstead House and the hosting of events described above reveal the extent of William and Catherine's excessive expenditure. This no doubt contributed to mounting financial troubles that were made even worse by the landscape improvements commissioned around the same time.

Humphry Repton's landscape improvements at Wanstead

In April 1813, Humphry Repton (1752–1818) was employed by William and Catherine to carry out improvements to the Wanstead landscape. Repton was an obvious candidate for employment. By the late 18th century he had become the leading landscape designer of the period, responsible for major improvements at Holkham (1789), Wentworth

Woodhouse (1790) and Harewood (1799). He had also authored several influential publications on landscape gardening.[31]

Wanstead was of great importance to Repton. The Napoleonic Wars, taxes and inflation had led to a steep decline in the type of major commissions from aristocratic patrons that had catapulted his early career. In contrast, commissions during the early 19th century were few and far between, not to mention modest.[32] In January 1811, his career was further blighted by a carriage accident that damaged his spine and confined him to a wheelchair for the remainder of his life. When Repton was invited to improve Wanstead, he enthusiastically accepted. On 23 June 1813, a frail Repton visited the estate with his son John Adey. A letter from Repton's sister Dorothy to her son, William, comments that the landscape designer spent three to four hours touring Wanstead after which he restored himself with a glass of wine provided by a Mrs Danvers. Repton made his second visit on 28 June 1813, presumably to finalise his designs.[33]

That September, Repton submitted his proposals for Wanstead. The report included several watercolour views depicting 'before' and 'after' scenes. The production of such views, bound together in red morocco, was a fundamental aspect of Repton's practice. Named on account of their presentation, the 'Red Books' were highly regarded as luxury commodities. Extracts from these proposals for various country houses were frequently included in his published treatises on landscape design. The title page for his 1816 publication, *Fragments on the Theory and Practice of Landscape Improvements*, states that the ideas put forward were 'collected from various manuscripts in the possession of the different noblemen and gentlemen for whose use they were originally written.'[34] Such publications provided a public platform from which Repton could exhibit his latest designs and ideas.

William, however, declined the opportunity to have a Red Book for Wanstead. This was a significant blow for Repton: 'I must confess I am a little mortified that it should be your wish not to have it seen, because it is a subject I am not a little vain of.'[35] The production of one of these publications devoted to Wanstead would have allowed Repton to include his designs for the property in detail, advertising his return to the kind of aristocratic commission on which he had established his career.[36] Instead, Repton could only include a small selection of his proposals for Wanstead in *Fragments* (1816), under the generic heading 'A place near the Capital'.[37] Although he did not directly refer to Wanstead, the views included were instantly recognisable to those familiar with what he described as 'one of the most magnificent places in this country.'[38] Why William declined to have a Red Book produced is unclear; however, their production was an additional expense, prepared only once payment for it had been guaranteed.[39] This suggests a certain lack of commitment and hints at the financial restrictions already facing Wanstead's new owners.

Humphry Repton and the picturesque debate

Repton's proposals for Wanstead were intended to modernise and revive the grounds for its new owners. They were also an opportunity for Repton to demonstrate his ability to engage with the recent debates on the picturesque and landscape gardening. When setting out as the nation's leading landscape designer in the late 18th century, Repton had sought to imitate the 'natural'-appearing landscapes made popular by his predecessor, Lancelot 'Capability' Brown (1716–83).

Repton's early commissions, in particular that at Tatton Park in Cheshire in 1791, showed Brown's influence, and so came under fire by supporters of the picturesque movement, Richard Payne Knight (1751–1824) and Uvedale Price (1747–1829), who argued that Brown's designs (and Repton's imitation of them) were highly unnatural. They instead argued that a garden should imitate the Italian landscape paintings by Nicolas Poussin (1594–1665), Claude Lorrain (c 1600–82) and Salvator Rosa (1615–73), free from human intervention and habitation.[40] They rejected the need for practical gardening skills and thus, in a sense, the idea of a controlled estate landscape.

Repton, however, perceived the rugged, romantic landscapes advocated by Knight and Price as an inappropriate setting for a country house. He argued that an estate landscape should be designed to be lived in, and to combine beauty and utility, calling for a 'greater affinity betwixt Painting and Gardening.'[41] This could not be achieved in the kind of rough, picturesque terrains praised by Knight and Price: 'the most beautiful scenes in nature may surprize at first sight, or delight for a time, but they cannot long be interesting unless made habitable; therefore the whole Art of Landscape Gardening may properly be defined as the pleasing combination of Art and Nature adopted for the use of Man.'[42]

The arguments from the two sides were exchanged through a series of publications between 1794 and 1798.[43] Despite originally positioning himself as a follower and defender of Brown, Repton's published writings indicate a gradual shift away from the Brownian style. In his 1806 publication, *An Enquiry into the Changes of Taste in Landscape Gardening*, Repton argued that 'the fashion of English gardening was in danger of becoming more tiresome, insipid and unnatural.'[44] Evidently, Repton no longer perceived an entirely Brownian landscape as wholly appropriate for an estate landscape:

> Extremes are equally to be avoided; and I trust that the taste of this country will neither insipidly slide into the trammels of that smooth shaven 'genius of the bare and bald,' which he [Knight] so justly ridicules; nor enlist under the banners of that shaggy and harsh-featured spirit, which knows no delight but in the scenes of Salvator Rosa; scenes of horror, well calculated for the residence of the banditti.[45]

The Wanstead commission was therefore an opportunity for Repton to demonstrate an approach that sought a balance between the manmade garden and the natural world that Brown, Price and Knight valorised, albeit in different ways. This was achieved by combining two different styles, referred to throughout the Wanstead report as the 'modern' and 'ancient' style. The 'modern' referred to the Brownian elements, which presented the natural landscape as 'the chief object' to follow.[46] The 'ancient' style, meanwhile, derived from Le Nôtre's landscape at Versailles, made popular in England by London and Wise during the early 18th century, and represented in Kip and Knyff's engravings of Wanstead in c 1708 (*see* Fig 1.2–1.4).[47]

Significantly, Repton refused to allow the 'modern' Brownian style to dominate his designs for Wanstead. He claimed that restoring the true character of the landscape was more important than following fashion: 'It is therefore an object worthy of consideration whether the original or the more recent Style be most advisable; and how far both may be admitted.'[48] Having retained some aspects of the early 18th-century landscape, Wanstead was already furnished with 'examples of the Geometric Style of Gardening'.[49] In his report, Repton writes to William, 'I could not but rejoice at the instructions I received, that it is your wish not to destroy, but rather to preserve the original style of the place ... I must congratulate you on the good taste displayed in such a wish.'[50] Not only was this economically more practical, but to seek out the site's original character was another means of negotiating recent debates around the role of art and nature in landscape gardening.

The Wanstead report

The June 1822 sale catalogue records lot 447 as 'Repton's Drawings of Plans for Improving the Grounds at Wanstead House (15).'[51] The report's pages were unbound and comprised of 15 hand-written pages with four grey-wash sketches of fencing and bridges at Wanstead and 9 watercolour views. Seven of these watercolour views featured overlays to reveal before and after scenes. The proposals were purchased, alongside a portfolio of drawings of clocks and stands, by 'Lightfoot' for nine guineas. Mr Lightfoot was William Wellesley's solicitor, who may have purchased the views on William's behalf. Indeed, William attempted to hold back several family portraits and views of Wanstead at the sale in 1822. Perhaps Repton's views were among the works Wanstead's owners attempted to hold onto. The whereabouts of the report were unknown until it resurfaced for sale in 2002 from a private collection. The views were purchased for the library of the late Sir Paul Getty at the Wormsley estate, where they are currently held.[52]

The approach

Three of the watercolour views produced for the Wanstead report depict the approach. The first view is taken from the central avenue running towards the house and laid out in the late 17th century by Josiah Child. In this view, the house occupies centre stage. Its magnificent Portland stone façade is reflected in the Basin, from which a grassy lawn extends towards the house. Urns and columns flank the forecourt. There are no figures or livestock in sight and the estate appears eerily deserted. This approach was recorded in early 18th-century views of the estate such as John Rocque's 1735 plan and an anonymous view entitled 'A view of Wanstead House, Epping Forest', produced around the same time (*see* Figs 4.1 and 5.1). The existing view appears unchanged by 1813 and was therefore among the features considered for improvement.

Lifting the flap to reveal Repton's proposals, we see that the empty forecourt has been transformed into private gardens with shrubbery, closing the house off from the approach road. The decision to close the house off will be addressed in the discussion of Repton's view from the portico. Suffice to say, it represented an important change in William and Catherine's relationship with the Wanstead locale and their growing desire for privacy.

In approaching the House, this road is far preferable to that on the North side of the bason, because it shews the House & the Park to greater advantage.

Fig 9.2

'In approaching the house, this road is far preferable to that on the North side of the bason, because it shows the House and park to greater advantage' (1813) by Humphry Repton, watercolour, 35.3 × 20.8 cm. [© The Trustees of The Wormsley Fund]

Repton's second view of the approach is taken from the southern road surrounding the Basin (Fig 9.2). Repton's text describes the southern approach as superior to the northern side 'because it shows the house and the Park to greater advantage.'[53] A visitor could take in a sweeping view of the landscape to the south and revel in the full beauty of Wanstead's façade. The livestock grazing by the Basin and other visitors taking in the view of the landscape evoke a sense of Wanstead as a revived estate.

The third approach depicted by Repton is taken from the public road which ran south-west of the house, between the Reservoir Pool and the Lake (now Blake Hall Road). The proposed improvements, which included the removal of the overgrown plantations south of the Basin and along the banks by the 'pool', were intended to restore Wanstead's presence in the wider landscape. Furthermore, it provided the western and southern staterooms with more pleasing scenes of the surrounding gardens as well as a view of London in the distance. The improved view for this approach depicts a bridge over the water, suggesting that Repton intended to join the Reservoir Pool and Lake together. These modifications, however, were not implemented and the waters remained separate.

Views from Wanstead House

Three watercolour views included in Repton's report are taken from the most prized rooms of the house, the Grand Hall, the Ballroom and the Saloon. Improving these views was critical for impressing the many guests William and Catherine expected to entertain at their newly refurbished seat.

The view from the Portico

Repton's view to the west is taken from the portico fronting the Grand Hall, looking out onto Wanstead's forecourt, where an open lawn lies immediately beneath the house (Fig 9.3). Paths on either side of the lawn lead toward the Basin and continue into the far distance. The lawn represents what Repton refers to as the 'modern' style. Repton criticises the view, stating 'we can see nothing natural, except the materials which Nature has furnished of land, trees and water; but all of these have been so forcibly under the control of Art, that they are no longer considered as natural objects any more than the stones and masonry of the house can be considered as natural rocks.'[54]

For Repton, the 'modern' Brownian style was unsuitable for this setting. He argues, 'Among the absurdities of the modern Style, is that of placing the house in the centre of its domain; from which every thing is

Fig 9.3
View towards the west from the house (1813) by Humphry Repton, watercolour, 36.7 × 21.4 cm.
[© The Trustees of The Wormsley Fund]

View towards the West from the House.
Looking down from the Portico on the Before-court — & supposing the scene unobstructed by any moving objects.

banished, but the beasts of the forest.'[55] He continues, 'we do not expect near a Metropolis any thing like perfect seclusion from mankind.'[56] Repton argued that the front gardens at Wanstead ought to serve as a public space, much like those belonging to Carlton House or St James' in London.[57] As the existing view illustrates, the front gardens at Wanstead were far from the public space Repton recommended. Instead they were 'unenliven'd by any moving objects', with no visitors coming or going and no livestock.[58]

This deserted scene was due to William's recent decision to reduce the frequent passing of 'unseemly carriages' directly beneath his window by erecting a gate to restrict access to the public highway, which, until then, had run through the estate. The public was displeased, and his actions were brought to the attention of the Chelmsford Assizes, who demanded access to be resumed.[59] These events are likely to have troubled Repton, who had developed concerns over the growing detachment between landowners and rural communities. His representation of a 'dull and unenliven'd scene' was therefore intended to illustrate the impact of restricting public access upon Wanstead's appearance.

Lifting the flap of this subdued watercolour view, a considerably more enlivened scene is revealed (Fig 9.4). The plain lawn has been replaced by a set of parterres laid out in a Union Jack design. The parterres are enclosed by shrubbery with access to the main pathways leading towards the Basin provided through arches on either side. The parterres to the left feature 'Cordbeilles of Roses and flowers mixed' and to the right 'more formal Embroidery Work with box &c.'[60] Each quarter of the parterre

Fig 9.4
View of the west parterre (1813) by Humphry Repton, watercolour, 36.7 × 21.4cm. [© The Trustees of The Wormsley Fund]

This side shews Parterres with Corbeilles of Roses & flowers mixed.   This side shews the more formal Embroidery Work with box &c.

garden features statuary at its centre, much like those planted by George London for Richard Child in *c* 1706. At the centre of the 'Union Jack' is a fountain pool. The scene is populated. A gentleman in the foreground is engaged in discussion with his female companion about the parterres, while other figures can be seen seated or taking a walk. Surrounding the Basin, two carriages with horses make their approach towards the house while livestock graze nearby.

Repton's view suggests that the parterre garden was intended to separate the spaces adjacent to the house, designed for friends and family, from the wider public. The design successfully accommodated both William's desire for privacy and a wider concern for the types of social space expected of an estate situated so close to London.

Repton proudly described the introduction of a parterre garden as 'a dereliction of all the modern notions of taste in landscape gardening' and criticised the existing lawn as 'too small to be fed by flocks and herds, too large to be considered as a bowling green.'[61] As a prominent feature of Wanstead's early 18th-century landscape, their introduction here offered Repton an opportunity to apply the 'ancient style' and by doing so, restore Wanstead's original character.

To the north of the parterre appears a tiered amphitheatre, much like those introduced at Wanstead during the early 18th century. Repton provides no comment in the text on this feature, and archaeological evidence for it is lacking, suggesting that not all features proposed in this view were executed. Another example of the 'ancient' gardening style in Repton's proposed view to the west is visible at the opposite end of the Basin where a balustrade or low wall with a pedimented centrepiece (possibly containing a grotto), backed by shrubbery, breaks up the original view of the wide sweeping avenue. Repton's proposal for this view reflects a growing confidence in his approach to landscape design, adopting the style best suited to the setting. Had Repton been permitted to publish the design, he would have been able to demonstrate publicly his ability to negotiate between 'ancient' and 'modern' gardening styles.

The view from the Saloon

Turning his back on the view to the west, Repton would have proceeded through the Grand Hall, entering the Saloon from where he made his next view 'looking down from the balcony of the Saloon, upon the square shaped lawn … without anything to enliven it' (Fig 9.5).[62] Once again, he presents a rather uninteresting scene, with little to focus on. A simple wooden fence separates the house from a square lawn that leads the eye towards the canal and the avenue of trees in the distance. Trees to either side of the lawn obscure much of the surrounding landscape.

The proposal for this vista demonstrates Repton's attempts to fuse the 'modern' and 'ancient' styles in order to rectify the landscape's appearance (Fig 9.6). One of the ways in which he attempted to do so was by improving the square lawn situated beneath the Saloon, which he described as 'one of the least pleasing specimens of the Ancient Style.'[63] Richard Child, 1st Earl Tylney, had introduced this lawn in *c* 1730 to replace the parterre gardens, canal and bowling green that

View towards the East.

Looking down from the Balcony of the saloon, upon the square shaped Lawn &c. explain'd in page 5

Fig 9.5
View towards the east
(1813) by Humphry Repton,
watercolour, 37.9 × 20.2 cm.
[© The Trustees of The
Wormsley Fund]

had formed London's formal gardens in the early 18th century. Repton perceived the lawn, which did in fact retain its overall square form, as a poor compromise between the 'ancient' and 'modern' styles, 'neither natural, nor of sufficient importance to be acknowledged as artificial.'[64] In this view, it is not so much the presence of the 'ancient' style that is problematic, but rather its appearance. Repton therefore applied the 'modern' principles of landscape gardening in order to correct the feature. The improved view shows the proposal to soften the lawn's geometric form by removing the trees on either side, opening up the garden in a manner typical of the 'modern' style.

Further examples of the 'ancient' style in this view include the avenue of trees and canal visible in the distance. Repton considered this area too large to undergo alterations, and thus retained its original form. This decision illustrates Repton's practical approach as a gardener. Unlike Brown's seemingly endless landscapes, the preservation of the garden's earlier symmetry could assist the viewer by providing objects on which to focus when looking out from the Saloon and thus were worthy of maintaining.

Like the view to the west, Repton's concern for the relationship between public and private spaces in an estate landscape is uppermost. The improved view to the east, however, shows only three figures admiring the landscape from behind the balustrade fence. This was because different spaces in the estate landscape served different purposes. The landscape at the front of the house, for example, served as a public environment, while that situated at the rear was a more private space, and not expected to conform to the same degree of public demand. The figures in the improved view show that the gardens immediately beneath the

Shewing the effect of admitting deer on this side & of a terrace & balustrade as a foreground to the landscape. also the artificial square nefs of this lawn is in some degrees altered & corrected

Fig 9.6
'View towards the east
showing the effect of
admitting deer on this
side and of a terrace and
balustrade as a foreground
to the landscape' (1813)
by Humphry Repton,
watercolour, 37.9 × 20.2 cm.
[© The Trustees of The
Wormsley Fund]

Saloon acted much like the enclosure of the Wanstead interior, intended primarily for family and friends, with public access only being granted on special occasions.

The view from the Ballroom

The view towards the south (Fig 9.7), 'looking down from the centre window of the long room [the Ballroom]', once again presents a bland scene. Repton's report provided little commentary for the view, but lifting the flap, a more pleasing scene is revealed (Fig 9.8).[65] This would have been achieved by the removal of the plantations to provide a view of the reconfigured waterworks and the introduction of new plantations on the field beyond to make the park and wider landscape of Epping Forest appear as one.

Perhaps most importantly, the proposed view presents a more pleasing frame to the view of the city of London in the distance. Repton considered Wanstead's relationship with the capital as one of the estate's most important characteristics: 'it must be classed with those Royal and Princely Residences which form the Retreats of the Great. From the Court or city' and argued that 'those who would treat this splendid Palace like the seat of an English Country Gentleman, at an hundred miles distance, would rob it of all its importance, and more than half its interest and beauty.'[66] The improvement of this view meant that visitors to the Ballroom at Wanstead could admire the beauty of the surrounding landscape while being reminded of Wanstead's close relationship with London, the source of its creation.

Fig 9.7
View towards the south (1813) by Humphry
Repton, watercolour, 33.2 × 13.9 cm.
[© The Trustees of The Wormsley Fund]

Fig 9.8
'View towards the south ... showing the manner in which
the water may be finished' (1813) by Humphry Repton,
watercolour, 33.2 × 13.9 cm.
[© The Trustees of The Wormsley Fund]

The Pleasure Ground

Repton's report for Wanstead described the gardens as offering 'great interest and novelty.'[67] This element of variation was one that Repton intended to enhance by connecting 12 distinct landscape features to form a Pleasure Ground. The 12 features are numbered in the text, suggesting that a plan identifying their location was originally included. The Pleasure Ground included a combination of pre-existing and new features that represented Repton's 'ancient' and 'modern' gardening principles.

Among the 'ancient features' were the Parterre Garden planted to the west, the Maze and Quincunx Cabinet de Verdure, the East Terrace and Vista, the Berceau Walk and the Fruit Wall. While the Parterre Garden and East Terrace and Vista were features introduced by Repton, little is known about the Maze and Quincunx Cabinet de Verdure. They do, however, appear on John Doyley's map of 1815–16, north of the parterre garden (Fig 9.9).

The Berceau Walk and the Fruit Wall predate Repton's employment at Wanstead. The wall is recorded as early as *c* 1708 when Kip and Knyff produced their view of Wanstead to the east (*see* Fig 1.2). This shows a boundary wall north of the formal gardens, behind the greenhouse. This is likely to have been that which Repton intended for his proposed fruit wall. Rocque recorded this wall in 1735 with a trellis walk running in parallel. The trellis walk is likely to have been what Repton refers to as the 'Berceau Walk.' The term 'berceau walk' derived from the use of trees or shrubs trained over it in an upended cradle shape. Repton's proposals recommended that the walk be pruned to allow the south side of the existing wall to receive more sunlight and accommodate the growing of fruits. To what extent this was implemented is unclear but the wall itself survives, now forming the boundary between residential gardens on The Warren Drive and Raynes Avenue.[68]

Fig 9.9

Plan of the manors of Wanstead, Woodford, Ruckholt and Aldersbrook (1815–16) by John Doyley. [Essex Record Office]

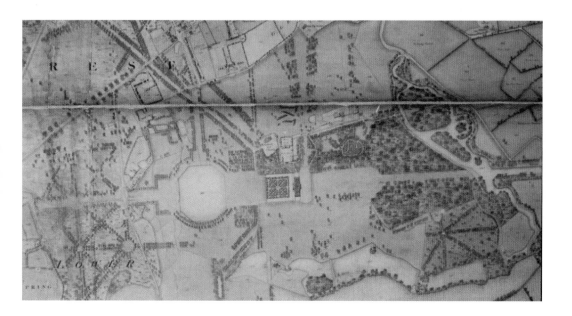

The 'modern' landscape features in Repton's Pleasure Ground included the American Garden, the Grotto Garden, the Island Garden, Wood Walk, Sheep Walk and the gardens at Highlands. The American Garden was laid out north-east of where the former greenhouse stood until 1799. It is unclear when the American Garden was introduced, but its outline can be identified in Searles' 1779 map of Wanstead (*see* Fig 6.2). Repton's report proposed that the garden 'may be increased in apparent size, without actually enlarging it', but offers no further detail as to how this would be achieved.

From the improved east terrace, Repton proposed Wood Walk. This path was intended to guide visitors from the house and its 'ancient' gardens towards a feature 'totally different in Character and Scenery', the Grotto Boathouse. Built by the 2nd Earl Tylney in *c* 1760, Repton expressed his appreciation for the Grotto by describing it as a 'sumptuous specimen.'[69] His report proposed to improve the Grotto Garden by enlarging it and providing 'a new character to its scenery.'

Repton also proposed Sheep Walk, a path designed to run from the Grotto garden alongside the banks of the Ornamental Waters, terminating at the end of the Berceau Walk. The path was designed to better incorporate the Grotto into the existing landscape while providing views of the islands, which he criticised for their association 'with many Puerile Conceits' and regarded by Repton as 'not worth restoring or preserving.' Repton did, however, describe them as 'now beautifully cloathed' and thus suggested they be maintained in their overgrown state. The islands feature in the report as two grey-wash sketches. Repton even proposed the use of a ferry to transport visitors between the islands and designed several rustic bridges to connect the islands and provide pleasing views of the Grotto.

The final feature to be incorporated into Repton's Pleasure Ground was the Highlands Garden. This was situated to the east, beyond the river Roding. It is the final watercolour featured in the report and the only one to be produced for the Pleasure Ground. This garden appears in John Doyley's 1815–16 survey (*see* Fig 9.9), but it is unclear whether this was an existing feature in 1813 and, if so, to what extent Repton's improvements were carried out. The Pleasure Garden celebrated many of Wanstead's existing features. It is an example of Repton's attempt to improve existing features rather than to create an entirely new scheme for the landscape. Crucially, it is perhaps the final account of the wider Wanstead landscape before the demolition of the house a decade later.

The current overgrown state of Wanstead's landscape makes it difficult to establish which of Repton's proposals were implemented. William and Catherine were slow to pay the designer, suggesting that not all the designs illustrated in Repton's report were executed. The proposed alterations to the approach road to Wanstead House do not seem to have been carried out. John Doyley's 1815–16 survey of the estate does, however, depict the four parterres proposed in Repton's view to the west (*see* Figs 9.4 and 9.9). Further evidence for the parterres can be found in archaeological research into the current landscape where their outline can be detected on the greensward when conditions are dry and in the Lidar scan of the park made in 2012 (*see* Fig 0.8).

Later views of the estate reveal evidence of new plantations around the lakes and around the Grotto, where new radiating walks, including Sheep Walk, were introduced. Repton's proposal for Wood Walk, which was to connect the east terrace with the Grotto Gardens, does not seem to have been implemented. It is not clear if the rustic bridges illustrated by Repton were erected to connect the islands, but the discovery of stone footings submerged just below the surface of the waters surrounding the Grotto Boathouse suggest that work may have begun on them before William and Catherine's mounting debts brought works to a halt. Even if the designs were not fully executed, the report offers valuable insight into how the estate appeared in 1813 and demonstrates the ways in which Repton engaged with contemporary trends and debates in landscape design through his proposals for Wanstead.

For Repton, the Wanstead commission was a bitter disappointment. In 1816, Repton wrote to his brother that he considered the Wanstead commission to be one, which, like the Brighton Pavilion and Carlton House, should have brought him fame and financial income.[70] William and Catherine's inability ultimately to pay for his extensive work meant that Wanstead was one of a number of Repton's final commissions that left the designer in financial ruin. It is also indicative of the financial troubles that were starting to take their toll on the young couple.

William and Catherine continued to live luxuriously, making further improvements to the estate. In 1818, they employed garden designer Lewis Kennedy (1789–1877) to improve the existing American Garden.[71] Kennedy's proposals for the American Garden roughly correspond to where the American Garden was recorded on Doyley's map. It appears bounded to the north by the Berceau Walk (referred to by Kennedy as the Arbour Walk) and featured an Italian rock garden at its centre. Other features of Kennedy's proposed garden included a Rustic Alcove and a Sinarium and Pheasantry. By 1820, however, it was becoming impossible to turn a blind eye to mounting financial troubles and no further works on the gardens were commissioned or proposed.

Exile from Wanstead

The costs incurred by the major improvement schemes to the house and grounds during the early 19th century were considerable, and no doubt had a major impact on William and Catherine's finances. Further debts were accrued by Catherine's decision in 1815 to share her £7,500 pin money with her husband.[72] William spent recklessly on carriages, thoroughbreds, entertainment and liaisons with other women in the capital, plunging the couple further into debt. His affair with actress and singer Maria Kepple caused further devastation when Maria gave birth to William's illegitimate son in 1818. Distraught by the betrayal, Catherine nonetheless attempted to take control by providing maintenance of £500 per annum on the condition that Maria did not reside within 50 miles of Wanstead.[73]

It was only his position as Member of Parliament for St Ives between 1812 and 1818 and for Wiltshire between 1818 and 1820 that prevented William from being prosecuted and sent to a debtors' prison. The costs of the 1820 election campaign for Wiltshire, however, were beyond

William's means, preventing him from running again and forcing him into exile. *The Essex Review* reported 'he was compelled to escape from his unsatisfied creditors in an open boat down the Thames, thereby adding one stain more to his already tarnished name by leaving his poor wife and three children to shift for themselves as best they might.'[74] Contrary to *The Essex Review*'s report, Catherine's pin money and claim to the Tylney estates, as arranged in the marriage settlement, gave her the right to remain in England with their three children, while William resided abroad in France.

In May 1820, William's solicitor, Mr Lightfoot, visited him in Calais to discuss the worsening financial matters and the Wanstead House deed was executed that month. The deed stated that £30,000 worth of goods from Wanstead House was to be held by creditors for the next two years.[75] If debts were not settled by the end of the two years, creditors would be entitled to seize the said assets. The terms laid out in the agreement suggest that William was confident his solicitors would soon settle his debts and that a return to England was imminent. Time passed and William became increasingly anxious and lonely. He frequently wrote to Catherine, begging her to join him in France. Catherine followed, accompanied by their three children and butler. Supported by Catherine's income, the family spent the next two years travelling in Europe, residing first in Paris before heading south to Naples.

Back in England, William and Catherine's solicitors were desperately trying to settle the extortionate debts by disposing of the family's assets such as the public houses that stood on Wanstead estate, William's prized thoroughbreds and the estate's timber. England's recession at this time, following the Napoleonic Wars, meant that the economic climate was poor, and few could afford such purchases. Debts continued to grow while the two-year grace period laid out in the deed of Wanstead House moved inexorably to a close.

In February 1821, A R Blake of Lincoln's Inn advised William that to maintain the house interiors 'in justice' would cost £10,000.[76] Significantly, it was brought to William's attention that Wanstead was no longer a desirable country seat: 'the local advantages which induced the original properties to create it – do not now exist.'[77] There was little alternative but to sell off Wanstead's contents and pull the house to the ground: 'This expensive establishment should be got rid of, by disposing of the Materials and furniture, which might produce £25,000.'[78] The gravity of the situation gave Catherine little choice but to agree to the solicitor's proposals. Within a decade of being married, her hopes and dreams for the ancestral seat came crashing down and arrangements for the sale of Wanstead House were made.

Notes

1   NA PROB 11/1253/199, Will of Sir James Tylney Long, 24 December 1794.
2   See Sevelinges 1820, II. Thanks to Richard Arnopp for a transcript of this correspondence. The obituary for the Prince de la Condé, Duke of Bourbon, refers to a letter written by the prince while at Wanstead to Altesse Serénissime Madame la Princesse Louise de Condé, Feb 3 1805. See Bowyer 1830; Chambers 1862, 56–59; Winter 1905, 213–22; Stead, 62 and 98.

3 Sevelinges, passim.
4 *The Morning Post*, 9 August 1816, np.
5 ERO D/DB f116/4, Bullock to Miss Tylney Long, From Wanstead House, 18 October 1810.
6 BL Add MS 52483, f.112, Bullock to Catherine at Draycot House, letter 2, February 1811.
7 *Morning Chronicle*, 2 July 1811, np.
8 BL Add MSS 36, 362 ff.115–16, John Buckler, drawings of the ground and principal floors from 1822. Special thanks to Kate Retford for sharing this material with me.
9 *Examiner*, 9 January 1814; Roberts 2015, 109–10.
10 NA C104/57/4; *Wanstead House Sale*, day 12, lot 66; *Wanstead House Sale*, lot 26.
11 Rowell 2007, 267–92.
12 *Wanstead House Sale*, day 12, no. 25, lot 37; now displayed at Chatsworth House in Derbyshire.
13 Rowell 2007, 267–92.
14 NA FO 610; See *Wanstead House Sale*, day 13, lots 50 and 51; day 4, lot 25; day 2, lots 43 and 44; Cator 2007, 237–35.
15 Davis 2016, 131.
16 Ibid.
17 *Wanstead House Sale*, day 17, lot 33.
18 Cator 2007, 233.
19 Rowell 2007, 267–92.
20 *The New Monthly Magazine and Universal Register*, February 1814, 96.
21 'Court of King's Bench', *Glasgow Herald*, 27 November 1827, np.
22 'Fete at Wanstead House', *The Morning Post*, 1 July 1814, np.
23 Ibid.
24 Ibid.
25 *The Morning Post*, 9 August 1816, np.
26 Ibid.
27 See *The New Monthly Magazine and Universal Register*, February 1814, 96; 'Fete at Wanstead House', *The Morning Post*, 1 July 1814, np.
28 WSHC 2062/4, Settlement giving Miss Catherine Tylney Long an independent income after marriage.
29 'ENTERTAINMENTS AT WANSTEAD HOUSE', *The Morning Post*, 9 August 1816, np.
30 ERO D/DQs/12, Will of John, 2nd Earl Tylney, 1784, 23.
31 See Repton 1794b; Repton 1803; Repton 1806; Repton 1816.
32 Daniels, 'Repton, Humphry'.
33 Jeffery 2018, 23.
34 Repton 1816, frontispiece.
35 Daniels 1999, 252.
36 Rogger 2007, 26.
37 Repton 1816, 129–36.
38 Repton 1816, 129.
39 Rogger 2007, 48.
40 For literature on the picturesque debate, see Fryer 1994, 162–74; Daniels 1999, 103–47; Daniels, 'Repton, Humphry'; Williamson 1995, 141–59.
41 Repton 1794a, 5.
42 Repton 1816, xxvi.
43 See Knight 1795; Price 1798.
44 Repton 1806, 7.
45 Repton 1806, 135.
46 PGL Repton 1813, 4.
47 PGL Repton 1813, 2.

48 Ibid.
49 Repton 1816, 129.
50 PGL Repton 1813, 1.
51 *Wanstead House Sale*, day 23, lot 447.
52 Special thanks to Georgina Green, who made the important discovery of Repton's proposals for Wanstead House in 2002. Thanks also to Bryan Maggs of the Sir Paul Getty Library for kindly providing me with access to this material. See also Jeffery 2005, 98–101.
53 PGL Repton 1813, 21.
54 PGL Repton 1813, 8.
55 Ibid.
56 Ibid.
57 Ibid.
58 PGL Repton 1813, 19.
59 'Interesting Trial', *The Weekly Entertainer: or, Agreeable and instructive repository*, 22 April 1813, 293–96. For a detailed discussion of the closure of Wanstead Park, see Roberts 2012.
60 PGL Repton 1813, 19.
61 PGL Repton 1813, 8.
62 PGL Repton 1813, 16.
63 PGL Repton 1813, 6.
64 Ibid.
65 PGL Repton 1813, 18.
66 PGL Repton 1813, 8.
67 PGL Repton 1813, 10.
68 Jeffery 2018, 26.
69 PGL Repton 1813, 12.
70 Daniels 1999, 254. Daniels quotes letter from Huntingdon Library HM 40878, Humphry Repton to William Repton, 31 March 1816.
71 See PGL Kennedy 1818.
72 Roberts 2015, 129.
73 Roberts 2015, 148.
74 Stead, 227.
75 Roberts 2015, 172.
76 ERO D/DB f116/4, A R Blake to William Pole Tylney Long Wellesley, 27 February 1821.
77 Ibid.
78 Ibid.

10 The great sales of Wanstead House, 1822–4

The June 1822 sale

In the spring of 1822, George Henry Robins, a London auctioneer renowned for his skill in selling country estates, was employed to conduct a 32-day sale of the contents of Wanstead House, commencing on 10 June. Newspapers across the nation wasted no time in advertising the upcoming sale, notifying readers when and how they could get their hands on a copy of Robins' catalogue.[1] The catalogue was a sizeable publication, occupying three volumes and 400 folio pages. Its frontispiece whetted the public's appetite with the promise of 'magnificent and costly furniture, grand costly bedsteads with rich velvet, silk, damask, beautiful Axminster carpets, brilliant plates of glass, rare old china, a variety of Parisian and Buhl cabinets and bookcases' as well as 'a valuable collection of fine paintings and sculpture, bronze casts from the Antique, splendid Gobelin Tapestry' and 'a Library of Ancient and Modern Books' (*see* Fig 0.5).[2]

The release of the catalogue in advance of the sale gave prospective buyers the opportunity to identify items of interest from the array of 'splendid and magnificent furniture' listed for this 'superb mansion.'[3] Robins' catalogue itemised lots of furniture by room, highlighting the most valuable pieces with ornate bold lettering and flowery detailed descriptions. Significantly, it was not just luxurious, costly furnishings that were on offer. Newspapers informed the public that items for 'villas, cottage residences or even servants' apartments' were to be sold, underlining the severity of William's debts. Robins catalogued items from Wanstead's service rooms alongside its spectacular state apartments. The first day of the sale, for example, included lots from two servants' bedrooms on the third floor, the Principal Grand Floor's Green Damask Velvet Sitting Room, as well as the Land Steward's Sitting Room, Housemaids' Closets, Butler's Pantry and Servants' Hall on the Rustic Ground Floor and Basement level.[4] Similarly, contents from Wanstead's outhouses such as the Game Keeper's Cottage, Brew House and Carpenter's Shop were catalogued alongside the landscape's most prized features such as the Grotto Boathouse. Interspersing the mundane with the grandiose helped to maintain public interest and ensure that the wealthiest buyers attended throughout the duration of the sale.

When necessary, the sale was arranged to attract a specialist clientele. Days 9, 10 and 11 were dedicated solely to Wanstead's collection of 'Fine Paintings and Sculpture by Italian, Flemish and English Masters', while Wanstead's collections of books, silverware, chinaware and fine wines were also grouped together and sold on specific days.[5] The variety of furnishings on offer thus formed 'an assemblage of the most valuable property ever offered for public sale and worthy of every Gentleman's attention.'[6]

Wanstead's high profile and William and Catherine's celebrity status made the sale a highly anticipated event and, when its doors were opened to the public in May 1822, crowds flocked to gaze in awe at the ill-fated Wanstead House. *The Literary Chronicle* reported, 'Wanstead House, with all its possessions, has been thrown open to the public, and has been the most attractive resort of the fashionable world, who have deserted the west end of the town in shoals, and made Whitechapel more travelled than Whitehall.'[7]

A sale at a country house was an opportunity to acquire second-hand goods but also to gaze at the belongings of the wealthy and see 'how the other half lived'. Although country house tourism provided regular access into the great houses of England, this was usually a controlled experience, guided by the steward of the house and revealing only the most public and impressive spaces. The sale, which was to take place throughout the entire palace, was therefore a distinct and rare touristic opportunity.[8] A letter from Merrick Shawe to William highlights the public interest in the sale:

> I went to Wanstead on Friday last but the crowd was so great that I could do nothing but give some directions for the security of the property in the House and also to protect the Gardens and Grotto from Damage. This required a reinforcement of Police officers – Robins' people exerted themselves very much and no mischief was done – but we were obliged to apply for 10 more Police men in addition to 9 already there. On Saturday the crowd was greater, but the force was sufficient to keep them in order. Mr Bertram Robins' man assured me there were 30,000 to view the House on Saturday – they were excluded from the Gardens & pleasure grounds on that day.[9]

At 11 o'clock on Monday 10 June 1822, the wait was finally over, and the great sale of Wanstead House began.

Major buyers at the Wanstead House sale

Given the extent of public interest and excitement, it comes as little surprise that the sale attracted an aristocratic clientele as well as some of the early 19th-century's most notable collectors, all of whom were eager to get their hands on the range of luxurious goods on offer. William Kent's heavy baroque furniture, the rich crimson genoa velvet hangings and the distinguished collection of French Boulle furnishings were among the most sought-after items. An annotated copy of the June 1822 sale catalogue held in the National Art Library at the Victoria and Albert Museum in London records the names of buyers and the prices paid for each lot sold, helping to establish the value of particular goods, who purchased them and where they were dispersed to.

Bristol ship owner, sugar baron and banker, Philip John Miles, is just one of the many names to feature prominently throughout the annotated sale catalogue. Like many of the wealthiest buyers at the sale, Miles' purchases reflect the taste for French furniture at the time, spending £89 5s on the 'GRAND PARISIAN CLOCK, *In costly Antique Buhl and Tortoise-Shell case*, by MYNUEL, à *Parie*' on display in the Grand Drawing Room.[10]

In addition, Miles purchased several pieces of furniture by Kent from the Ballroom, Grand Dining Room, Drawing Room and Library, as well as many of the genoa velvet curtains belonging to the state apartments, a state bed from the Chints State Bed Chamber, some statuary, and urns.[11] These lots were acquired for Leigh Court in Bristol, which Miles had purchased in 1811 and remodelled extensively.

Identifying other notable buyers from the Wanstead sale catalogue can be complicated by the fact that many aristocratic customers acquired items through their personal agents. This saved them the inconvenience of having to attend the sale on multiple days and to suffer the indignity of mingling with the large, unruly crowds. Retaining some degree of anonymity was also thought to help keep prices from becoming competitively high. The 2nd Earl of Grosvenor, for example, sent his agent, the cabinetmaker John Davis, to purchase items for Eaton Hall, including a pair of Kentian 'COSTLY VEINED MARBLE PIER TABLE[S]' from the Grand Hall and a 'MAGNIFICENT SQUARE ROSE WOOD LIBRARY TABLE … *WITH BEAUTIFUL BUHL AND TORTOISE SHELL, HONEY SUCKLE BORDER*' from the Grand Ballroom for £141 15s.[12] Similarly, James Gomme attended the sale on behalf of Fiennes Wykeham-Martin of Leeds Castle who 'requested me to look thro the splendid Catalogue and go there and select and purchase such Things I shd. deem suitable for Leeds Castle I attended five Weeks and have bought many curious Articles.'[13] Among the items Gomme purchased were an '*elegant cut glass Chandelier*' and the Louis XIV 'PARISIAN ARMORIE' from the Ballroom, as well as 'A GRAND MASSIVE CARVED AND GILT FRAME PIER TABLE' by Kent from the adjoining Anteroom.[14]

Perhaps the most significant buyers to attend the sale, however, were William Cavendish, 6th Duke of Devonshire, and George Herbert, the 11th Earl of Pembroke and his second wife, Catherine Woronzow, daughter of the Russian ambassador, whose acquisitions purchased from the June sale have remained intact at Chatsworth House in Derbyshire and Wilton House in Wiltshire, in settings of similar grandeur to those in which they were originally. Now accessible to the visiting public, these collections offer the Wanstead enthusiast a rare opportunity to experience a fragment of the lost interior of Wanstead House.

At the time of the sale, the 11th Earl of Pembroke, and his wife, Catherine, were engaged in a major improvement scheme at Wilton. Like many of the sale's wealthiest buyers, the Pembrokes were keen to acquire works by Kent, purchasing several pieces by the designer, including the carved gilt wood settees from the Ballroom, upholstered in costly crimson Genoa velvet, the frame ornamented with a mask of Diana on its crest and mermaids and festoons of flowers between the scroll legs.[15] One of these settees appears in Hogarth's 1728 conversation piece, *An Assembly at Wanstead House*, set in the Ballroom (*see* Fig 4.8). They also purchased the suite of eight large carved gilt wood and gesso side chairs upholstered in genoa crimson, depicted in Nollekens' portrait of the Tylney family in the Saloon, and two carved, painted and parcel gilt wood console tables with marble tops (*see* Fig 4.12).[16] The introduction of Kent's furniture into the Pembrokes' state apartments proved so successful that many would be forgiven for thinking they had been originally intended for Wilton.[17]

Similarly, the 6th Duke of Devonshire was carrying out extensive and costly improvements to his ancestral seat at Chatsworth House in Derbyshire. According to the annotated sale catalogue, the duke's agent, George Spencer Ridgeway, purchased three tables designed by Kent for Wanstead House, the 'magnificent square library table' for £92 8s from the Grand Hall, and two 'SUPERB BLACK PORPHYRY PIER TABLE[S], on a splendid massive carved and gilt frame' from the Ballroom, for around £26 each.[18]

Ridgeway also made purchases from Wanstead's art collection, including the antique statue of Apollo from the Saloon, as well as statues of Domitian and Agrippina from the Hall (*see* Fig 4.7).[19] These works, reportedly recovered from the ruins of Herculaneum, had been acquired by John Child, 2nd Earl Tylney, and formed important additions to the duke's growing collection of Classical sculpture at Chatsworth.[20] Nowhere is the 6th Duke of Devonshire's 'love of marble' more apparent than in the sculpture gallery he created at Chatsworth, which was illuminated by the magnificent bronze chandeliers designed by Vulliamy for William and Catherine in *c* 1813 (Fig 10.1).[21] Ridgeway's purchase of the two chandeliers for around £300 each, was the most expensive of the sale. Once installed at Chatsworth, alterations were made to the Tylney crest that adorned the chandeliers and which, according to the duke, gave 'such offence, as an indignity to my crest, that I was compelled to remove the much respected reptiles, and make the eagles support the termination of their chains instead.'[22] Although highly valued for their luxurious craftsmanship,

Fig 10.1
The Sculpture Gallery.
[The Devonshire Collections, Chatsworth/Bridgeman Images]

the duke would have been keen to disassociate himself from the recently disgraced Tylney name.

Despite the scandal surrounding the Tylney family and Wanstead House, the purchases made by prominent collectors such as the 6th Duke of Devonshire, the 11th Earl of Pembroke and Lady Pembroke, the 2nd Earl Grosvenor and Fiennes Wykeham-Martin suggest that Wanstead's furniture, particularly the works produced by William Kent in the early 18th century and the recently acquired collection of French furniture, were desirable commodities, fit for furnishing an ancestral seat during the early 19th century.

Wanstead's fine-art collection

The extent of Wanstead House's collection of paintings, sculpture and tapestries was such that their dispersal lasted for three entire days. The collection was predominantly made up of landscape scenes and family portraits; other themes included mythological, biblical and historical subjects. The sculptures on offer were largely those purchased by John Child, 2nd Earl Tylney, after 1750. The Gobelin tapestries from Wanstead's state apartments were on sale on day 10, but received no buyers and were deferred until a later date.[23] Albeit vast, Wanstead's collection of fine art was somewhat typical and there is little to suggest that Wanstead's owners demonstrated any connoisseurship. Moreover, visitor accounts drew little attention to Wanstead's artworks, mentioning only Kent's ceiling paintings, Casali's historical scenes, Schalken's portrayal of Portia over the fireplace in the Saloon, and the 2nd Earl's antique statues. Crucially, it is these works that appear to have been among the highest-selling works that summer.

For example, five of the seven historical scenes painted by Casali for the 1st Earl Tylney in *c* 1741 sold for between £60 and £90. Their importance in the sale was made clear by Robins' detailed listings for them, which described the works as 'all equally rich and varied in composition, bold and masterly in drawing, and splendid in colour'.[24] Mr Davis, agent to the 2nd Earl Grosvenor, purchased *Alexander presenting his Mistress Campaspe to Apelles*, *The Continence of Scipio* and *Sophonisba Presented with a Cup of Poison* for a total sum of £259 7s. The works were subsequently hung in the entrance hall at Eaton Hall.[25] Casali's 'noble gallery picture' of *Coriolanus Overcome by the Entreaties of his Mother, Wife and Children* (see Fig 4.6), *Pompey taking Leave of his Wife Cornelia* and *The Return of Cloelia* were sold for £63 each to James Gomme for Fiennes Wykeham-Martin of Leeds Castle.[26] Although the sale catalogue notes 'the works of this excellent modern Italian Artist are little known in this country', the prices for which they sold indicate they were considered among the more noteworthy works in Wanstead's fine-art collection.

After the great sale of June 1822, auction houses selling works from the former Tylney collection took care to draw attention to a Wanstead provenance. When Colonel Hugh Baillie sold Andrea Casali's painting of Pandora at Christie's in March 1824, the sale catalogue noted 'painted for Wanstead House, where bought'.[27] Similarly, when Schalken's painting of *Portia Destroying Herself by Fire* was sold at Christie's on 30 June 1835, the catalogue drew attention to its provenance, 'the capital picture formerly in the Wanstead House collection' (*see* Fig 4.11).[28] When the painting reappeared in another London saleroom one year later, its provenance was again remarked upon, presumably in the hope that this would attract greater public interest.[29]

There is one name listed among the buyers of Wanstead's art collection that features most prominently in the sale catalogue. A buyer named 'Jones' appears to have attended all three days of the art sale, purchasing around 30 works, mostly portraits and estate views of Wanstead. Another annotated copy of the sale catalogue held in the Redbridge Museums and Heritage Centre records the same paintings as being purchased by Wellesley.[30] This reveals that 'Jones' was not purchasing the works for his own collection, but rather acting as agent for William and Catherine to ensure that particular paintings remained within the family.

Many aristocrats perceived it as their duty to maintain, consolidate and continue their family's portrait collections and believed that such collections were capable of inspiring future generations, enforcing claims to heritage and respectability.[31] Moreover, family portraits were highly valued, not necessarily because of their material worth, but rather because they provided symbolic continuity. As a result, they would often be the final possessions to be disposed of when a family was faced with the task of selling inherited goods.[32] A letter from Lieutenant Colonel Merrick Shawe, private secretary to the Wellesley family, written to William on the first day of the auction, regarding the paintings intended for safeguarding, reads as follows:

> We went over Wanstead House with old Molly who pointed out the family pictures … it would be wrong to suffer one of these to be sold and they would not be anything worth considering … I have desired Robins to buy them all in and I dare say it will not make £100 difference, and you would be justly blamed for letting them go.[33]

The paintings acquired by 'Jones' included important family portraits such as lot 171, William Hogarth's 'A VIEW OF THE INTERIOR OF THE BALLROOM OF WANSTEAD HOUSE, WITH A NUMEROUS ASSEMBLAGE OF LADIES AND GENTLEMEN. A highly curious and interesting Picture by this inimitable and immortal Artist', for £147 (*see* Fig 4.8), and lot 318, 'Nollikins, Interior of the Saloon of Wanstead House, with an assemblage of Ladies and gentlemen. *A Conversazione*' for £127 1s (*see* Fig 4.12).[34] These were the most expensive paintings of the art sale, though their high price was likely fixed to deter other buyers. Other paintings 'acquired' by Jones included three of six portraits attributed to Geoffrey Kneller, described by Lybbe Powys in 1781 and listed as lot 20, 'A Portrait of a lady with a dog'; lot 29, 'A Portrait of a Gentleman, with a blue mantle'; and lot 74, 'A Portrait of a Lady in Blue, with a red mantle.'[35] Portraits by Willem Wissing, Joseph Highmore and Jonathan Richardson (*see* Fig 2.1) and views of the estate attributed to Charles Catton the Elder were also held back (*see* Figs 4.1 and 5.5–5.6).

The severity of William's debts was so grave that the paintings were never retrieved from Robins and instead placed in storage, only to resurface when Robins' collection was sold after his death in 1852.[36] While many are now untraceable, the efforts to save the family portraits highlight the importance of preserving such images, even at a time of crisis.[37]

The outcome of the June 1822 sale

Despite the quantity of goods on offer and the large crowds who flocked to Wanstead, the sale failed to raise the funds anticipated by William and Catherine. Instead, the total takings amounted to just half the amount required to pay off William's debts. This is likely to have been due to the sale taking place when England was suffering a deep recession brought about by the Napoleonic Wars. Few had the means to purchase Wanstead's luxurious and costly goods at their true value. Moreover, William's decision to employ Robins to conduct the sale proved problematic. Robins' primary aim was to make as much money as possible for himself, and instead of just agreeing to receive a percentage of the sales, he managed to set himself a rather bold commission of £10,000.[38] This gave Robins little incentive to fetch the highest prices, instead selling goods to friends and associates for a fraction of their worth and holding certain items aside for himself.

For William and Catherine, the outcome of the June sale was devastating. Not only had the collection of precious family heirlooms been lost, there was not sufficient improvement of William's debts, forcing him to remain in exile. Ignoring her pleas to place the children in education back in England and to visit her ailing mother, William pressurised Catherine to remain by his side in France, fearing that she would abandon him if he permitted her return.

The September 1822 sale

Following the disappointment of the June sale, William appointed his father, now Lord Maryborough and Master of the Mint, as the fourth trustee to assist with his affairs. His father's renowned financial acumen gave William reason to believe that his debts could be quickly resolved. However, on 16 August 1822, Maryborough wrote to William informing his son that he could not realistically expect to return home for at least another five years.[39] Maryborough urged William to consider the absolute necessity of the strictest economy while he attempted to settle with creditors.[40] As William's frustration grew, arrangements for a second sale were made. The sale took place between 9 and 11 September 1822 and was intended to dispose of the items deferred and unsold from the June sale.

Robins' listings for the September sale catalogue reveal that some of Wanstead's most valuable items, such as the rich collection of tapestries and damask hangings, as well as some of its most costly furniture, fine paintings, antique sculptures, china and glassware had failed to sell.[41] The catalogue also reveals that some of Wanstead's outhouses still needed stripping of their contents. Items from the

Grotto Boathouse, such as marble slab pier tables, bamboo Chinese-frame elbow chairs, stained glass windows, petrified stones and other curiosities, were still available for purchase, as were vases, stone pedestals and Egyptian stone ornaments from the American Garden. The listings for the most basic of goods such as an ironing table and drying horse from the washhouse and four dog kennels from the gamekeeper's cottage emphasise the extent of William and Catherine's desperation by this stage.

Like the June sale, the September sale offered a variety of goods to a range of buyers, and yet the funds raised were still insufficient. By the autumn, public interest in Wanstead House had waned and the sale failed to attract anything like the crowds that had flocked to the estate earlier in the summer. Instead, the September sale was a sombre and poorly attended affair that did little to resolve the crisis engulfing Wanstead: 'A melancholy gloom pervaded the mansion, and exhibited a striking example of the mutability of human greatness. The company consisted of about forty persons and exhibited very little of the spirit of a public sale.'[42]

Sic transit gloria mundi: the demolition of Wanstead House, 1823–4

After the failure of the September sale, William, Catherine and their three children left Paris and moved south to Naples. Soon after their arrival, Catherine received news of her mother, Lady Catherine's, death. While Catherine grieved for her mother, William is likely to have felt some private relief in the knowledge that his mother-in-law's allowance would revert to Catherine and increase her annual salary. Although the couple's finances were to some extent improved, the magnificent family seat remained a heavy burden, made worse by the revelation that Draycot Cerne, the Tylney Long manor house in Wiltshire, where Lady Catherine resided, had reverted to Catherine.[43]

As stated, the terms of William and Catherine's marriage settlement of 1812 restricted William to life interest of the Tylney estates only and under no circumstances was he permitted to sell the family seat. Baron Maryborough's efforts to find a tenant for Wanstead House had met with little success. The costs of running the estate were extortionate and the dispersal of its goods through the 1822 sales made the prospect of furnishing the enormous empty shell of a palace unappealing.

As the situation grew ever more desperate, the proposal to demolish Wanstead House became unavoidable. Thus, on 24 September 1822, *The Kaleidoscope* announced that now 'every vestige of its [Wanstead House] former splendour [is] dispersed'; the demolition of Wanstead House was imminent. The article lamented this state of affairs and drew comparisons to Cannons, the seat of the 1st Duke of Chandos and Cassandra Brydges, Richard Child, 1st Earl Tylney's half-sister, which had been demolished in 1747, stating 'Sic transit gloria mundi'; 'thus passes the glory of the world.'[44]

On 12 May 1823, Robins set up his rostrum for the third time at Wanstead House, this time in the Saloon, and proceeded to sell its building fabric as one whole lot to a group of Norwich tradesmen, Messrs. Stannard, Athow, de Carle, Wright and Coleman, for £10,000.[45] Conditions of the sale demanded that all materials, including the building's foundations, were to be sold and cleared from the site by Lady Day, 1825.[46] The materials acquired included the 'many Thousand feet of the finest wainscot, in Floors and Linings of Rooms; elegant carved work in Figures of Noble Design and Mouldings; splendid chimney pieces, of the finest and most valuable sculpture', as well as glass windows and doors, carved oak frame doors and string courses.'[47] For several months, Stannard and Athow lived on the premises, selling the material in large and small lots to suit the needs of a variety of buyers eager to pick up a bargain and/or relish a souvenir of Wanstead.[48] Landed aristocrats, such as Lord Tankerville of Chillingham Castle in Northumberland and the Revd Savill Ogle of Kirkley Hall in Newcastle, purchased four marble fireplaces for £426.[49] Meanwhile, locals in possession of a considerably smaller budget could purchase more affordable fabric such as wainscot floors for about £5 per square foot or doors for around £2.[50]

With its interior stripped away, the dismantling of Campbell's former masterpiece could commence. The absence of a surviving structure or even its foundations makes it difficult to imagine quite how enormous a task dismantling Wanstead House would have been. The outer walls themselves were 4½ feet thick, of brick clad with Portland stone. The closest that we can get today to imagining the scale of Wanstead House is to stand beneath the looming portico of Wentworth Woodhouse. Doing so makes it clear that Wanstead's demolition was no small feat. Indeed, pulling down Wanstead House proved to be a most precarious and dangerous task, resulting in some labourers reportedly falling to their deaths in the process.[51]

The final sale of Wanstead's building fabric took place on 29 June 1824 and lasted for three days. Sale catalogues were available in advance from the auctioneer Wooley Simpson's premises at Bucklersbury in the City of London or various inns across the country, suggesting that buyers travelled far and wide to claim Wanstead's celebrated architectural features. Most notable among these was the famous stone portico, complete with its eight Corinthian columns, superb capitals, grand pediment and finely carved modillions. *The Morning Post* urged prospective buyers to salvage the portico, arguing (sadly, in vain) 'it would be much indeed to be deplored should this unrivalled portico not be perpetuated as a national specimen of architectural beauty and taste, in some one of the public or private structures now in progress throughout the Kingdom.'[52]

As many took sorrow in the demolition of Wanstead House, others like satirist Isaac Robert Cruickshank perceived it as a lesson in the pitfalls of the elite's extravagant lifestyle. '*This truly designed Corinthian auctioneer a going like lightning through a gooseberry bush, gone*', published in September 1824, depicts Wooley Simpson driving a fashionable two-wheel trap with a groom seated alongside him (Fig 10.2). Behind them stands the ill-fated façade of Wanstead House and a signpost pointing left to Bucklersbury [passage], the site of Simpson's auction

This truly designed CORINTHIAN AUCTIONEER *a Going like lightning through a Gooseberry bush Gone*

Fig 10.2

This truly designed Corinthian Auctioneer a going like lightning through a Gooseberry bush, gone (1824) by Isaac Robert Cruikshank, hand-coloured etching, 23.9 × 38.6 cm. [The British Museum]

house, and right to Wanstead. A second signpost positioned alongside that for Wanstead reads, 'To be sold by auction by Mr W.W. Simpson this truly designed Corinthian portico Jun 29 1824.' The use of 'Corinthian' here is a reference to advertisements which stressed the Corinthian stone portico, as well as to the literary character Corinthian Tom created by Pierce Egan in 1821, who, much like Wanstead's owners, was famous for his extravagant spending and luxurious lifestyle.[53]

The total dispersal of Wanstead's building fabric was of significant financial advantage for its creditors. In October 1824, one newspaper reported that 'some of the creditors, we think would be well paid by half a crown in the pound, as may be collected from some of their charges.'[54] Another announced, 'The proceeds of the sale of Wanstead House and its furniture have been greater than was expected by the creditors, who are now receiving 10s. in the pound, and are in expectation of a further dividend of 5s. in the course of a month or two.'[55] For Catherine, the demolition of her 100-year-old ancestral seat was nothing short of devastating.

Notes

1   *The Morning Post*, 11 March 1822, 1.
2   See ERO SALE/B284, frontispiece.
3   *The Morning Post*, 11 March 1822, 1.
4   *Wanstead House Sale*, day 1.
5   *The Morning Post*, 11 March 1822, 1; see ERO SALE/B284, frontispiece.
6   *The Morning Post*, 21 May 1822, np.
7   *The Literary Chronicle and Weekly Review*, 15 June 1822, 379–80.

8 MacArthur and Stobart 2010, 175–95.
9 ERO D/DB f116/4, Merrick Shawe to William Wellesley Pole, *c* 22 June 1822.
10 *Wanstead House Sale*, day 17, lot 34.
11 For examples of Kent furniture purchased by Miles, see *Wanstead House Sale*, day 2, lots 11 and 12; day 4, lot 22; day 11, lots 5–7; day 13, lots 29 and 30; day 17, lot 18. For urns, see day 10, lot 369.
12 *Wanstead House Sale*, day 12, lot 31; day 13, lot 14.
13 Oxford, Bodleian Libraries MS. Eng. Misc.d.165, f.197, letter from James Gomme to Revd Mark Noble of Barming, 18 July 1822. Special thanks to Michael Cordwell James for providing me with a transcript of this correspondence.
14 *Wanstead House Sale*, day 13, lots 26, 37 and 7.
15 *Wanstead House Sale*, day 13, lot 38.
16 *Wanstead House Sale*, day 13, lots 39–46.
17 Robinson 2009, 42–7.
18 *Wanstead House Sale*, day 12, lot 26 and day 13, lots 15 and 16.
19 *Wanstead House Sale*, day 9, lots 239, 245 and 246.
20 The 6th Duke of Devonshire's, *Handbook of Chatsworth and Hardwick* (1845) records the statues of Domitian and Agrippina on display in the North Entrance Hall, where they remain to this day. The statue of Apollo was recorded in the West Corridor and is now displayed in the Chapel corridor.
21 *Wanstead House Sale*, day 12, lots 37 and 38.
22 Keeling 1997, 10.
23 The annotated June sale catalogue held in the NAL records none of the buyer's names alongside the listings for the Gobelin tapestries. Their listing in the September 1822 sale catalogue indicates that the tapestries were deferred and sold again that autumn. See BNF CVE 39280, *A Catalogue of the superb Gobelin tapestry*.
24 *Wanstead House Sale*, day 9, lot 228.
25 *Wanstead House Sale*, Day 9, lots 228–30. These works are now displayed at Runcorn Town Hall.
26 *Wanstead House Sale*, day 10, lots 362–4, 124. Casali's *Coriolanus* is now displayed at Burton Constable Hall in East Yorkshire.
27 Christie's, 5–6 March, 1824, lot 35.
28 Christie's, 'A Gentleman, deceased [and] Sir James Stuart, Bart.', 30 June 1835, lot 81.
29 Messrs. E Foster and Son, May 11–12, 1836, lot 175.
30 See RHC annotated copy of *Wanstead House Sale*.
31 Retford 2006, 340.
32 Pointon 1993.
33 *Parliamentary Papers, House of Commons and Command*, Vol. 23 (1838); ERO D/DB f116/4, Shawe to Wellesley, 10 June 1822.
34 *Wanstead House Sale*, day 9, lot 171 and day 10, lot 318.
35 Climenson 1899, 205; *Wanstead House Sale*, day 8, lots 20, 29 and 74.
36 Roberts 2015, 192.
37 Miles Barton's article for the *Georgian Group Journal* discusses a portrait thought to depict Richard Child, Viscount Castlemain and 1st Earl Tylney, listed as lot 328 on day 10 of the sale as 'Richardson – A portrait of a Gentleman in blue.' The painting was among those bought in at the 1822 Wanstead sale, but its whereabouts after 1822 are unknown. The painting resurfaced in 2001 attributed to 'a follower of Michael Dahl', and as having belonged to Richard Child, but further enquiries have proven unsuccessful. This is currently the only known verified portrait of a Wanstead family member. See Barton 2011, 184–5. Tim Couzens has carried out extensive research, tracing the furnishings and artworks of Wanstead House that were sold in the 1822 sale. Special thanks to Tim Couzens for a conversation regarding the tracing of the sale items and the collection of family portraits put aside for Wellesley in the 1822 sale.

38   Roberts 2015, 193.
39   RHC 20127 (f.20) Baron Maryborough to William Wellesley Pole, 16 August 1822.
40   Ibid.
41   'Multiple Advertisements and Notices', *The Morning Post*, 2 September 1822, np.
42   'London', *Caledonian Mercury*, 16 September 1822, np.
43   Roberts 2015, 206.
44   'Chit-Chat', *The Kaleidoscope: or, Literary and Scientific Mirror*, 24 September 1822, 95–6.
45   *The Times*, 12 May 1823, np.
46   Ibid.
47   The Times, 14 May 1823, np.
48   Ibid.
49   Stead, 78.
50   Ibid.
51   'Multiple News Items', *The Bury and Norwich Post: Or, Suffolk and Norfolk Telegraph, Essex, Cambridge, & Ely Intelligencer*, 21 January 1824, np.
52   *The Morning Post*, 28 June 1824, np.
53   Ibid. Brailsford, 'Egan, Pierce'.
54   'NEWSPAPER CHAT', *The Examiner*, 31 October 1824, np.
55   'Sunday's Post', *The Bury and Norwich Post*, 3 November 1824, np.

11 | Return from exile

As Wanstead's magnificent edifice was torn apart, equally dramatic events were unfolding on the Continent. The past two years of exile in Calais, Paris, Naples and Florence had subjected Catherine to misery. Not only had she witnessed her ancestral seat come to ruin, her marriage was crumbling to pieces. William's ongoing love affair with Helena Bligh *née* Paterson, the rumoured illegitimate daughter of the Duke of Wellington and wife of Thomas Bligh of the Coldstream Guards, whom the couple had met one year earlier in Florence, had at last proven too much to bear.[1] In September 1824, Catherine announced her intention to separate and returned home to England with their three children, William (1813–63), James (1815–51) and Victoria (1818–97). In April 1825, she filed for divorce. Intent on protecting their children and preserving what remained of the Tylney fortune and estates, Catherine made the valiant decision to file for legal custody. In an age when men held all power over their children, Catherine perhaps seemed naive. However, the marriage settlement that had been so painstakingly drawn up a decade earlier perhaps provided her with the necessary security to take such drastic action.

On 12 September 1825, Catherine died, just one month short of her 36th birthday. Since returning to England, her health had deteriorated, suffering repeated seizures and chest pains. The cause behind her illness is uncertain, but newspapers were quick to point the finger at William. When *The Times* reported Catherine's death on 19 September 1825, the cause of illness was described as 'too private and delicate a nature to be alluded to in a public journal', but noted 'the unexpected intrusion into her family circle ... was not of a nature to alleviate her last afflictions.'[2] Fortunately, Catherine had the foresight to make amendments in her will and ensure her children were made wards of court after her death, with the Duke of Wellington (William's uncle) acting as guardian. Her loyal sisters, Emma and Dora, also acted according to her sister's wishes, fiercely protecting the children from William.

The custody trial began in February 1826 and lasted an entire year.[3] Meanwhile, Captain Bligh had taken William to court for adultery, or 'criminal conversation' as it was more commonly known, with his wife Helena. The case of *Wellesley v. Bligh* found William guilty and Bligh was awarded damages of £6,000.[4] It was instrumental in cementing the Lord Chancellor's decision over the custody battle, deeming William unfit to parent and permanently placing the children in the legal guardianship of Wellington, who as a national figure is sure to have felt great embarrassment over his nephew's scandalous behaviour. The case made William the first man to be denied custody of his own children and was a significant turning point in British legal history.

William died in 1857, in destitute circumstances at his lodgings in Piccadilly, an outcast from polite society. His funeral at Kensal Green Cemetery was a low-key affair and obituaries lambasted his infamous character. *The Morning Chronicle* described him as 'redeemed by no single virtue, adorned by no single grace.'[5] His legacy, as the infamous culprit responsible for bringing the Tylney seat to ruin, has earned him the nickname 'Wicked William' among Wanstead historians. Although he played a major role in the family's downfall, it is important to consider the other factors that played a part in Wanstead's demise.

A significant amount of scholarship on 18th-century estates more broadly reveals that it was not uncommon for landowners to be heavily burdened with financial debt for several generations.[6] The Tylney family ledgers at Hoare's Bank show that debt was already a concern in the 1760s when the 2nd Earl Tylney had neglected Wanstead to reside abroad in Italy.[7] Furthermore, evidence from various newspapers suggests that efforts were being made to sell off parts of Wanstead House prior to William and Catherine's ownership. On 16 April 1795, for example, *The Morning Post and Fashionable World* announced an auction of Wanstead's livestock and agricultural equipment and, in 1799, the contents of Wanstead's greenhouse, including an impressive collection of orange and lemon trees, as well as two hot houses, were also sold off.[8] On 12 June 1800, *The Whitehall Evening Post* announced a third sale of 'Feather Beds, Carpets & Attic Furniture &c. belonging to Wanstead House.'[9] Although the expense of William and Catherine's refurnishing of Wanstead and landscape improvements carried out in the early 19th century, combined with William's already existing personal debts, contributed significantly to the financial decline, there were clearly other factors that contributed to Wanstead's ruin.

Upon his death in 1857, William and Catherine's eldest and only surviving son, William Richard Arthur, inherited the title of 5th Earl of Mornington. Five years later, he died unmarried and childless in Paris. *The Gentleman's Magazine*'s obituary reported 'he succeeded to the family honours, but through the extravagance of his father, to a greatly diminished patrimony.'[10] Victoria, the youngest of the three children, continued to reside with her aunts at Draycot Cerne in Wiltshire and remained unmarried until her death in 1897. In default of any male heirs, the family's Irish titles were merged into the long list of honours enjoyed by the Duke of Wellington and the remaining land at Wanstead was bequeathed to their father's cousin, Henry Wellesley, 1st Earl Cowley (1804–84). Not only was the Wanstead estate lost, the Tylney bloodline had now been completely extinguished.

Notes

1   For a detailed account of the relationship between William and Catherine Wellesley-Pole-Tylney-Long and their time in exile, see Roberts 2015.
2   *The Times*, 19 September 1825, np.
3   See Parliamentary Archives HL/PO/JO/10/8/758 *Wellesley v. Wellesley*, which incorporates trial transcripts and affidavits from *Wellesley v. Beaufort*.
4   *Stead, Bligh v Wellesley*.
5   *The Morning Chronicle*, 2 July 1857, np.
6   Habakkuk 1994, 17; Mackley and Wilson 2000, 25–6.
7   HB/8/T/11/392, Private letter book commencing 5th March 1778, Letter to Sir James Tylney Long, 14 November 1779, 45–6. Thanks to Pamela Hunter for her assistance at Hoares Bank Archive and for providing me with access to this material.
8   *Morning Post & Fashionable World*, 16 April 1795, np; ERO SALE/B284.
9   *Whitehall Evening Post*, 12 June 1800, np.
10 *The Gentleman's Magazine*, September 1863, 375.

12 Epilogue: tracing the lost relics of Wanstead House and its gardens

The demolition of Wanstead House must have felt dramatic for those accustomed to its colossal structure dominating views of the landscape. In 1842, Wooley Simpson, the auctioneer of Wanstead's building fabric ruminated, 'little did I dream I would see its proud columns prostrated in the dust', and decried its removal from the peripheries of the capital, describing Wanstead as 'the most attractive object (of its kind) near London and a national ornament.'[1] Shortly after the sale of its building material in 1824, around 2,000 trees on the estate were felled and the land leased for grazing, further eradicating the estate from view. In 1861, William Coller wrote, 'As we look upon the mansionless park – for all that remains is the steward's house [the Temple] – the overgrown walks, and once almost elysian pleasure grounds, now let out for pasturage, we cannot but sigh over this sad page of patrician history.'[2]

The land at Wanstead remained under Cowley's ownership until 1882, when a substantial part of the gardens was sold to the Corporation of the City of London to incorporate into Epping Forest. While one newspaper perceived this as 'the final effacement of what was once one of the most glorious domains in England', many delighted in the City's decision to permit public access to 'this beautiful and romantic corner of Epping Forest', perceiving it as a benefit 'particularly of the East-end population'.[3] On the August Bank Holiday that year, 'several thousand persons' descended on the new public park.[4] In 1893, Wanstead Park Golf Club purchased the remaining land (and the site of the former palace) from Cowley's family, the former stables now accommodating the club house.

As a sports ground and public park, the former Georgian estate took on a new lease of life. Postcards from the early 20th century captured scenes of the Grotto Boathouse and the central avenue (now known as the Glade), as pleasing landscape features and vistas despite their separation from the 'princely mansion' to which they were originally associated (Figs 12.1 and 12.2). Yet much of the pleasure gardens that Wanstead's owners had invested so much in to create became increasingly hidden from view and there was concern among some that the story of the house and its owners would be lost. In 1900, a memoir dedicated to Catherine sorrowfully enquired, 'How many of those who wander through its thick woods and linger round its lakes, watching the herons and moorhens, or gaze upon the costly grotto, ever give thought to the sorrows of Catherine Long or the wicked recklessness of Wellesley Pole?'[5] The author of the memoir may yet have taken heart by the knowledge that despite the sale and demolition of Wanstead House and the subsequent decline of its

Fig 12.1
Postcard of the Grotto
Boathouse, Wanstead Park.
[Wanstead Image Archives]

landscape, the memory of this once glorious Georgian estate endures, its ruins igniting curiosity among the many walkers who wander the avenues of the park, or stand by the ruins of the Grotto Boathouse, overlooking the early 18th-century Ornamental Waters.

Interest in the lost estate has resulted in several measures being taken to protect the historic landscape. In 1954, the National Heritage List for England identified several important relics of the former Georgian estate.

S 9024   THE GLADE, WANSTEAD PARK.

Fig 12.2
Postcard of the Glade,
Wanstead Park.
[Wanstead Image Archives]

These included: the Portland stone piers at the junction of Overton Drive and Blake Hall Road (c 1715), which received Grade II* status, and the Temple and Grotto Boathouse (both c 1760), which received Grade II status in 1979; the Wanstead Golf clubhouse, which occupies one of the late 18th-century stables, was also granted Grade II status and, in 1987, the park was recognised for its special historic interest and made a Grade II* Park and Garden. In 2009, English Heritage added Wanstead Park to the Heritage at Risk Register in response to concerns that the park was losing many of the features which contributed to its historic value. The landscape has attracted much archaeological fieldwork over the years, and seminal reports such as the extensive survey of the park by the Debois Landscape Survey Group of 1990 and that produced by Compass Archaeology for English Heritage in 2013 have been critical in drawing attention to the site's historic status and the need for conservation measures.

In addition, the landscape has received considerable local support, most notably through the Friends of Wanstead Parklands, which was established in 1980. Among the committee's objectives is to advance public education in the character, archaeology and history of Wanstead Park. The committee has undertaken considerable work to achieve its objectives. The Temple has been converted into a visitor centre to inform the public about the site's history. Historic walks of the park are offered on occasion and members of the Friends of Wanstead Parklands frequently share new research findings on the landscape, house and its owners on their website. Their collaboration with conservation groups has been instrumental to the ongoing preservation of the landscape and surviving structures.

Currently there are two areas of concern for the parklands. The first is the condition of the early 18th-century lake system commissioned by Richard Child, 1st Earl Tylney. This is one of the main features of the historic landscape. Of the original seven lakes, five survive, albeit in varying states of poor condition. The Heronry Pond, situated to the south of where Wanstead House once stood, and the Ornamental Waters, to the east, are of the greatest concern, leaking considerable amounts of water. The Perch Pond, Shoulder of Mutton and Basin are also leaking, but to a slightly lesser degree. The historic value and conservation measures that the lake system requires were first brought to attention in 1978 in a survey by Alan Cornish and James Berry. Efforts to protect these historic waterworks is ongoing; however, the actions put in place have only offered temporary solutions and there remains grave concern that the ponds will eventually dry out, erasing one of the most important features of the 18th-century landscape.

More recently, there have been positive developments towards the preservation of the Grotto Boathouse built by the 2nd Earl Tylney in c 1760. A Conservation Management Plan written by Alan Baxter in 2019 identified many sections of the structure that require attention.[6] In December 2020, the Heritage of London Trust commissioned London Stone Conservation to carry out a survey of the site.[7] The survey identified the landing stage of the Grotto Boathouse as being in the most critical condition, with one side of this area partially collapsed. Its condition puts at risk the main masonry wall of the structure overlooking the Ornamental Waters. The Heritage of London Trust has most generously offered a grant to The Friends of Wanstead Parklands to restore the Grotto's landing stage.[8] The restoration of the landing stage is critical to the structure's survival and necessary for any future work towards repairing its façade and recreating its once spectacular interior. The project is an important step towards the preservation of one of Wanstead's most prized historic monuments.

The restoration of the Grotto Boathouse landing stage is a welcome intervention in helping to maintain features of the 18th-century landscape. Recent archaeological technologies such as a Lidar scan of Wanstead Park reveal that, while obscured by undergrowth, many early 18th-century landscape structures, such as the Amphitheatre and Fortification Island, survive (*see* Fig 0.8). This presents exciting possibilities for Wanstead's future and strengthens the case for the site's ongoing preservation.

In contrast to the landscape, the house itself will remain fundamentally lost, with its building fabric dispersed and largely unidentified. Coming into close contact with a fragment of Wanstead House is a rare and uncanny experience. The largest known collection of building fabric from Wanstead is housed in an early 19th-century town house on Hills Road in Cambridge. The house was owned and built by a carpenter and builder named Richard Woods, using fabric purchased from the Wanstead building sale in 1823–4. Woods had formerly acted as clerk of works for the building of William Wilkins' Downing College in 1818 and Queen's College in 1823. Given his architectural interest and expertise, it is unsurprising that he sought items from the Wanstead sale for use at Hills Road.[9] Entering the building through one of Wanstead's Corinthian door cases (Fig 12.3), one encounters the fine wrought iron balustrade, probably from Wanstead's Grand Staircase, and two fully panelled rooms where the original marble fireplace and overmantel recorded in

Fig 12.3
Front elevation, Hills Road
Cambridge.
[Hannah Armstrong]

Nollekens's portrait of the Saloon is displayed (Fig 12.4; *see* Fig 4.16). Hills Road represents only a fraction of what existed at Wanstead. A window pediment, embellished with the Tylney coat of arms, prompts us to wonder where such details may appear in buildings elsewhere across the country.

The tradesmen who purchased the single lot of Wanstead fabric in 1823 worked on several buildings designed by the architect William Wilkins (1778–1839). For example, in 1824, Joseph Stannard (1771–1855), an architect and builder, along with his son of the same name and profession, signed the contract to build the New Court at

Fig 12.4
Wrought iron balustrade, Hills Road Cambridge.
[Hannah Armstrong]

Cambridge designed by Wilkins. This has led to speculation that some of Wanstead's building fabric has been repurposed there and on Kings Parade (*see* Appendix I). John de Carle (1750–1828) was a stonemason and worked on Wilkins' Downing College, where fabric on Wanstead may have been relocated, but this remains speculative.[10]

Like Wanstead's building fabric, its contents are widely dispersed. On occasion, however, new discoveries about its furnishings are made when an item from a private collection resurfaces in today's sales rooms, their association with the former lost palace generating additional interest to the object itself. In 2011, for example, a giltwood side table designed by Kent for Wanstead's Saloon sold at Christie's for £73,250.[11] More recently, a pine conversation stool, designed by Kent and also displayed in the Saloon, sold at Christie's for £92,500.[12] The high value of these items reflects an ongoing interest not only in the craftsmanship of Kent's early furniture designs, but in the fascinating story behind the objects' provenance. Although this study's investigation into the Grand Hall, Ballroom and Saloon has reconstructed how the most prized spaces of Wanstead House appeared, the sheer quantity of furniture listed in the 1822 sale catalogue highlights how much is left to discover.

The whereabouts of certain paintings listed in the 1822 sale catalogue remains something of a mystery. On day 9 of the sale, lot 284 was recorded as 'SIBERECHTS, JAN – A Landscape, View of Wanstead House and surrounding Country.'[13] Siberechts, an established Flemish artist renowned for his views of country estates, died in 1703. The view of Wanstead would therefore depict the Elizabethan manor purchased by Josiah Child in 1673 and would provide us with further information regarding the late 17th- and early 18th-century landscape schemes. Equally intriguing is lot 311 on day 10 of the sale, recorded as 'Nollikins – *Females Bathing, in a Landscape, with a distant View of Wanstead House*' and the numerous family portraits attributed to Godfrey Kneller, Willem Wissing, Joseph Highmore and Jonathan Richardson.[14] Locating these paintings would provide new evidence, furthering our understanding of Wanstead and its owners.

Just as we will never be able to wander through the magnificent interiors of Wanstead House, neither can we travel back in time to meet with its owners and ask some of the burning questions that remain. The nature of investigating a lost estate means that sometimes we are unable to access the types of archival sources that would contribute to our understanding of the estate's development and the lives of its owners. The dispersed nature of evidence for Wanstead, however, gives hope that there is more material to be discovered.

Josiah Child's associations with the Atlantic slave trade, for example, certainly demands further research. In 2020, Historic England carried out a research audit on the transatlantic slave economy and England's built environment and called for further studies to analyse the importance of archaeological sites and demolished buildings in understanding the reach and depth of transatlantic slavery's legacy on the shaping of Great Britain's landscape.[15] While this study of Wanstead has gone some way in addressing the financial input Josiah's participation in the East India Company and Royal Africa Company had on Wanstead's early development, there is still much to be learnt.

In addition, out of the ownerships discussed, only one concerns a female member of the family: Catherine Tylney Long. The female voice at Wanstead has effectively been silenced over time and we know little about the wives and daughters who lived there. Country house historians have pointed to the neglect of the subject of women and the country house, which marginalises their contribution.[16] Were the necessary evidence to surface, we could gain insight into the relationships between Wanstead's owners and their wives and the role these women played in the administration, management and development of Wanstead. The search for Wanstead House is, therefore, ongoing, presenting a range of exciting possibilities for future research.

We know little of the personal sentiments of Wanstead's owners, but it is certain they would have witnessed the demise of their ancestral seat with heavy hearts. This study of one the great estates of Georgian England has sought to illuminate what has been lost. It is hoped that it can play a part in ensuring the preservation of this historic site for generations to come.

Notes

1. Simpson 1842, 1.
2. Coller 1861, 473.
3. *Globe*, 26 April 1882, np; *Shoreditch Observer*, 1 April 1882, np.
4. *Hackney and Kingsland Gazette*, 9 August 1882, np.
5. Winter 1905, 222.
6. Baxter 2019.
7. London Stone Conservation, *Wanstead Grotto Make Safe and Consolidation of Masonry on Landing Stage: Condition Survey and Report* (December 2020). Thanks to John Sharpe, chairman of the Friends of Wanstead Parklands, for a discussion on this project, and Nicola Stacey, Director of Heritage of London Trust.
8. Special thanks to Nicola Stacey and Hilary Brigden of the Heritage of London Trust for sharing their findings with me.
9. See Baggs 1996, 131–3; Anon 'Wanstead House'; Bradley and Pevsner 2015, 327.
10. Baggs 1996, 131–3.
11. Christie's, 'The Exceptional Sale', 7 July 2011, lot 51.
12. Christie's, 'The English Collector', 22 May 2014, lot 1191.
13. *Wanstead House Sale*, day 9, lot 284.
14. *Wanstead House Sale*, day 10, lot 311.
15. Wills and Dresser 2020.
16. Lewis 2009, 336–63; Arnold 2003.

Appendix: locations of the contents and building fabric of Wanstead House

This appendix lists the current whereabouts of the surviving outbuildings belonging to Wanstead House, its building fabric and collection of furniture, paintings and sculpture.

Outbuildings and other structures belonging to the former Wanstead estate

The table below lists the name of the building, its location, date of construction and, where applicable, its listed status.

Wanstead Park

Portland stone gate piers with RC initials	Junction of Overton Drive/ Blake Hall Road	*c* 1715–50	Grade II*
Wanstead Golf Clubhouse (former stable house)	Overton Drive	*c* 1760–80	Grade II
The Grotto Boathouse	Ornamental Waters	*c* 1760	Grade II
The Temple (formerly the Pheasantry/Menagerie)	Visitor Centre	*c* 1760	Grade II

Location of building fabric and architectural structures

The table below lists the item of building fabric, its location, date of production and, where applicable, the listed status of the building in which the item is displayed.

2 Hills Road, Cambridge

Front door and architrave	Front elevation	*c* 1715	Grade II*
Wrought iron balustrade	Hall	*c* 1715	
Fireplace and overmantel	East reception room	*c* 1715	
Fireplace and overmantel	West reception room	*c* 1715	
Panelling and pilasters	Hall	*c* 1715	

Hendon Hall Hotel, North London

Four Corinthian capitals	Front elevation	*c* 1715	Grade II

Chillingham Castle, Northumberland

Two white marble fireplaces	The Great Hall	*c* 1715–20	Grade I

The Warren, Loughton, Essex

Obelisk from Wanstead's forecourt	(Purchased from the 1747 sale of Cannons, Essex)	*c* 1713–24	

West Ham Park, Portway, Newham, London

Coade stone urns	Terrace above the tennis courts	*c* 1760	

15 King's Parade, Cambridge

Window pediments	Front elevation	*c* 1715	Grade II

Furniture

The table below lists the location of where the item of furniture is displayed, designer, item description and date of production.

Chatsworth House, Derbyshire

William Kent	Black porphyry pier tables	*c* 1730
William Kent	Centre table, for the Great Hall	*c* 1730
William Kent	Square library table	*c* 1730
Vulliamy & Sons	Two bronze chandeliers with Tylney crest	*c* 1811

Wilton House, Wiltshire

William Kent	Suite of eight side chairs, carved gilt wood and gesso, Genoa crimson upholstery	*c* 1725–30
William Kent	Suite of six settees, carved gilt wood, red velvet upholstery	*c* 1725–30
William Kent	Console table, carved, painted and parcel-gilt wood, marble top	*c* 1730

Wallace Collection, London

Attributed to André-Charles Boulle	Side table, oak, pinewood, walnut, gilt bronze, brass and première- and contre-partie Boulle marquetry of brass and turtleshell	c 1705

Paintings and sculpture from Wanstead House in public collections

The table below lists name of artist, title of work, date of production (if known) and object's current location.

Andrea Casali	*The Continence of Scipio*	c 1743	Runcorn Town Hall, Cheshire
Andrea Casali	*Coriolanus Beseeched by his Wife and Mother to Spare the City of Rome*	c 1743	Burton Constable Hall, Yorkshire
Andrea Casali	*Sophonisba Taking Poison*	c 1743	Runcorn Town Hall, Cheshire
Anonymous	Antique statue of Agrippina		Chatsworth House, Derbyshire
Anonymous	Antique statue of Apollo		Chatsworth House, Derbyshire
Anonymous	Antique statue of Domitian		Chatsworth House, Derbyshire
Anonymous (formerly attributed to Charles Catton the Elder)	*A Prospect of the Park and House at Wanstead*	c 1730	Newham Archive (formerly Passmore Edwards Museum), London
Anonymous (formerly attributed to Charles Catton the Elder)	*A View of Wanstead House, Epping Forest*	c 1730	Parham House, West Sussex
Joseph Frans Nollekens	*Portrait of a Family*	1740	Yale Centre for British Art, New Haven
Joseph Frans Nollekens	*Richard Child, 1st Earl Tylney*	1740	Fairfax House, York
Joseph Frans Nollekens	*Children Playing with a Hobby Horse*	1741–7	Yale Centre for British Art, New Haven
Joseph Frans Nollekens	*Portrait of Two Boys*, probably Joseph and John Joseph Nollekens	c 1745	Yale Centre for British Art, New Haven

Joseph Frans Nollekens	*Children at Play*, probably the artist's son Jacobus and daughter Maria Joanna Sophia	1745	Yale Centre for British Art, New Haven
Jonathan Riley	*Portrait of Sir Josiah Child*	*c* 1685	National Portrait Gallery, London
Laurent Delvaux	Statue of Hercules	*c* 1720	Waddesdon Manor, Buckinghamshire
Laurent Delvaux	Two white marble urns, a Bacchanalian and the Sacrifice to Diana	*c* 1721–8	Anglesey Abbey, Cambridgeshire Currently on display at the Victoria and Albert Museum, London
Peter Scheemakers	Two white marble urns depicting Sacrifice to Hercules and Sacrifice to Apollo	*c* 1721–8	Anglesey Abbey, Cambridgeshire Currently on display at the Victoria and Albert Museum, London
William Aikman	*Portrait of William Kent*	1720	National Portrait Gallery, London
William Hogarth	*An Assembly at Wanstead House*	*c* 1728–31	Philadelphia Museum of Fine Art/The John Howard McFadden Collection, 1928

References

Archives

Bibliothèque Nationale de France

CVE 39280, *A Catalogue of the superb Gobelin tapestry, beautiful damask and velvet hangings, and other articles, of the princely mansion, Wanstead house, deferred at the late sale, together with various uncleared lots* (London, 1822)

Bodleian Libraries, University of Oxford

MS. Eng. Misc.d.165, f.197, Letter from James Gomme to Revd Mark Noble of Barming, 18 July 1822

The British Library

Add MS 27 995 f.1, William Hogarth's 'Account taken January first 1731 of all ye Pictures that Remain unfinish'd'

Add MSS 36, 362 ff.115–6, John Buckler, drawings of the ground and principal floors from 1822

Add MS 52483, f.112, Bullock to Catherine at Draycot House, letter 2, February 1811

Add MS 752, f.54v, Smart Lethieullier to Dr Charles Lyttelton, 19 October 1756

BL Maps Collection, K.Top.13.30.a.11TAB, John Rocque, *A Plan of the House, Gardens, Park, and Plantations of Wanstead, the Seat of the Earl of Tylney*, 1735

BL Maps Collection, K.Top.13.2, Henry Overton, *A New Map of the County of Essex*, 1713

BL Maps Collection Crace Port.19.18, John Rocque, *An exact survey of the city's of London, Westminster ye borough of Southwark and the county near ten miles round begun in 1741 and ended in 1745*

General Reference Collection 191.g.15-16, Leonard Knyff and Johann Kip, *Britannia Illustrata or views of several of the Queens Palaces and also of the principal Seats of the Nobility and Gentry of Great Britain, curiously engraved in eighty copper plates*, 1720

MS 752, f.54v, Smart Lethieullier to Dr Charles Lyttelton, 20 August 1751

Stowe MS 752, f.102v, Smart Lethieullier to Dr. Charles Lyttleton, 25 September 1759

Essex Record Office

D/DB f116/4, A R Blake to William Pole Tylney Long Wellesley, 27 February 1821

D/DB f116/4, Bullock to Miss Tylney Long, From Wanstead House, 18 October 1810

D/DB f116/4, Merrick Shawe to William Wellesley Pole, c 22 June 1822

D/DB f116/4, Shawe to Wellesley, 10 June 1822

D/DCw P59, L Searles, *A Survey of Wanstead Park*, 1779

D/DCW P7, J Cradock, *Plan of Wanstead Park*, 1725

D/DCY P2A, J Doyley, *Plan of Wanstead*, c 1815–16

D/DGn 181, Conveyance, 5 December 1661

D/DK F1, Part of a Diary of a Wanstead Quaker, c 1707–15

D/DQs/12, Will of John 2nd Earl Tylney

D/DU 546/2, An antiquary's notebook kept by Alfred Savill of Chigwell Hall, 1761–2

I/Mp 388/1/57, Rough plan of Saloon at Wanstead House

SALE/B284, *Wanstead House sale of contents of the whole house and sale of greenhouses, 2 hothouses and contents including orange and lemon trees* (London, 1799)

T/B 39 W.H.L

TA/404, Letter to Miss Catherine, from Oatlands, 24 November 1811

Hoares Bank Archive

HB/8/T/11/392, Private letter book commencing 5th March 1778, Letter to Sir James Tylney Long, 14 November 1779

Hoares & Co to Lord Tylney, 14 November 1779

Lewis Walpole Collection Online

Horace Mann to Horace Walpole, 9 November 1753

Horace Mann to Horace Walpole, 25 October 1768

Horace Mann to Horace Walpole, 15 February 1777

Horace Mann to Horace Walpole, 28 June 1777

Horace Walpole to Richard Bentley, the Earl of Strafford, 17 July 1755

National Archives

C104/57/4, VULLIAMY v VULLIAMY (?1825): Shop books of clock- and watchmaker; Particulars of silverware and ornaments: London

C 111/215, LONG v PHIPPS: Inventories of household furniture, plate, linen, china, books, wines and effects of Sir James Tilney-Long, deceased, at Draycot House near Chippenham, Wilts, and Wanstead House, Essex

FO 610, Foreign Office: Chief Clerk's Department and Passport Office: Passport Registers

PROB 11/1253/199, Will of Sir James Tylney Long, 24 December 1794

PROB 11/451/289, Will of Sir Josiah Child of Wanstead, Essex, 1696

National Art Library

Fougeroux, P F 1728, *Voiage d'Angleterre, d'Hollande et de Flandre, fait en l'annee 1728*

Newham Archive

Hiram Stead Collection, 1823

Parliamentary Archives

HL/PO/JO/10/8/758 *Wellesley v. Wellesley* which incorporates trial transcripts and affidavits from *Wellesley v Beaufort*

Redbridge Museums and Heritage Centre

Baron Maryborough to William Wellesley Pole, 16 August 1822

Letter to Earl Tylney dated 25 February 1764 from Draycot

YW301, Charlotte Fermour to her mother, Countess of Pomfret, 13 October 1743 20127 (f.20)

Box 4, Vol. 1, Letter Nos. 1–13

Letter from Lord Tylney to his brother, Sir Robert Long, 11 June 1760

William Wellesley Pole to William Wellesley, 19 November 1811, Vol. 1, Letter 8

Sir Paul Getty Library

Repton, H 1813 *Report on Wanstead Landscape*

Kennedy, L 1818 *Nottiae on American Gardens, Wanstead, Essex*

Wiltshire and Swindon History Centre

2062/4, Settlement giving Miss Catherine Tylney Long an independent income after marriage

2246, William IV – photocopies and transcripts of letters written by the Duke of Clarence (William IV) during courtship

947/2114, John Child 2nd Earl Tylney to Sir Robert Long, 20 September 1752

947/2114, Sir Robert Long to Lord Tylney, 20 August 1764

947/2114, John Child to Sir Robert Long, 20 August 1765

947/2114, John Child 2nd Earl Tylney to Sir Robert Long, 20 November 1765

947/2116 Letter to James Tylney Long, 25 June 1764

947/2116, Sir Robert Long to Dolly/Dorothy, 29 July 1765

947/2117, James Tylney Long to Sir Robert Long, 13 March 1764

947/2121, John Child 2nd Earl Tylney to Sir James Tylney Long, 24 October 1775

Primary sources

Anon 1712 *Flora Triumphans: Wanstead Garden, An Heroick Poem Most Humbly Addrest to the honourable Sir Richard Child*. London: Redmayne and Morphew

Anon 1794 *Ambulator, or, A Pocket Companion in a Tour round London*. London: J Scatcherd

Anon 1800 *Topographical and Statistical Description of the County of Essex*. London: C Cooke

Bentham, J 1785 *Offences against one's self: Paederasty*. London

Campbell, C 1715 *Vitruvius Brittanicus*, **I**. London

Chambers, E 1728 *Cyclopaedia: or an Universal Dictionary of Arts and Sciences*, **I**. London: D Midwinter

Chambers, W 1791 *Treatise on the Decorative Part of Civil Architecture*. London

Child, J 1668 *Brief Observations Concerning Trade*. London

Child, J 1690 *Discourse about Trade*. London

Defoe, D 1724 *A Tour Thro' the Whole Island of Great Britain*, **I**. London

Defoe, D 1727 *The Complete English Tradesman in familiar letters, directing him in all the several parts and Progressions of Trade*. London: Charles Revington

Edwards, G 1751 *A Natural History of Birds*. London

Edwards, G 1764 *Gleanings of Natural History: Exhibiting Figures of Quadrupeds, Birds, Insects, Plants, &c Most of which have not, till now, been either Figured or Described WITH DESCRIPTIONS of Eighty-five different Subjects Designed, Engraved, and Coloured after Nature, On FIFTY-TWO COPPER-PLATE PRINTS*. London

Finberg, A J 1934 'Vertue Notebooks'. *The Walpole Society*, **XVIII**. Oxford: Printed for the Walpole Society by Frederick Hall at the University Press

Fores S 1789 *New Guide for Foreigners*. London: S W Fores

Harris, J 1702 *Leighton-Stone Air*. London

Jackson, W 1776 *Sodom and Onan*. London

James, J 1712 *Theory and Practice of Gardening*. London: G James

Knight, R P 1795 *The Landscape: A Didactic Poem in three books addressed to Uvedale Price Esq*. London: Bulmer & Co

Langley, B 1728 *New Principles of Landscape Gardening or, The laying out and planting parterres, groves, wildernesses, labyrinths, avenues, parks, &c*., London: A Bettesworth and J Batley

London, G and Wise, H 1706 *The Retir'd Gardener*, **I**. London

Lucas, J 1892, *Kalm's Account of his visit to England on his way to America*. London: Macmillan & Co

Macky, J 1722 *A Journey through England. In familiar letters. From a gentleman here, to his friend abroad*, **I**. London: J Hooke

Mollet, A 1670 *The Garden of Pleasure*. London: John Martin and Henry Herringham

Morant, P 1768 *History of Essex*. London: William Boyer

Muilman, P 1771 *A New and Complete History of Essex*, **IV**. Chelmsford: Lionel Hassell

North, R 1713 *A Discourse of Fish and Fishponds*. London

Papillon, A F W 1887 *Memoirs of Thomas Papillon, of London, Merchant (1623–1702)*. Reading

Parliamentary Papers, House of Commons and Command, **23**, 1838

Peach, R E 1885 'Ralph Allen, Prior Park and Bath'. *The Antiquary* **12**, November. London

Price, U 1798 *A letter to Humphry Repton, Esq. On the application of the practice as well as the principles of Landscape Gardening*. Hereford

Rapin, R 1672 *Of Gardens*. London: Thomas Collins and John Ford

Repton, H 1794a *A letter to Uvedale Price, Esq*. London: G. Nicholl

Repton, H 1794b *Sketches and Hints on Landscape Gardening*. London: J & J. Boydell

Repton, H 1803 *Observations on the Theory and Practice of Landscape Gardening*. London: T Bensley

Repton, H 1806 *An Enquiry into the Changes of Taste in Landscape Gardening*. London: J Taylor

Repton, H 1816 *Fragments on the Theory and Practise of Landscape Gardening*. London: T Bensley & Son for J Taylor

Serres de Latour, A 1788 *Londres et ses environs*. Paris: Buisson

Sevelinges, C (ed) 1820 *Condé, Memoires de la maison de Condé imprimes sur les manuscrits autographes et d'apres l'autprisation de S.A.S Monseigeur le duc de Bourbon: contenant la vie du Grand Condé, ecrite par feu Mgr.le prince de Condé, la correspondence de ce prince avec tous les souverains et prices des familles royales de l'Europe, depuis 1789, jusqu'en 1814*, **II**. Paris

Shaftsbury, Cooper A 1732 'Letter concerning design', *Characteristicks of men, manners, opinions, times*, **III**. London

Shaw, S 1788 *Tour to the West of England in 1788*. London: Robson and Clark

Simpson, W 1842 *Professional excursions, by an auctioneer*. London: Alfred Greenland

Switzer, S 1718 *Ichnographia Rustica: OR THE Nobleman, Gentleman, and Gardener's RECREATION*, **I**. London: D Browne

Trapp, J 1791 *A Picture of Italy. Translated from the Original German of W. de Archenholtz*. Dublin: W Corbet

Vertue, G 1798 *The works of Horatio Walpole, Earl of Orford: Anecdotes of painting [and the other fine arts]*, **III**. London

Volkmann, J 1788 *Neueste Reisen durch England: Vorzüglich in Absicht auf die Kunstsammlungen, Naturgeschichte*

Walpole, H 1871 *Anecdotes of Painting in England by Horace Walpole*. Reprint of the edition of 1786. London: Alexander Murray

Watkins, R 2002 *Jerome Lalande, Diary of a Trip to England 1763*. Kingston, Tasmania

Young, A 1768 *A Six Week Tour through the southern Counties of England and Wales*. 3 edn London: W Nicoll

Newspapers and periodicals

'A Description of Wanstead House in Essex, the seat of the late Earl of Tilney'. *New London Magazine*, April 1789

'Chit-Chat'. *The Kaleidoscope: or, Literary and Scientific Mirror*, 24 September 1822, 95–6

'Court of King's Bench'. *Glasgow Herald*, 27 November 1827

'Description of TILNEY HOUSE, on EPPING-FOREST'. *The Oxford Magazine or Universal Museum* **8**, 1772, 242–3

'ENTERTAINMENTS AT WANSTEAD HOUSE'. *The Morning Post*, 9 August 1816

'Fete at Wanstead House'. *The Morning Post*, 1 July 1814

'INCIDENT'S OCCURRING IN AND NEAR LONDON, INTERESTING MARRIAGES, &c.'. *La Belle Assemblée: or Court and fashionable magazine*, March 1812, 164–6

'Interesting Trial'. *The Weekly Entertainer: or, Agreeable and instructive repository*, 22 April 1813, 293–6

'London'. *Caledonian Mercury*, 16 September 1822

'Mr Wellesley Pole and Lord Kilworth'. *The Examiner*, 18 August 1811, 536–7

'Multiple Advertisements and Notices'. *The Morning Post*, 2 September 1822

'Multiple News Items'. *The Bury and Norwich Post: Or, Suffolk and Norfolk Telegraph, Essex, Cambridge, & Ely Intelligencer*, 21 January 1824

'NEWSPAPER CHAT'. *The Examiner*, 31 October 1824

'Sunday's Post'. *The Bury and Norwich Post*, 3 November 1824

'To the printer of Town and Country Magazine'. *Town and Country Magazine*, 1770

'WANSTEAD FOREST'. *Saturday Review of Politics, Literature, Science and Art*, 7 August 1858

Addison, W 1753 *The Spectator*, **VIII** (Edinburgh)

Anon 1771 'Reflections on seeing Lord Tylney's House'. *Town and Country Magazine*, **3**

Bowyer, Nichols, J (ed) 1830 'Obituary – The Duke of Bourbon'. *The Gentleman's Magazine: and Historical Chronicle*, September, 271–3

Examiner, 9 January 1814

Gazetteer and New Daily Advertiser, 30 July 1764

General Evening Post, 2–4 December 1735

General Post, 27–9 August 1772

Gibson, J 1796 'A Short account of several gardens near London, with remarks on some particular is wherin they excel, or are deficient, upon a view of them in December 1691'. *Archaeologia* **XII**, 186–7

Hyrn, J 1823 'Wanstead House: Elizabeth'. *Calcutta Journal of Politics and General Literature* **1**, February, 599–600

Lethieullier, S 1779 'A letter from Smart Lethieullier, Esq; to Dr Charles Lyttleton, relating to some antiquities found in the county of Essex, Read November 27, 1746'. *Archaeologia: or miscellaneous tracts relating to antiquity* **I**, 73–4

Lloyds Evening Post, 1 July 1763

Morning Chronicle, 2 July 1811

Morning Post & Fashionable World, 16 April 1795

The Daily Post, 18 January 1720

The Gentleman's Magazine, 28 November 1794

The Gentleman's Magazine, and Historical Chronicle **70**, 1800

The Gentleman's Magazine, September 1863

The Globe, 26 April 1882

The Hackney and Kingsland Gazette, 9 August 1882

The Literary Chronicle and Weekly Review, 15 June 1822, 379–80

The Liverpool Press, 24 April 1812

The Merchant Princes of England, London Society, an illustrated Magazine of light and amusing literature for the hours of relaxation, **39**, March 1865

The Mirror of Literature, Amusement & Instruction, 16 November 1822, 33–5

The Morning Chronicle, 2 July 1857

The Morning Post, 9 August 1816

The Morning Post, 11 March 1822

The Morning Post, 21 May 1822

The Morning Post, 28 June 1824

The Morning Post, 22 November 1884

The New Monthly Magazine and Universal Register, February 1814

The Shoreditch Observer, 1 April 1882

The Times, 12 May 1823

The Times, 14 May 1823

The Times, 19 September 1825

Watson, W 1751–2 'An Account of the Bishop of London's Garden at Fulham; by Mr. William Watson, F.R.S', *Philosophical Transactions (1683–1775)* **47** (London), 241–7

Weekly Journal or Saturday's Post, 20 July 1717

Whitehall Evening Post, 12 June 1800

Sales catalogues

'A Catalogue of All the Materials of the Dwelling-house, out-Houses &c of His Grace James Duke of Chandos … At his Late Seat call'd Cannons … Sold by Auction by Mr. Cock', 16 June 1747

Christie's, 'Consigned from the Continent; and A Man of Fashion', 5–6 March 1824

Christie's, 'A Gentleman, deceased [and] Sir James Stuart, Bart.', 30 June 1835

Christie's, 'The Exceptional Sale', 7 July 2011

Christie's, 'The English Collector', 22 May 2014

Messrs. E. Foster and Son, 11–12 May 1836

Wanstead House, Essex. Magnificent Furniture, Collection of Fine Paintings and Sculpture, Massive Silver and Gilt Plate, Splendid Library of Choice Books, The Valuable Cellars of Fine-Flavoured Old Wines, Ales, &c., &c. (London, 1822)

Secondary sources

Ackerman, J 1990 *The Villa: Form, and Ideology of Country Houses*. London: Thames and Hudson

Adams, S (ed) 1995 *Household Accounts and Disbursement Books of Robert Dudley, Earl of Leicester 1558–1561, 1584–1586*. Cambridge: Cambridge University Press

Anon 1947 *Seven Centuries of Wanstead Church*. Wanstead: The Church

Anon 1990 *Runcorn Town Hall: A History and Description*. Halton: Halton Borough Council

Arciszewska, B 1992 'A Villa Fit for a King: The Role of Palladian Architecture in the Ascendancy of the House of Hanover under George I'. *Canadian Art Review* **19**, 41–58

Arnold, D 1996 *The Georgian Villa*. Stroud: Alan Sutton

Arnold, D 2003 *The Georgian Country House: Architecture, Landscape and Society*. Stroud: Sutton

Aspinall, A (ed) 1951 *Mrs. Jordan and her family: being the unpublished correspondence of Mrs Jordan and the Duke of Clarence, later William IV*. London: Arthur Baker

Atwell, G 1954 'Wanstead House'. *Essex Review* **LXIII**, 67–80

Baggs, A P 1996 'The After-life of Wanstead'. *Georgian Group Journal* **5**, 131–3

Baker, M 2000 *Figured in Marble: The Making and Viewing of Eighteenth-Century Sculpture*. London: V&A Publications

Baker, M 2014 *The Marble Index: Roubiliac and Sculptural Portraiture in Eighteenth-century Britain*. London and New Haven: Yale University Press

Balmori, D 1991 'Architecture, Landscape, and the Intermediate Structure: Eighteenth-Century Experiments in Mediation'. *Journal of the Society of Architectural Historians* **50**, 38–65

Barton, M 2011 'Sir Richard Child of Wanstead: A Portrait Revealed'. *Georgian Group Journal* **XIX**, 184–5

Beer de, E S (ed) 2000 *The Diary of John Evelyn*, 6 vols, **IV**. Oxford

Bingham, H 1939 *Elihu Yale: The American Nabob of Queen Square*. London: Anchon Books

Blackett-Ord, C (ed) 2001 'Letters from William Kent to Burrell Massingberd from the Continent, 1712–1719'. *Walpole Society Annual* **63**, 75–109

Bradley, S and Pevsner, N 2015 *Buildings of England: Cambridgeshire*. London and New Haven: Yale University Press

Breman, P and Addis, D (eds) 1972 *Guide to Vitruvius Britannicus: Annotated and Analytic Index to the Plates*. New York: Benjamin Blom Inc

Brindle S 2013 'Kent the Painter' *in* Weber, S (ed) *William Kent: Designing Georgian Britain*. London and New Haven: Yale University Press, 111–49

Brown L 2010 *The Slavery Connections of Marble Hill House*. Manchester: University of Manchester

Byrant, J 2013 'From "Gusto" to "Kentissime": Kent's Designs for Country Houses, Villas and Lodges' *in* Weber, S (ed) *William Kent: Designing Georgian Britain*. London and New Haven: Yale University Press, 183–242

Cabe Halpern, J 1992 'Uses of Paintings in Garden History' *in* Dixon Hunt, J (ed) *Garden History: Issues, Approaches, Methods*. Washington: Dumbarton Oaks, 183–202

Cartwright, J (ed) 1888 T*he Travels Through England of Dr Richard Pococke, Successively Bishop of Meath and of Ossory, During 1750, 1751 and Later Years*, **1**. London: Camden Society

Cator, C 2007 'French Furniture at Wanstead'. *Furniture History* **43**, 227–36

Chambers, W and R 1862 'The Last of the Condés'. *Chambers Journal of Popular Literature, Science and Arts* **421**, 25 January, 56–9

Chapman, G 1928 *The Travel Diaries of William Beckford of Fonthill*. London: Constable & Co

Clemenson, H C 1982 *English Country Houses and Landed Estates*. London: Croom Helm

Climenson, E J (ed) 1899 *Passages from the Diaries of Mrs Philip Lybbe Powys of Hardwick House, Oxon. AD 1756 to 1808*. Toronto: University of Toronto

Coller W 1861 *The People's History of Essex: Comprising a Narrative of Public and Political Events in the County*. Chelmsford: Meggy and Chalk

Colvin, H 1963 'Eythorpe House and its Demolition in 1810–1811'. *Records of Buckinghamshire* **16**, 219–27

Colvin, H 2008 *A Biographical Dictionary of British Architects 1600–1840*. London and New Haven: Yale University Press

Connor, T P 1977 'The Making of Vitruvius Britannicus'. *Architectural History* **20**, 14–30

Cornforth, J 2004 *Early Georgian Interiors.* London and New Haven: Yale University Press

Couch, S 1992 'The Practice of Avenue Planting in the Seventeenth and Eighteenth Centuries'. *Garden History* **20**, 173–200

Cowell, F 1998 'Adam Holt (1691–1750) Gardener: His Work at Coopersale House, Essex'. *Garden History* **26**, No. 2, 214–17

Craske, M 2007 *The Silent Rhetoric of the Body: A History of Monumental Sculpture and Commemorative Art in England, 1720–1770.* London and New Haven: Yale University Press

Dalton, C 2009 '"He that … doth not master the human figure": Sir John Vanbrugh and the Vitruvian Landscape'. *Garden History* **37**, No. 1, 3–37

Daniels, S 1999 *Humphry Repton: Landscape Gardening and the Geography of Georgian England.* London and New Haven: Yale University Press

Dixon Hunt, J 1987 *William Kent: Landscape Garden Designer.* London: Zwemmer

Dixon Hunt, J (ed) 1995 *The History of Modern Taste in Gardening/Horace Walpole.* New York: Ursus Press

Dixon Hunt, J 2013 'Landscape Architecture' *in* Weber, S (ed) *William Kent: Designing Georgian Britain.* London and New Haven: Yale University Press, 365–92

Dorment, R 1986 *British Painting in the Philadelphia Museum of Art.* Philadelphia: Philadelphia Museum of Art

Dunlop, I and Kimball F 1950 'The Gardens of Wanstead House, Essex.' *Country Life* **108**, 28 July 1950, 294–8

Earle, P 1989 *The Making of the English Middle Class: Business, Society and Family Life in London, 1660–1730.* London: Metheun

Eastment, W 1969 *Wanstead Through the Ages.* Letchworth: Essex Countryside

Einberg, E 1987 *Manners and Morals, Hogarth and British Painting 1700–1760.* London: Tate Publishing

Einberg, E 2017 *William Hogarth, A Complete Catalogue to his Paintings.* London and New Haven: Yale University Press

Emmison, F G and Skelton, R A 1957 '"The Description of Essex" by John Norden, 1594'. *The Geographical Journal*, **123**, No. 1, 43–61

Eustace, K 1982 *Michael Rysbrack: Sculptor 1694–1770.* Bristol: City of Bristol Museum and Art Gallery

Finn, M and Smith, K (eds) 2018 *East India Company at Home.* London: UCL Press

Fleming, J, Honour, H and Pevsner, N (ed) 1998 *The Penguin Dictionary of Architecture and Landscape Architecture*, 5 edn. London: Penguin Books

Fry, C 2003 'Spanning the Political Divide: Neo-Palladianism and the Early Eighteenth-Century Landscape'. *Garden History* **31**, No. 2, 180–92

Fryer, H 1994 'Humphry Repton's Commissions in Herefordshire: Picturesque Landscape Aesthetics'. *Garden History* **22**, No. 2, 162–74

Furbank, P N and Owens, W R (eds) 1991 *A Tour Through the Whole Island of Great Britain/Daniel Defoe.* London and New Haven: Yale University Press

George, M D 1952 *Catalogue of Political and Personal Satires in the British Museum*, **IX**. London: British Museum

Gibbs, V 1913 *Complete Peerage.* London: St Catherine Press

Girouard, M 1978 *Life in the English Country House.* Harmondsworth: Penguin

Goldring, E 2014 *Robert Dudley, Earl of Leicester, and the World of Elizabethan Art: Paintings and Patronage at the Court of Elizabeth I.* London and New Haven: Yale University Press

Goldring, E 2016 'Elizabeth in Essex'. *Historic Gardens Review* **34**, 16–21

Goodfellow G L M 1964 'Colen Campbell's Shawfield Mansion in Glasgow'. *Journal of the Society of Architectural Historians* **23**, No. 3, 123–8

Grassby, R 2001 *Kinship and Capitalism: Marriage, Family and Business in the English-speaking World*. Cambridge: Cambridge University Press

Habakkuk, J 1994 *Marriage, Debt and the Estates System: English Landownership 1650–1950*. Oxford: Clarendon

Harris, C 2001 *What's in a Name? Meanings of London Underground Stations*. London: Capital Transport Publishing

Harris, E 1979 *Arbours and Grottos: A Facsimile of the Two Parts of* Universal Architecture, 1755 and 1758, *with a Catalogue of Wright's Works in Architecture and Garden Design*. London: Scolar Press

Harris, E 1986 '*Vitruvius Britannicus* before Colen Campbell'. *Burlington Magazine* **128**, 340–5

Harris, E and Savage, N 1990 *British Architectural Books and Writers: 1556–1785*. Cambridge: Cambridge University Press

Harris, J 1979 *The Artist and the Country House: A History of Country House and Garden View Painting in Britain, 1540–1870*. London: Sothebys

Harris, J 1981 *The Palladians*. London: Trefoil Books, published in association with the Royal Institute of British Architects Drawings Collection

Harris J 1982 *William Talman, Maverick Architect*. London: Allen and Unwin

Harris, J 1986 'The Artinatural Style' *in* Hind, C (ed) *The Rococo in England, Georgian Group Symposium Proceedings*. London: Victoria & Albert Museum

Harris, J 1991 'Wanstead's Compelling Vista'. *Country Life* **22**, 22 August, 60–2

Harris, J 1994 *The Palladian Revival: Lord Burlington, His Villa and Garden at Chiswick*. London and New Haven: Yale University Press

Harris, J, Strong, R and Binney, M (ed) 1974 *The Destruction of the Country House 1875–1975*. London: Thames and Hudson

Hunt, M R 1996 *The Middling Sort: Commerce, Gender and the Family in England 1680–1780*. Berkeley: University of California Press

Ingamells, J 1997 *A Dictionary of British and Irish Travellers in Italy, 1701–1800*. London and New Haven: Yale University Press

Jacques, D 2014 'Our Late Pious Queen Whose Love to Gard'ning Was Not a Little': Queen Anne in her Parks and Gardens'. *Journal for Eighteenth-Century Studies* **37**, 199–216

Jeffery, S 2003 *The Gardens of Wanstead, Proceedings of A Study Day, 1999*. London: London Parks and Gardens Trust

Jeffery, S 2005 'How Repton saw Wanstead'. *Country Life*, 14 April, 98–101

Jeffery, S 2018 'Humphry Repton's Report on Wanstead' *in Repton in London: The Gardens and Landscapes of Humphry Repton (1752–1818)*. London: London Parks and Gardens Trust, 21–9

Jones, R 1982 'The First Indonesian Mission to London'. *Indonesia Circle. School of Oriental and African Studies* **10**, 9–19

Keeling, D F 1994 *Wanstead House, the Owners and their Books*. Wanstead: Tylney Press

Keeling, D F 1997 *Wanstead House and Chatsworth: Treasures from Wanstead House Acquired by the 6th Duke of Devonshire*. Wanstead: Tylney Press

Keeling, D F 2014 *William Kent, 1685–1748: His Work at Wanstead House*. Wanstead: Wanstead Historical Society

Keeling, D F 2015 *Sir Richard Child: Art Collector and Patron of the Arts.* Wanstead: Wanstead Historical Society

Keeling, D F and Page, B 2014 'William Kent, 1685–1748: His Work at Wanstead House'. *Wanstead Record* **2**, April

Kerr, H 1943 'East of Aldgate'. *Country Life* **94**, 22 October, 728–31

Kimball, F 1933 'Wanstead House, Essex'. *Country Life* **74**, 2 December, 605–6

Latham, R (ed) 2003 *The Diary of Samuel Pepys: A Selection.* London: Harper Collins

Laurence, A 2003 'Space, Status and Gender in English Topographical Paintings *c* 1660–*c* 1740'. *Architectural History* **46**, 81–94

Letwin, W 1959 *Sir Josiah Child, Merchant Economist.* Boston: Baker Library

Lewis, J 2009 'When a House is not a Home: Elite English Women and the Eighteenth-Century Country House'. *Journal of British Studies* **48**, 336–63

MacArthur, R and Stobart, J 2010 'Going for a Song? Country House Sales in Georgian England' *in* Stobart, J and Van Damme, I (eds) *Modernity and the Second-hand Trade. European Consumption Cultures and Practices, 1700–1900.* Basingstoke: Palgrave, 175–95

Mackley, A and Wilson, R 2000 *Creating Paradise: The Building of the English Country House 1660–1880.* London: Hambledon and London

Marks, A 1981 'Assembly at Wanstead House'. *Philadelphia Museum of Art Bulletin* **77**, 3–15

Montagu, M (ed) 1825 *The Letters of Mrs. Elizabeth Montagu with Some Letters of her Correspondence.* Boston: Wells and Lilly

Mowl, T 2000 *Gentlemen Players: Gardeners of the English Landscape.* Stroud: Sutton

Musson, J 2005 *How to Read a Country House.* London: Ebury

Myrone, M 2006 *Gothic Nightmares: Fuseli, Blake and the Romantic Imagination.* London: Tate Publishing

Nellis Richter, A 2008 'Spectacle, Exoticism, and Display in the Gentleman's House'. *Eighteenth-Century Studies* **41**, No. 4, 543–63

Parsons, M 1973 'Wanstead Manors' *in* Powell, W R (ed) *A History of the County of Essex,* Vol. VI. London, 322–7

Pevsner N 1969 *The Buildings of England: Essex.* London: Penguin Books

Pevsner, N and Bettley, J 2007 *The Buildings of England: Essex.* London and New Haven: Yale University Press

Pointon, M 1993 *Hanging the Head: Portraiture and Social Formation in Eighteenth-century England.* London and New Haven: Yale University Press

Retford, K 2006 'Patrilineal Portraiture? Gender and Genealogy in the Eighteenth-Century Country House' *in* Style, J and Vickery, A (eds) *Gender, Taste and Material Culture in Britain and North America 1700–1830.* New Haven and London: Yale University Press, 323–52

Retford, K 2013 'The Topography of the Conversation Piece: A Walk around Wanstead' *in* Retford, K, Perry, G and Vilbert, J (eds) *Placing Faces: The Portrait and the English Country House in the Long Eighteenth Century.* Manchester: Manchester University Press, 38–62

Roberts, G 2015 *The Angel and the Cad: Love, Loss and Scandal in Regency England.* London: Macmillan.

Robinson, J M 2009 'Regency Revival: The 19th Century Refurnishing of Wilton'. *Apollo Magazine* **170**, 42–7

Rogger, A 2007 *Landscapes of Taste: The Art of Humphry Repton's Red Books.* London: Routledge

Rowell, C 2007 'French Furniture at Uppark: Sir Harry Fetherstonhaugh and his Friends in Post-revolutionary Paris'. *Furniture History* **43**, 267–92

Savage, N 1998 'Colen Campbell: 1676–1729' in *Mark J Millard Architectural Collection. Volume II: British Books, Seventeenth through Nineetheenth Centuries.* Washington: National Gallery of Art

Sheridan, R B 1994 *Sugar and Slavery: An Economic History of the British West Indies, 1623–1775.* Barbados: Canoe Press

Skelton, A 2010 'The Greenhouse at Wanstead'. *Georgian Group Journal* **XVIII**, 49–64

Snodin, M (ed) 1984 *Rococo: Art and Design in Hogarth's England.* London: Victoria and Design

Stern, P 2011 *The Company-State: Corporate Sovereignty and the Early Modern Foundations of the British Empire in India.* Oxford: Oxford University Press

Stobart, J 2013 'Inventories and the Changing Furnishings of Canons Ashby, Northamptonshire, 1717–1819'. *Regional Furniture* **27**, 1–43

Stutchbury H 1967 *The Architecture of Colen Campbell.* Manchester: Manchester University Press

Summerson J 1977 *Architecture in Britain: 1530–1830.* London: Penguin

Summerson, J 1993 *Architecture in Britain: 1530–1830,* 9 edn. London and New Haven: Yale University Press

Tallis, N 2018 *Elizabeth's Rival: The Tumultuous Tale of Lettice Knollys, Countess of Leicester.* London: Michael O'Mara Books

Tasker, G E 1898 'Wanstead: Its Manor & Palace'. *Essex Review* **7**, 213–30

Thacker, C 1976 *Masters of the Grotto: Joseph and Josiah Lane.* Tisbury: Compton Press

Tuffs, J E 1988 *Wanstead House.* Wanstead: Wanstead Historical Society

Varley, J 1948 'John Rocque. Engraver, Surveyor, Cartographer and Map-seller'. *Imago Mundi* **5**, 83–91

Wall, C 1997 'The English Auction: Narratives of Dismantling's'. *Journal of Eighteenth-Century Studies* **31**, 1–26

Weber, S 2013 'Kent and the Georgian Baroque Style in Furniture: Domestic Commissions' *in* Weber, S (ed) *William Kent: Designing Georgian Britain.* London and New Haven: Yale University Press, 469–525

Williamson, T 1995 *Polite Landscapes: Gardens and Society in Eighteenth-century England.* Stroud: Alan Sutton

Wills, M and Dresser, M 2020 *The Transatlantic Slave Economy and England's Built Environment: A Research Audit.* Historic England

Winter, L 1905 'The Lovely Miss Long'. *Longman's Magazine 1820–1905*, 213–22

Wood, A C (ed) 1958 *The Continuation of the History of the Willoughby Family.* Eton: University of Nottingham

Worsley, G 1995 *Classical Architecture in Britain: The Heroic Age.* London and New Haven: Yale University Press

Worsley, G 2005 *England's Lost Houses: From the Archives of Country Life.* London: Aurum

Wrightson, K 2000 *Earthly Necessities: Economic Lives in Early Modern Britain, 1470–1750.* London and New Haven: Yale University Press

Zahedieh, N 2013 'An Open Elite? Colonial Commerce, the Country House and the Case of Sir Gilbert Heathcote and Normanton Hall' *in* Dresser, M and Hann, A (eds) *Slavery and the British Country House.* Swindon: English Heritage, 71–7

Webography

Anon, 'avenue, n.', *Oxford English Dictionary*, http://www.oed.com.ezproxy.lib.
bbk.ac.uk/view/Entry/13673?rskey=wy5eit&result=1&isAdvanced=false,
accessed 5 February 2016

Anon, 'Wanstead House, 2 Hills Road Cambridge', *Historic England*, https://
historicengland.org.uk/listing/the-list/list-entry/1099114, accessed 11 January
2020

Arnopp, R, 'The Owners of Wanstead Park', *Friends of Wanstead Parklands*,
https://wansteadpark.org.uk/history/the-owners-of-wanstead-park-
part-1-1086-1499/, accessed 14 May 2019

Brailsford, D, 'Egan, Pierce (1772–1849)', *Oxford Dictionary of National Biography*,
http://www.oxforddnb.com/view/article/8577, accessed 8 June 2015

Centre for the Studies of the Legacies of British Slavery, www.ucl.ac.uk/lbs/estates/,
accessed 5 April 2021

Coutu, J, 'Joseph Wilton', *Oxford Dictionary of National Biography*, https://www.
oxforddnb.com/view/article/29706, accessed 2 July 2019

Cruickshanks, E, 'CHILD, Sir Richard, 3rd Bt. (1680–1750), of Wanstead, Essex',
History of Parliament, www.historyofparliamentonline.org/volume/1715-1754/
member/child-sir-richard-1680-1750, accessed 10 April 2014

Daniels, S, 'Repton, Humphry (1752–1818)', *Oxford Dictionary of National Biography*,
www.oxforddnb.com/view/article/23387, accessed 6 February 2015

Denford, S 2015 'Temple over time', *Friends of Wanstead Parklands*, https://
wansteadpark.org.uk/wp-content/uploads/2015/08/TEMPLE-OVER-TIME-
EXHIB-small.pdf, accessed 3 March 2021

Ferris, J P, 'Child, Josiah (c.1630–99) of Wanstead, Essex', *History of Parliament*,
www.historyofparliamentonline.org/volume/1660-1690/member/child-
josiah-1630-99, accessed 6 February 2014

Gash, N, 'Wellesley [formerly Wesley],' *Oxford Dictionary of National Biography*,
https://www.oxforddnb.com.ezproxy.lib.bbk.ac.uk/view/29001, accessed
15 January 2020

Grassby, R, 'Child, Sir Josiah, first baronet', *Oxford Dictionary of National Biography*,
www.oxforddnb.com.ezproxy.lib.bbk.ac.uk/view/article/5290, accessed
8 March 2013

Harris, J, 'London, George (d. 1714)', *Oxford Dictionary of National Biography*,
http://www.oxforddnb.com/view/article/37686, accessed 5 February 2016

Hibbert, C, 'George IV (1762–1830)', *Oxford Dictionary of National Biography*, www.
oxforddnb.com/view/article/10541, accessed 24 May 2016

Johnson, J, 'Brydges, James, first duke of Chandos (1674–1744)', *Oxford Dictionary
of National Biography*, www.oxforddnb.com/view/article/3806, accessed
2 December 2015

Lindley, K, 'Glynne, Sir John (1603–1666)', *Oxford Dictionary of National Biography*,
www.oxforddnb.com/ezproxy.lib.bbk.ac.uk/view/article/10843, accessed
13 June 2014

Macaulay, J, 'Smith, James (1644/5–1731)', *Oxford Dictionary of National Biography*,
www.oxforddnb.com/view/article/63118, accessed 7 October 2015

McConnell, A, 'Beckford, William Thomas (1760–1844)', *Oxford Dictionary of National
Biography*, www.oxforddnb.com/view/article/1905, accessed 2 December 2015

Norgate, G, 'Pole, William Wellesley – [formerly Wesley –] third Earl of Mornington
(1763–1845', *Oxford Dictionary of National Biography*, https://doi-org.ezproxy.
lib.bbk.ac.uk/10.1093/ref:odnb/29010, accessed 15 January 2020

Phibbs, J, 'Lancelot Capability Brown', *Oxford Dictionary of National Biography*, https://doi.org/10.1093/ref:odnb/3635, accessed 15 November 2019

Sambrook, J, 'William Benson', *Oxford Dictionary of National Biography*, www.oxforddnb.com/view/article/2147, accessed 13 June 2014

Sullivan, M G, 'Nost, John (*d*. 1710)', *Oxford Dictionary of National Biography*, www.oxforddnb.com/view/article/69041, accessed 29 September 2015

Watson, P and Knights, M, 'CHILD, Sir Richard, 3rd Bt. (1680–1750), of Wanstead, Essex', *History of Parliament*, accessed 18 January 2021

White, R, 'Vardy, John (1717/18–1765)', *Oxford Dictionary of National Biography,* www.oxforddnb.com/view/article/28112, accessed 14 November 2014

Willis, P, 'Bridgeman, Charles (*d*. 1738)', *Oxford Dictionary of National Biography*, www.oxforddnb.com/view/article/3401, accessed 2 September 2014

Dissertations and theses

Armstrong, H 2016 'The Lost Landscapes and Interiorscapes of Wanstead House: Reconstructing the Eighteenth-Century Estate'. Unpublished PhD thesis, Birkbeck College, Univ of London

Davis, D 2016 'British Dealers and the Making of the Anglo-Gallic Interior, 1785–1853'. Unpublished PhD thesis, Univ of Reading

Hotson, A 2006 'Late Stuart Moneyed Men and their Patronage of Sculpture and Architecture, circa 1660–1720'. Unpublished PhD thesis, Courtauld Institute of Art

O'Hara, J 2010 'Colen Campbell and the Preparatory Drawings for *Vitruvius Britannicus*'. Unpublished PhD thesis, Univ of York

Roberts, G 2020 'Long-Wellesley & Publicity: The Role of Celebrity in the Public Sphere (1788–1832)'. Unpublished PhD thesis, Univ of Westminster

Rumble L 2001 '"Of Good Use or Serious Pleasure": *Vitruvius Britannicus* and Early Eighteenth Century Architectural Discourse'. Unpublished PhD thesis, Univ of Bristol

Weekes, R 2018 'The Architecture of Wanstead House: To What Extent were Colen Campbell's Designs a Reflection of his Reverence for Palladio and Inigo Jones in *Vitruvius Britannicus*'. Unpublished BA dissertation, Birkbeck College, Univ of London

Unpublished sources

Baxter, A 2019 *The Grotto, Wanstead Park, Conservation Management Plan, Prepared for the City of London Corporation*

Berry, A and Cornish, J 1978 *The Lake System of Wanstead Park and The Mystery of the Heronry Pond*

Compass Archaeology 2014 *Strategic Assessment and Conservation Measures for Wanstead Park, London Borough of Redbridge*

Debois Landscape Survey Group 1990 *Wanstead Park: A Survey of the Landscape*

London Stone Conservation 2020 *Wanstead Grotto Make Safe and Consolidation of Masonry on Landing Stage: Condition Survey and Report*

Roberts, G 2012 *Wanstead Park: 1813*

Index

Page numbers in **bold** refer to illustrations.